Nothing gets betw

Cardboard Crack

I can't imagine us ever being apart. Every moment we share together is so magical.

Hey, that happens to remind me. You should think about getting rid of some of these Magic cards you have everywhere.

SLAM

A collection of comics about the world's most addictive game.

Nothing gets between me and my Cardboard Crack

Check out these other Cardboard Crack books:
Cardboard Crack
I will never quit Cardboard Crack
Cardboard Crack anytime, anywhere
Cardboard Crack until the day I die
I'm always thinking about Cardboard Crack
Cardboard Crack is an intellectual sport

This book collects comics that originally appeared online between
August 10, 2015 and April 18, 2016, and can also be viewed at:
cardboard-crack.com
facebook.com/CardboardCrack

For information write:
cardboardcrack.mtg@gmail.com

Printed in the U.S.A.

For "A Place to Play," the Magic shop where my love for the game first began, and which shaped so much of who I am today. It's no longer there anymore in Willow Glen, California, but the memories of all the late nights I spent there, and all the people I shared those times with, will never be forgotten.

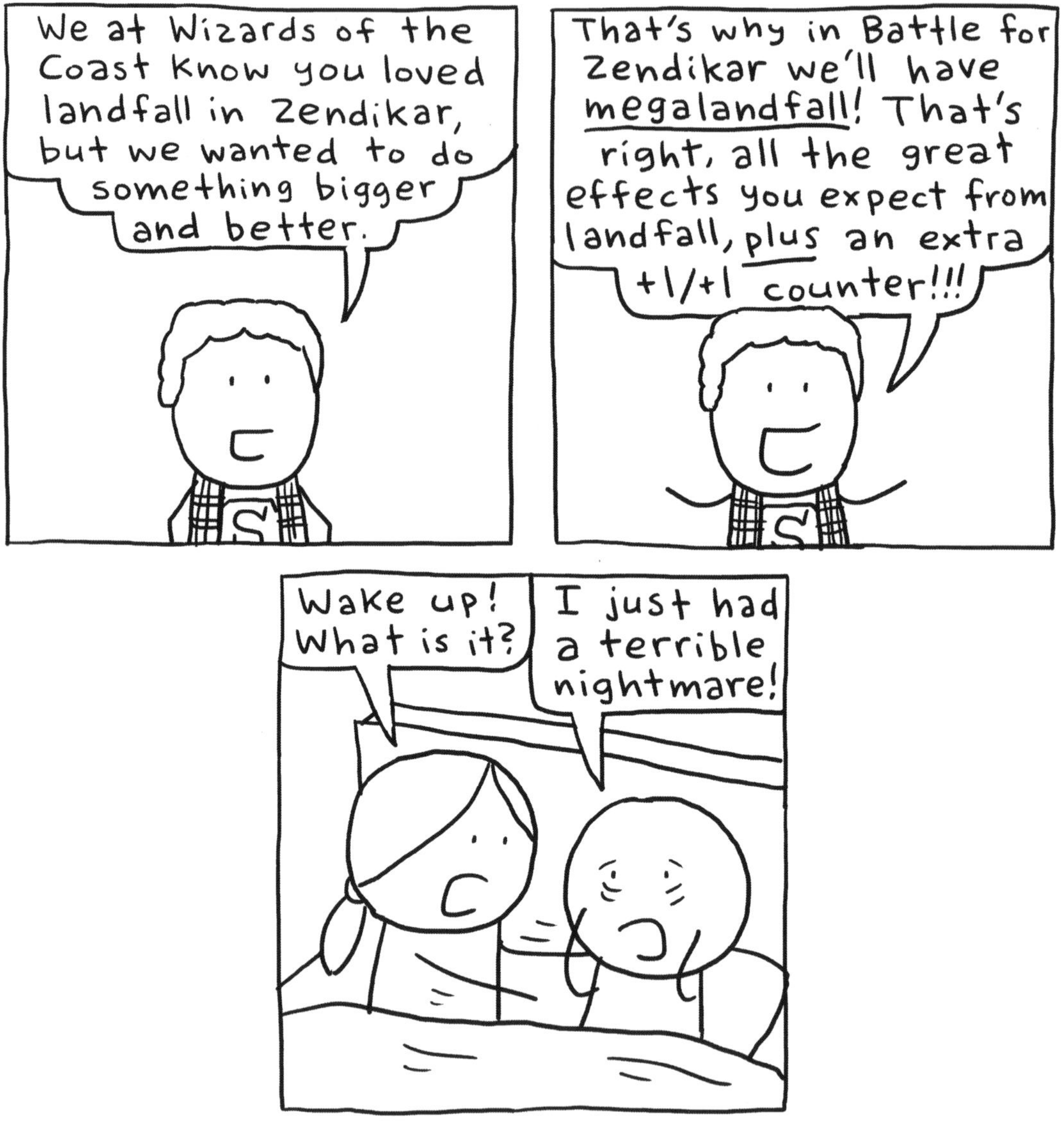
We at Wizards of the Coast know you loved landfall in Zendikar, but we wanted to do something bigger and better.
That's why in Battle for Zendikar we'll have megalandfall! That's right, all the great effects you expect from landfall, plus an extra +1/+1 counter!!!
Wake up! What is it?
I just had a terrible nightmare!

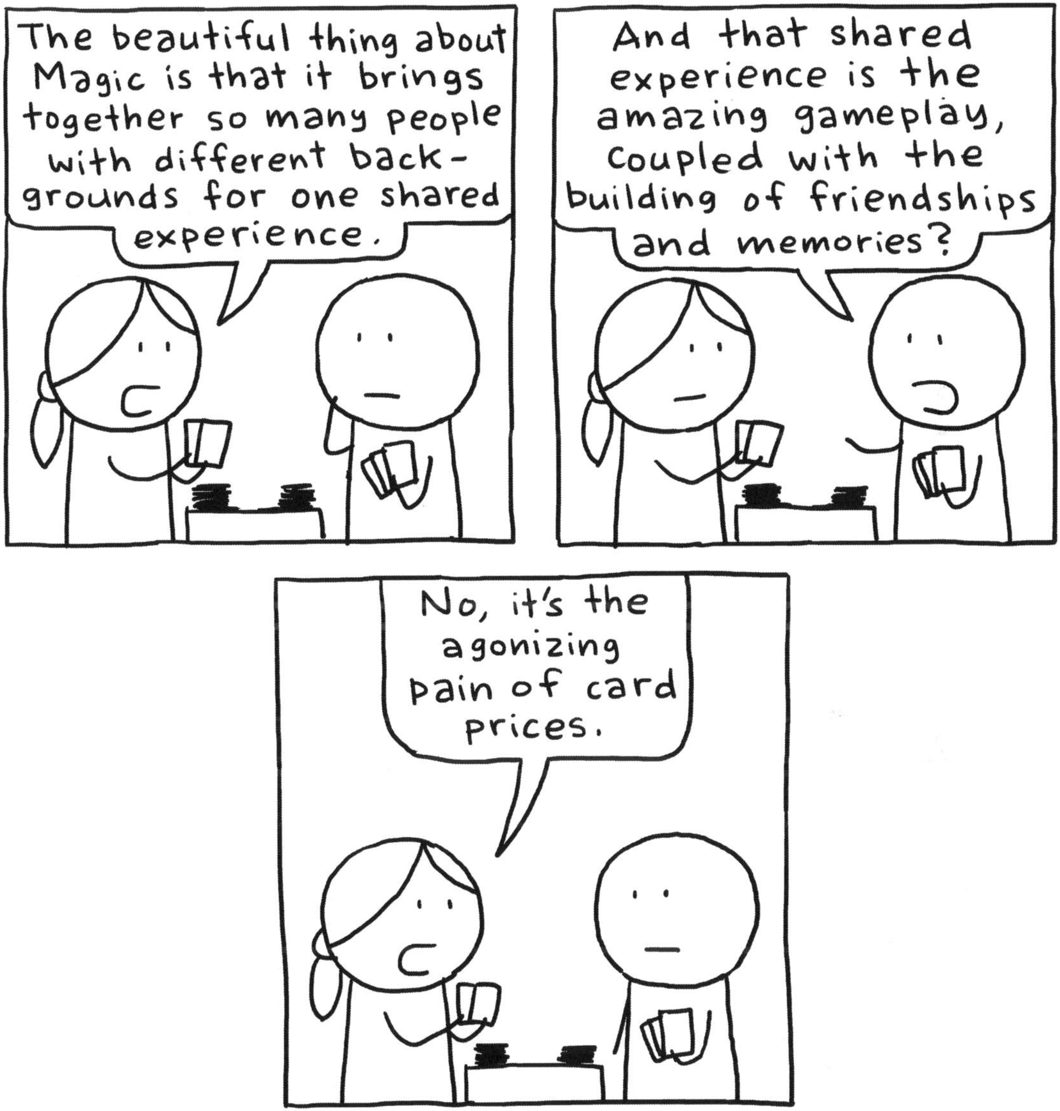
The beautiful thing about Magic is that it brings together so many people with different back-grounds for one shared experience.
And that shared experience is the amazing gameplay, coupled with the building of friendships and memories?
No, it's the agonizing pain of card prices.

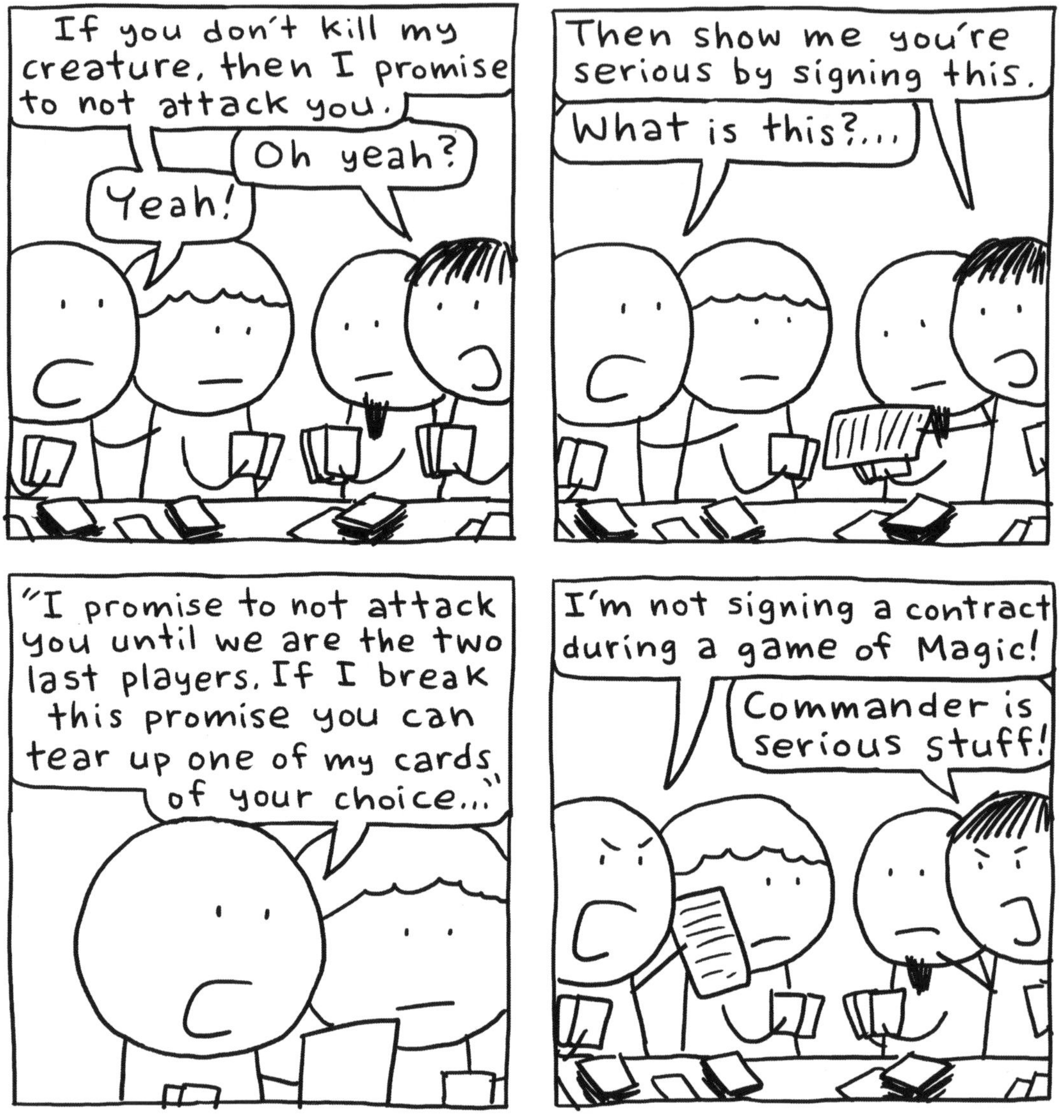
If you don't kill my creature, then I promise to not attack you.
Yeah!
Oh yeah?
Then show me you're serious by signing this.
What is this?...
"I promise to not attack you until we are the two last players. If I break this promise you can tear up one of my cards of your choice..."
I'm not signing a contract during a game of Magic!
Commander is serious stuff!

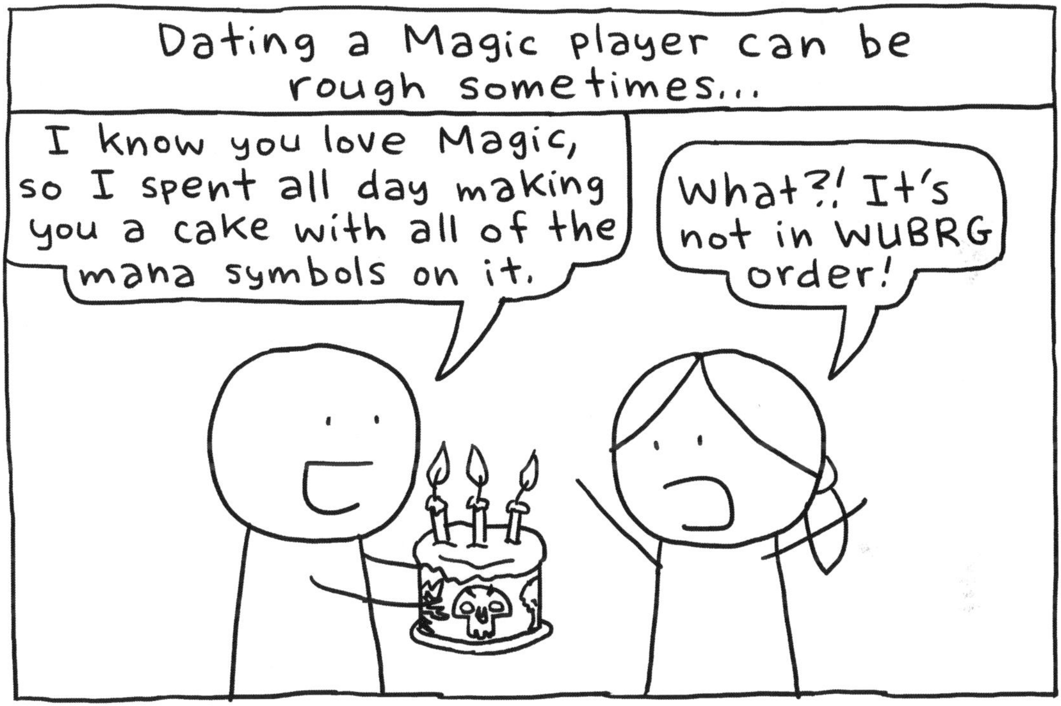
Dating a Magic player can be rough sometimes...
I know you love Magic, so I spent all day making you a cake with all of the mana symbols on it.
What?! It's not in WUBRG order!

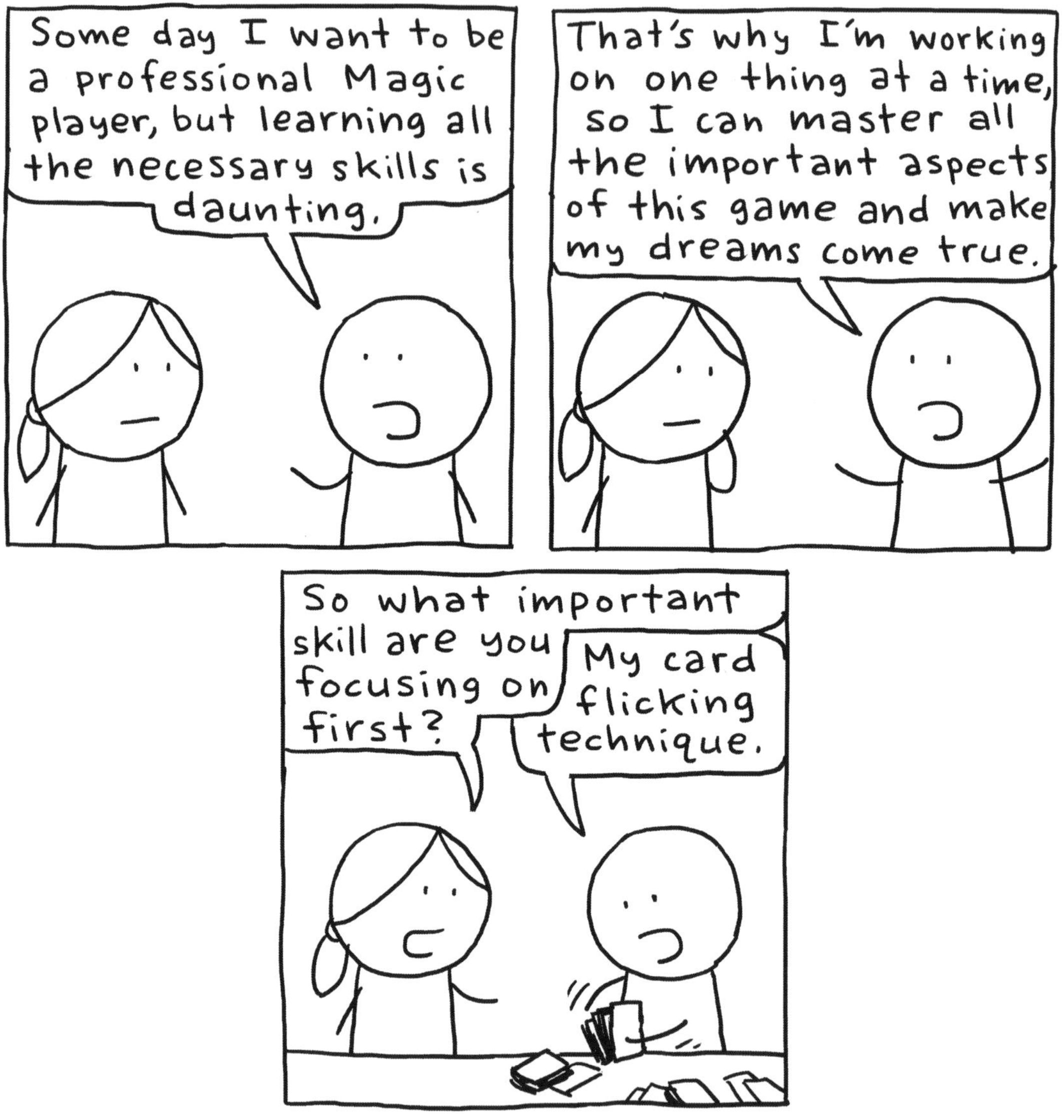
Some day I want to be a professional Magic player, but learning all the necessary skills is daunting.
That's why I'm working on one thing at a time, so I can master all the important aspects of this game and make my dreams come true.
So what important skill are you focusing on first?
My card flicking technique.

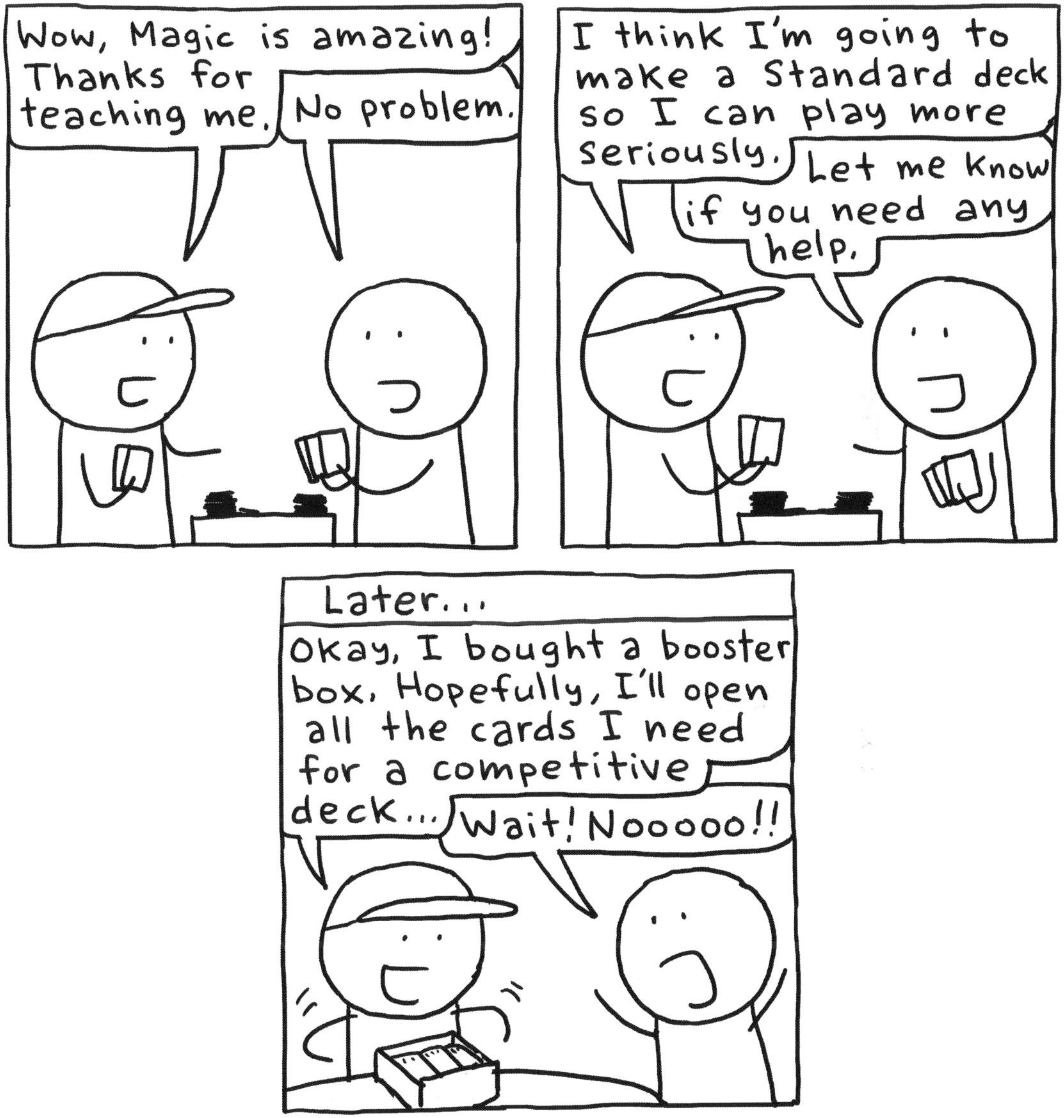
Wow, Magic is amazing! Thanks for teaching me.
No problem.
I think I'm going to make a Standard deck so I can play more seriously.
Let me know if you need any help.
Later...
Okay, I bought a booster box. Hopefully, I'll open all the cards I need for a competitive deck...
Wait! Nooooo!!

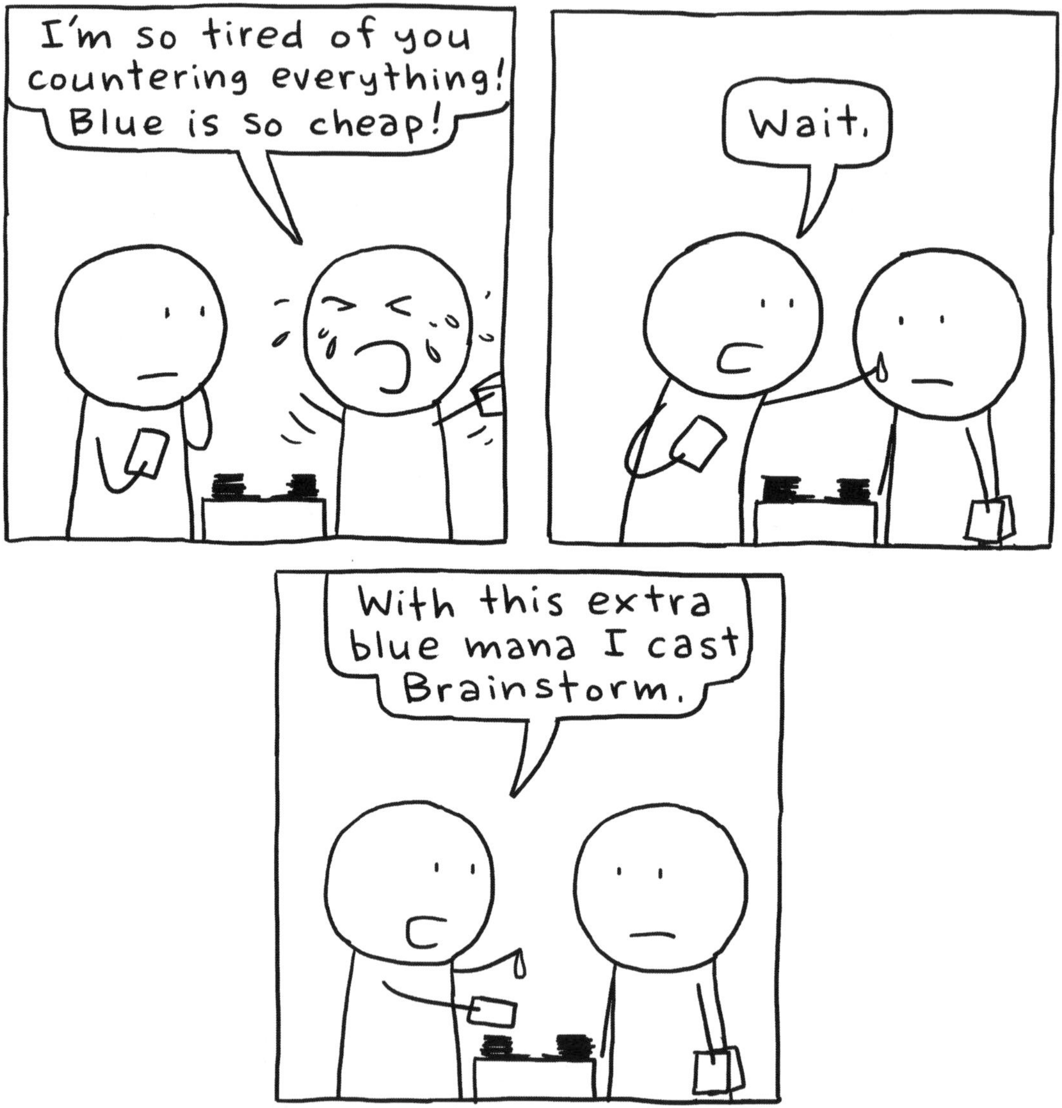
I'm so tired of you countering everything! Blue is so cheap!
Wait.
With this extra blue mana I cast Brainstorm.

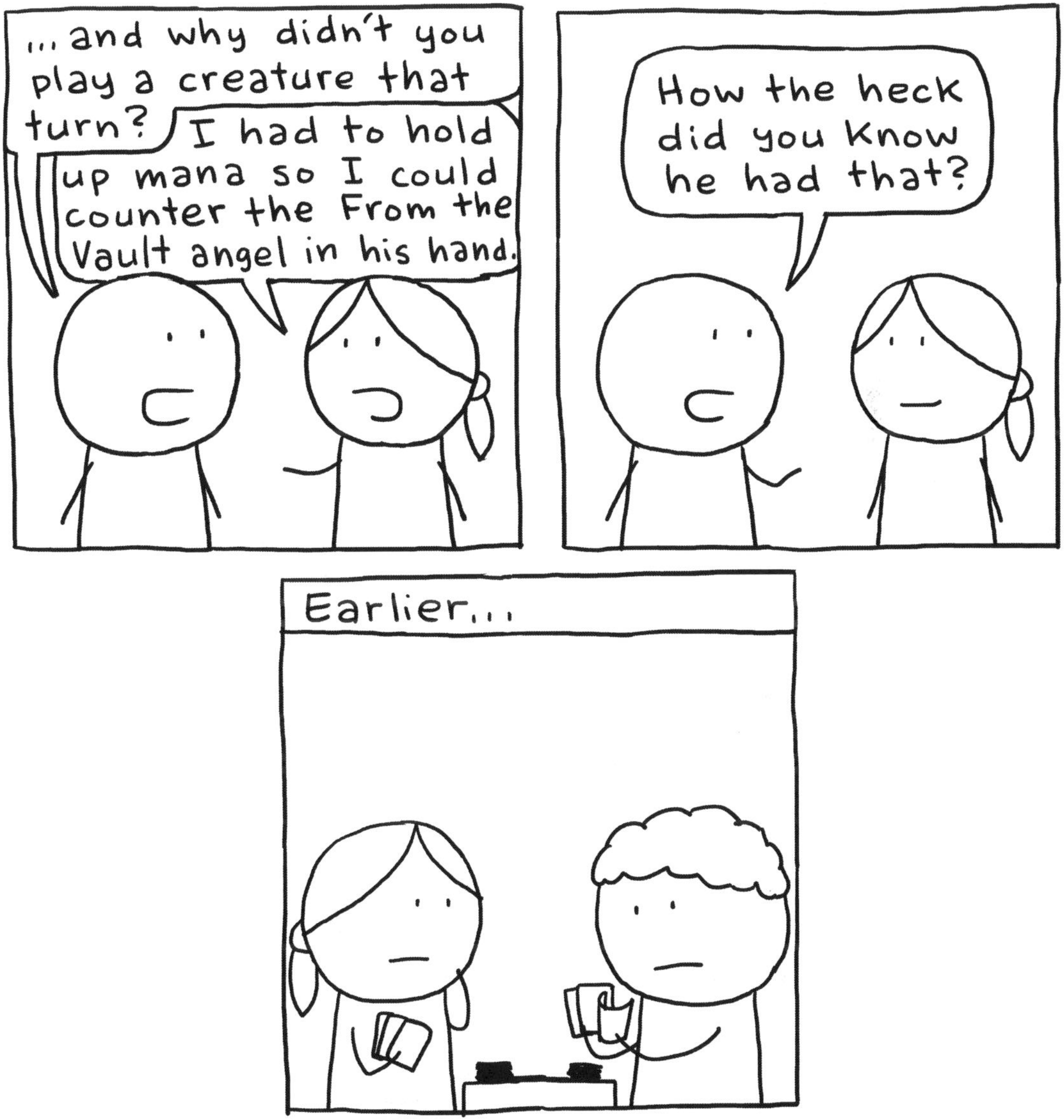
...and why didn't you play a creature that turn?
I had to hold up mana so I could counter the From the Vault angel in his hand.
How the heck did you know he had that?
Earlier...

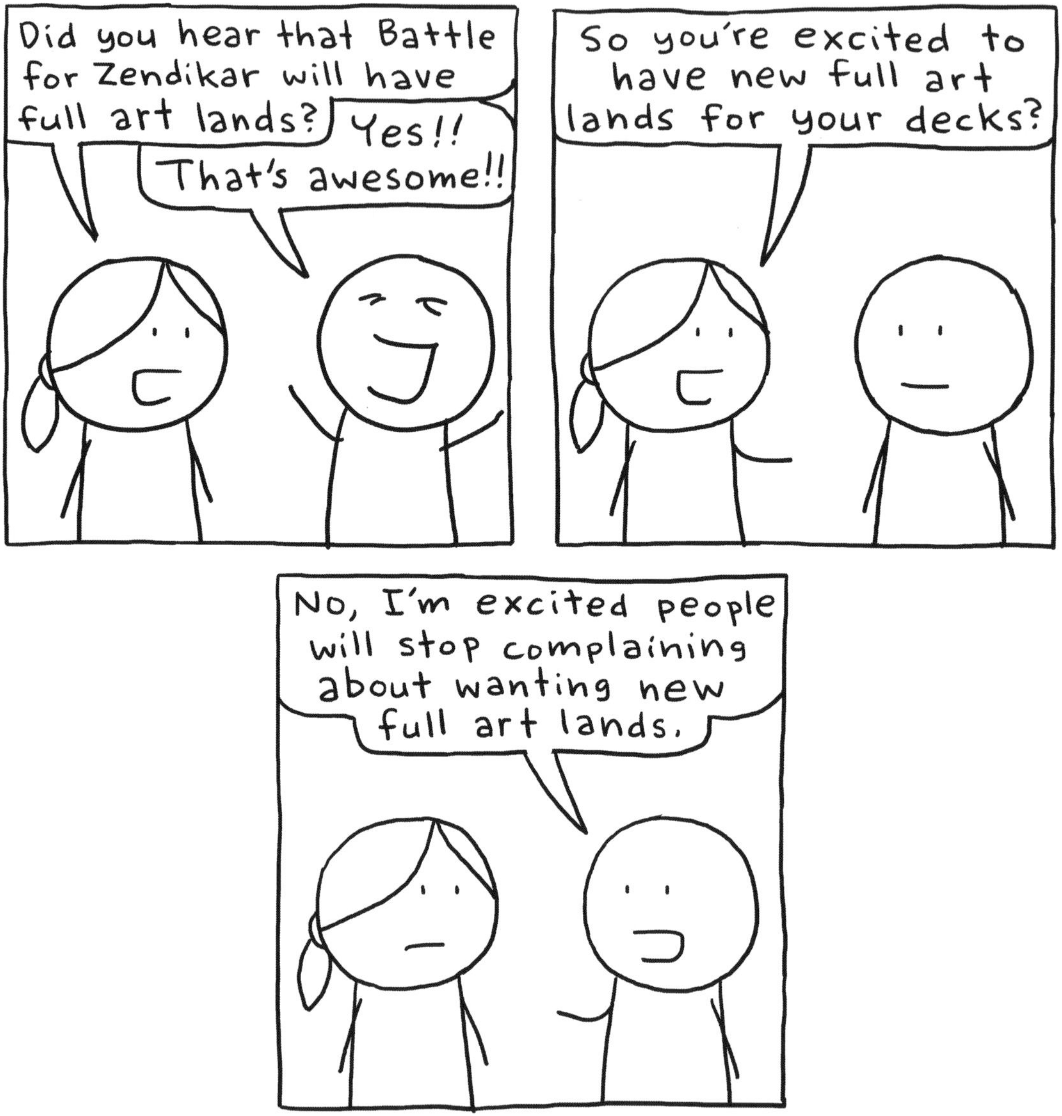
Did you hear that Battle for Zendikar will have full art lands?
Yes!! That's awesome!!
So you're excited to have new full art lands for your decks?
No, I'm excited people will stop complaining about wanting new full art lands.

In 2005...
Want this extra Sol Ring I have?
Why? It's useless in anything but Vintage which I don't even play.
Now...
Please trade me a Sol Ring!!
Don't you have like 20 of them already?
Yeah, but I need to build another Commander deck!!

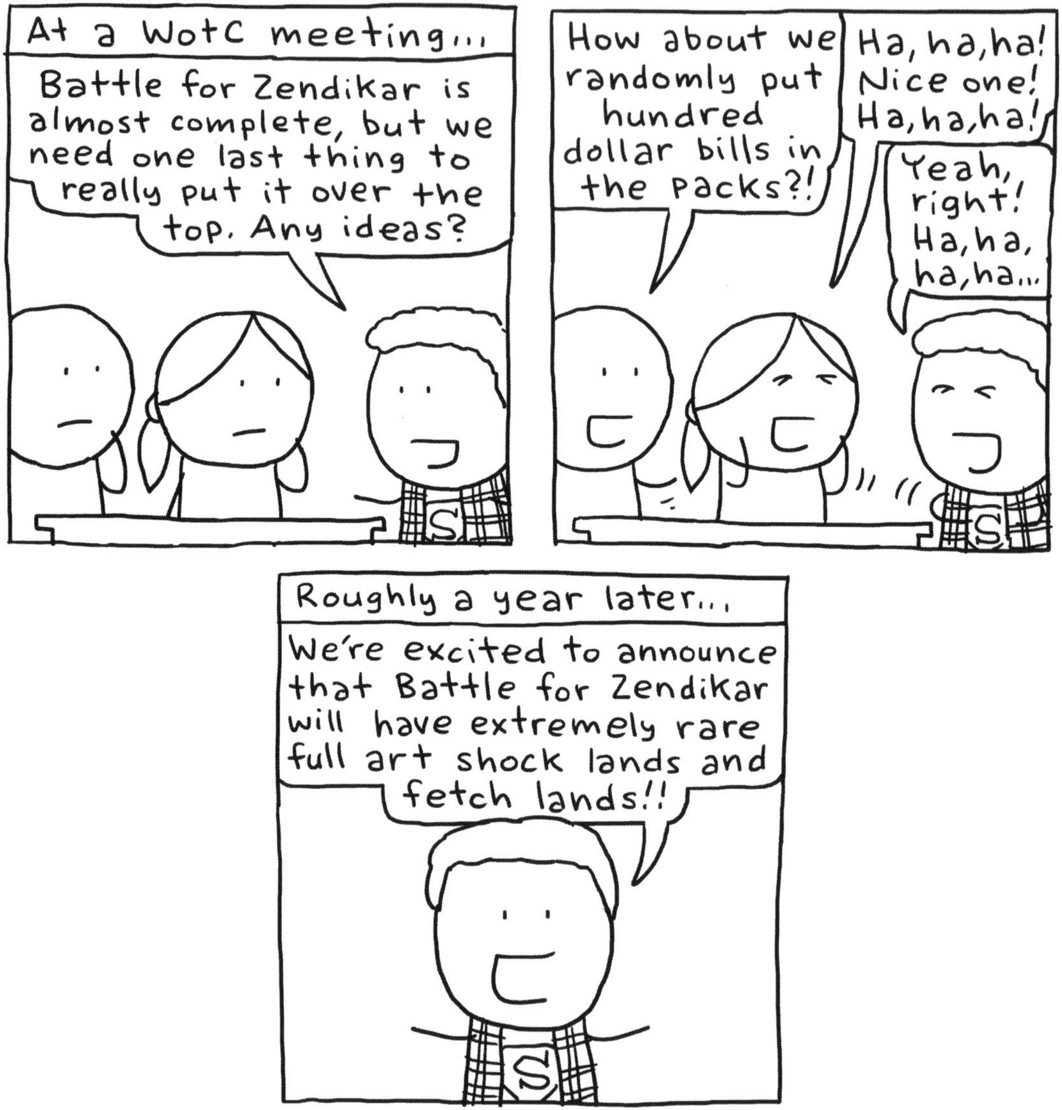
At a WotC meeting...
Battle for Zendikar is almost complete, but we need one last thing to really put it over the top. Any ideas?
How about we randomly put hundred dollar bills in the packs?!
Ha, ha, ha! Nice one! Ha, ha, ha!
Yeah, right! Ha, ha, ha, ha...
Roughly a year later...
We're excited to announce that Battle for Zendikar will have extremely rare full art shock lands and fetch lands!!

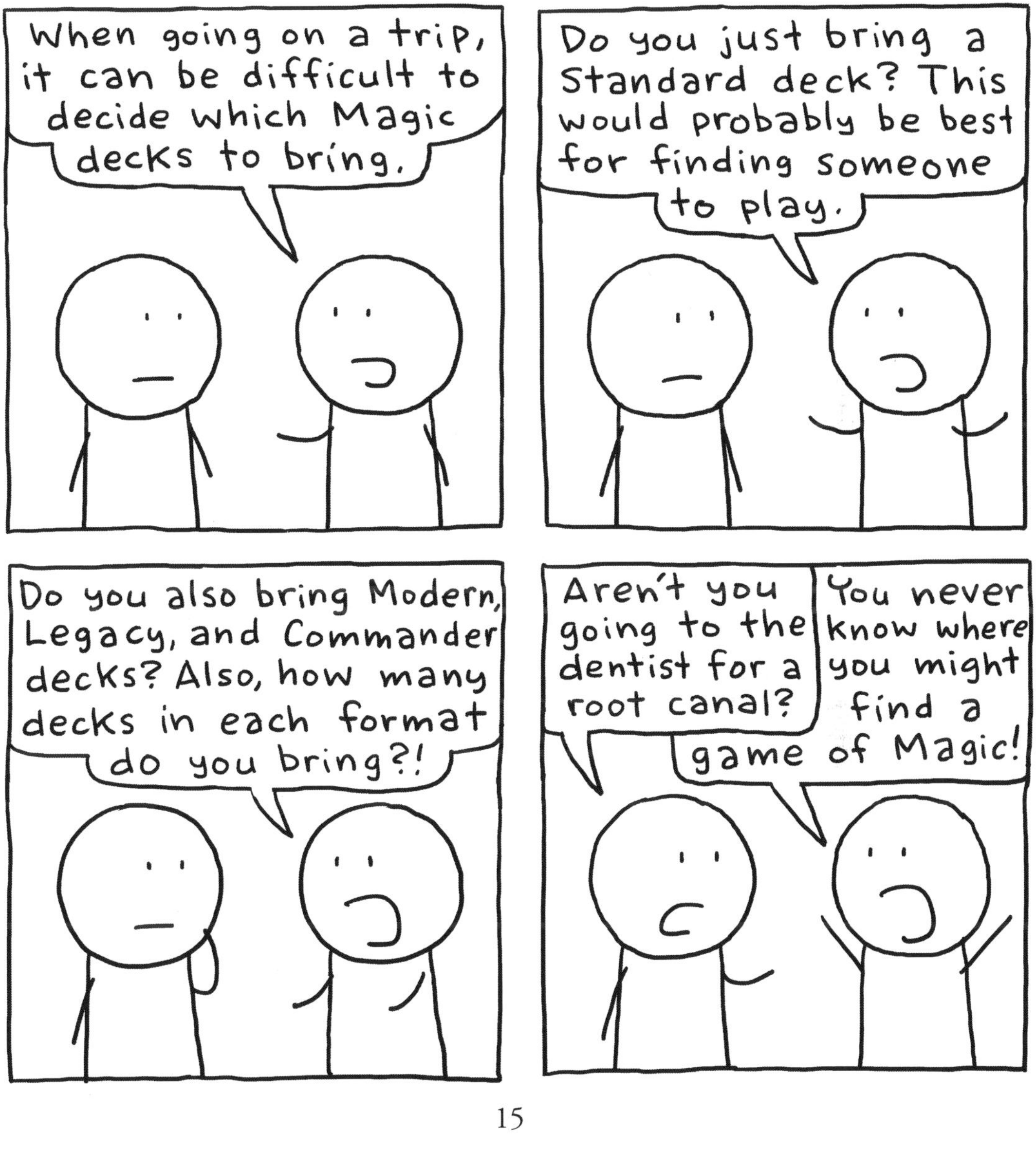
When going on a trip, it can be difficult to decide which Magic decks to bring.
Do you just bring a Standard deck? This would probably be best for finding someone to play.
Do you also bring Modern, Legacy, and Commander decks? Also, how many decks in each format do you bring?!
Aren't you going to the dentist for a root canal?
You never know where you might find a game of Magic!

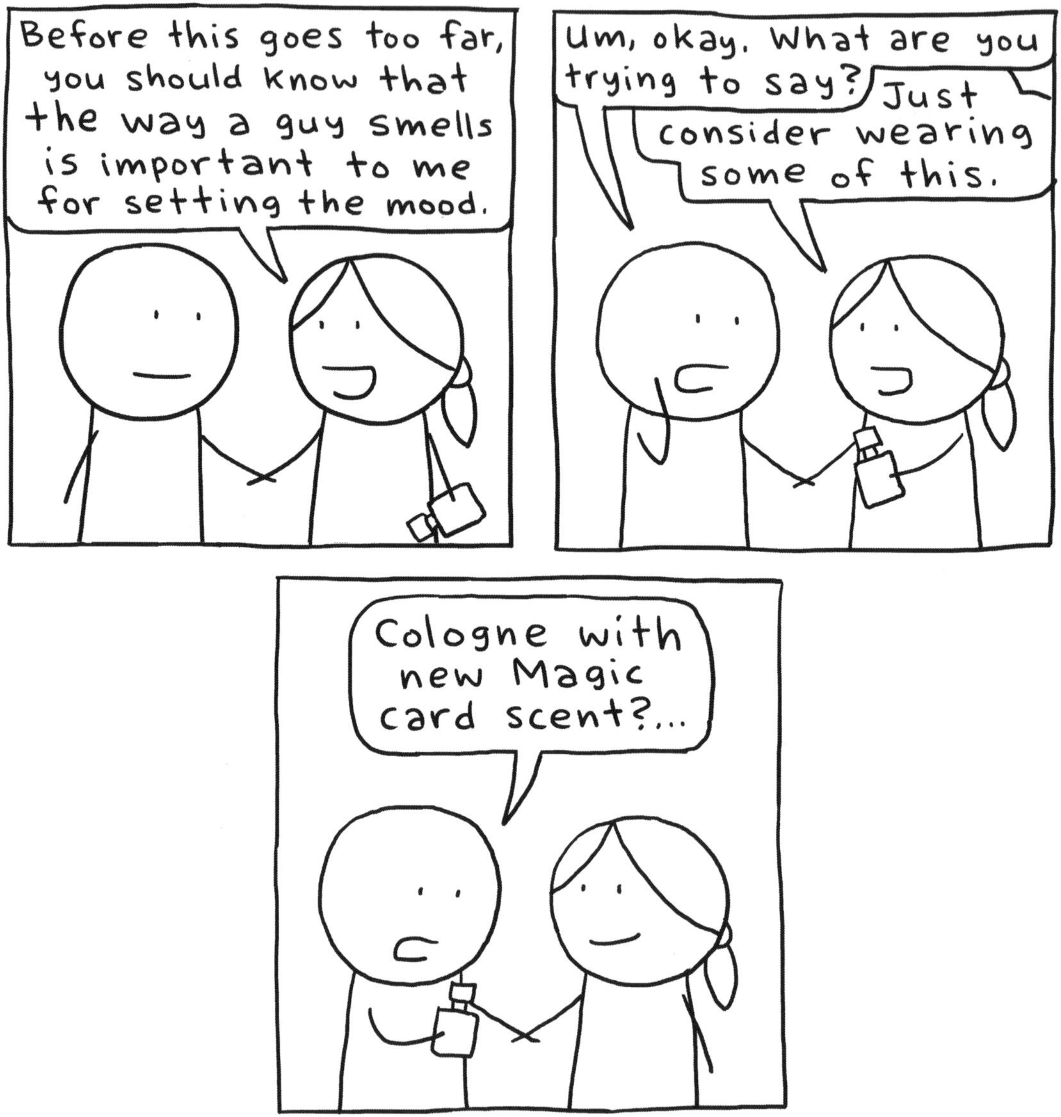
Before this goes too far, you should know that the way a guy smells is important to me for setting the mood.
Um, okay. What are you trying to say?
Just consider wearing some of this.
Cologne with new Magic card scent?...

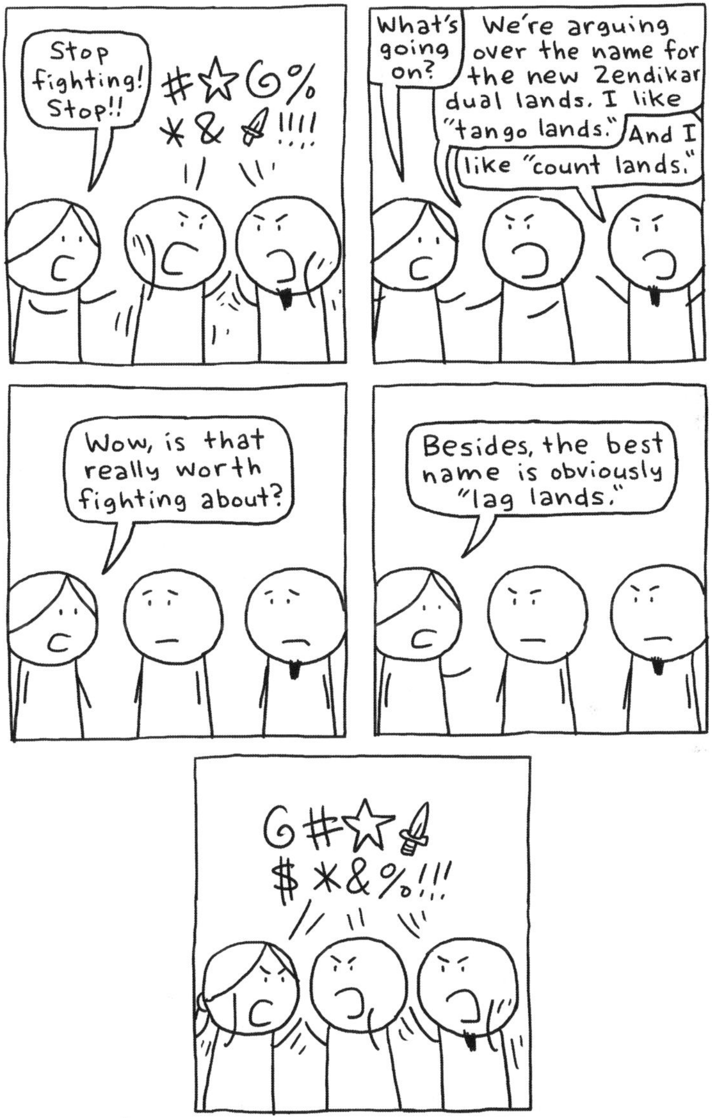
Stop fighting! Stop!!
#☆6%*&!!!!
What's going on?
We're arguing over the name for the new Zendikar dual lands. I like "tango lands."
And I like "count lands."
Wow, is that really worth fighting about?
Besides, the best name is obviously "lag lands."
6#☆$*&%!!!

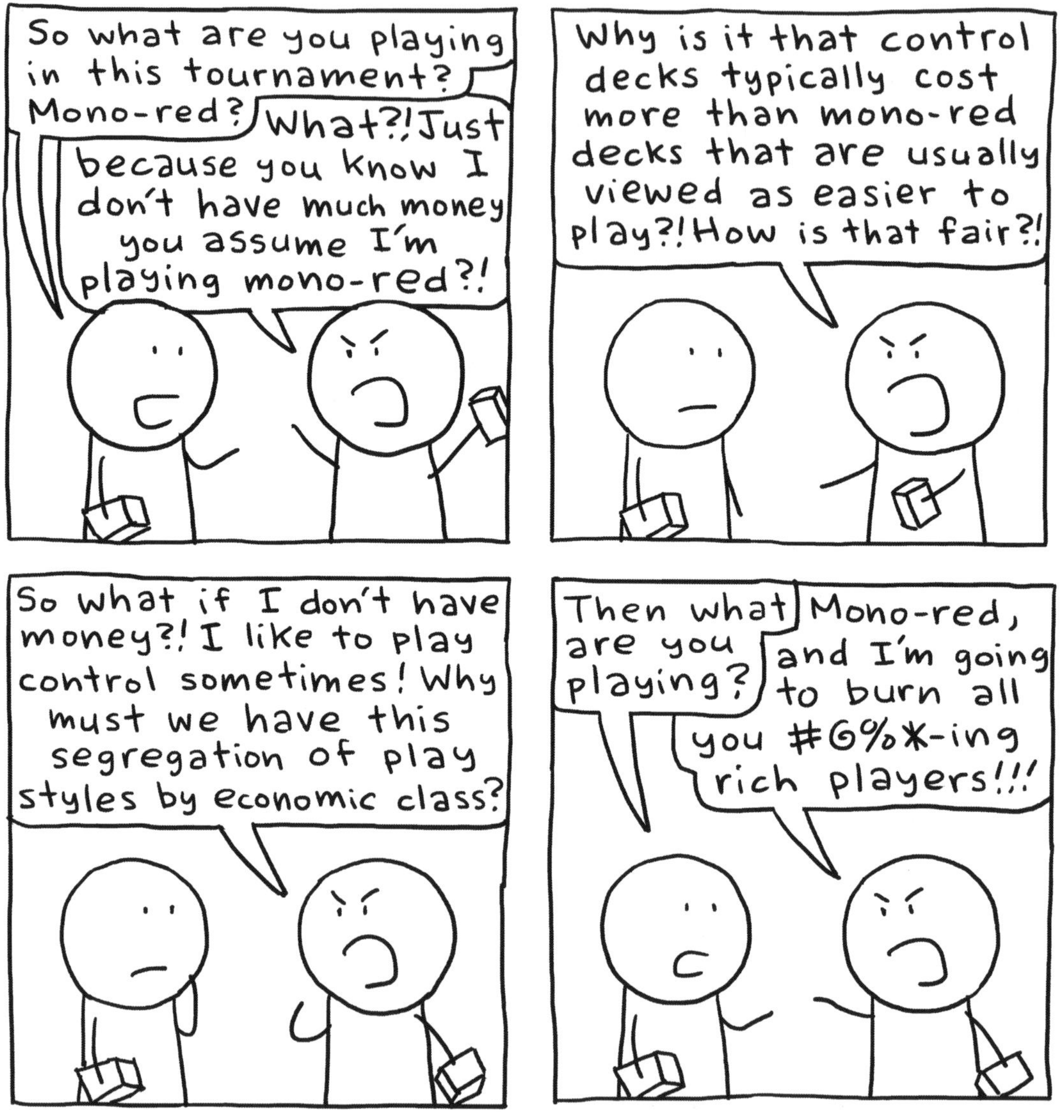
So what are you playing in this tournament? Mono-red?
What?! Just because you know I don't have much money you assume I'm playing mono-red?!
Why is it that control decks typically cost more than mono-red decks that are usually viewed as easier to play?! How is that fair?!
So what if I don't have money?! I like to play control sometimes! Why must we have this segregation of play styles by economic class?
Then what are you playing?
Mono-red, and I'm going to burn all you #@%*-ing rich players!!!

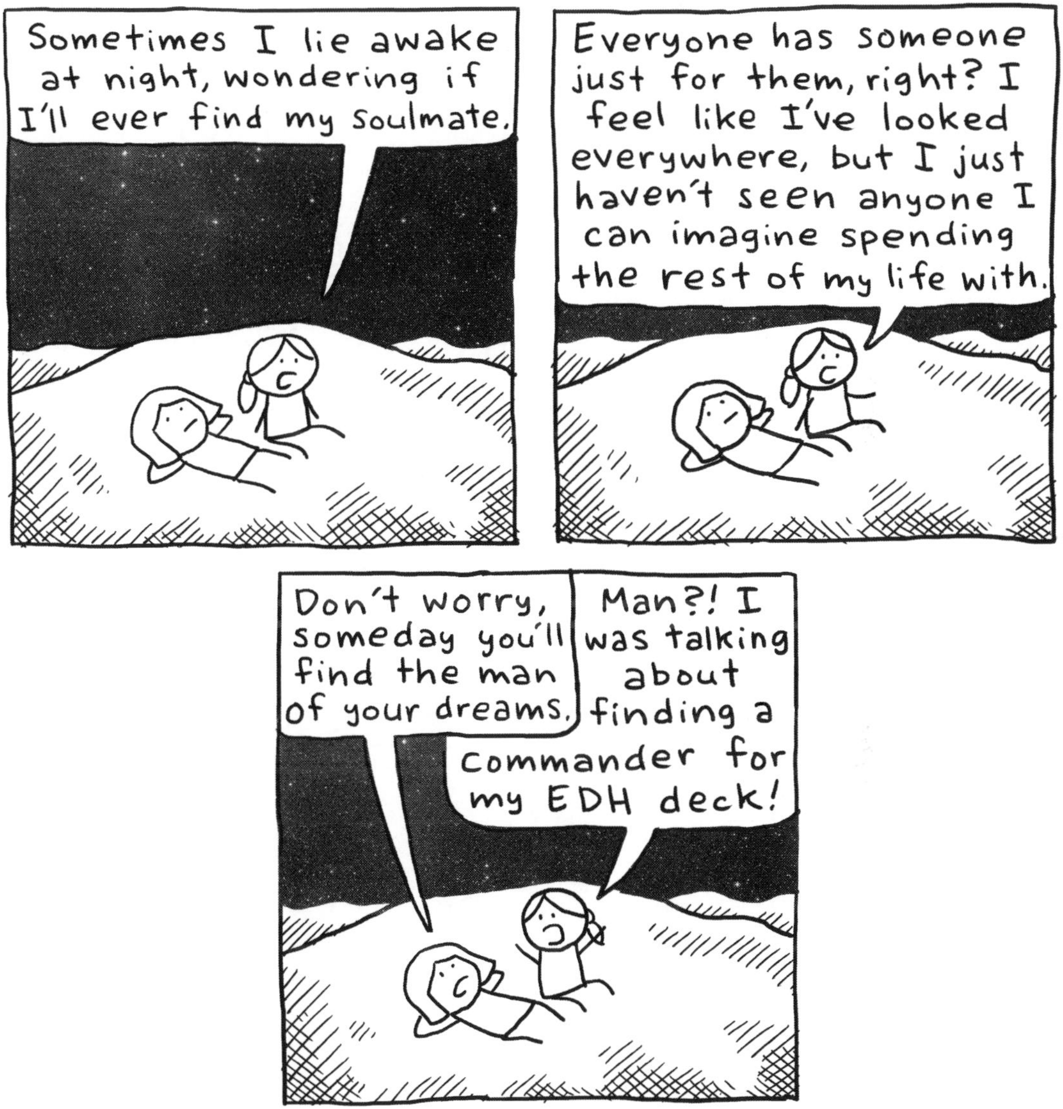

Sometimes I lie awake at night, wondering if I'll ever find my soulmate.
Everyone has someone just for them, right? I feel like I've looked everywhere, but I just haven't seen anyone I can imagine spending the rest of my life with.
Don't worry, someday you'll find the man of your dreams.
Man?! I was talking about finding a commander for my EDH deck!

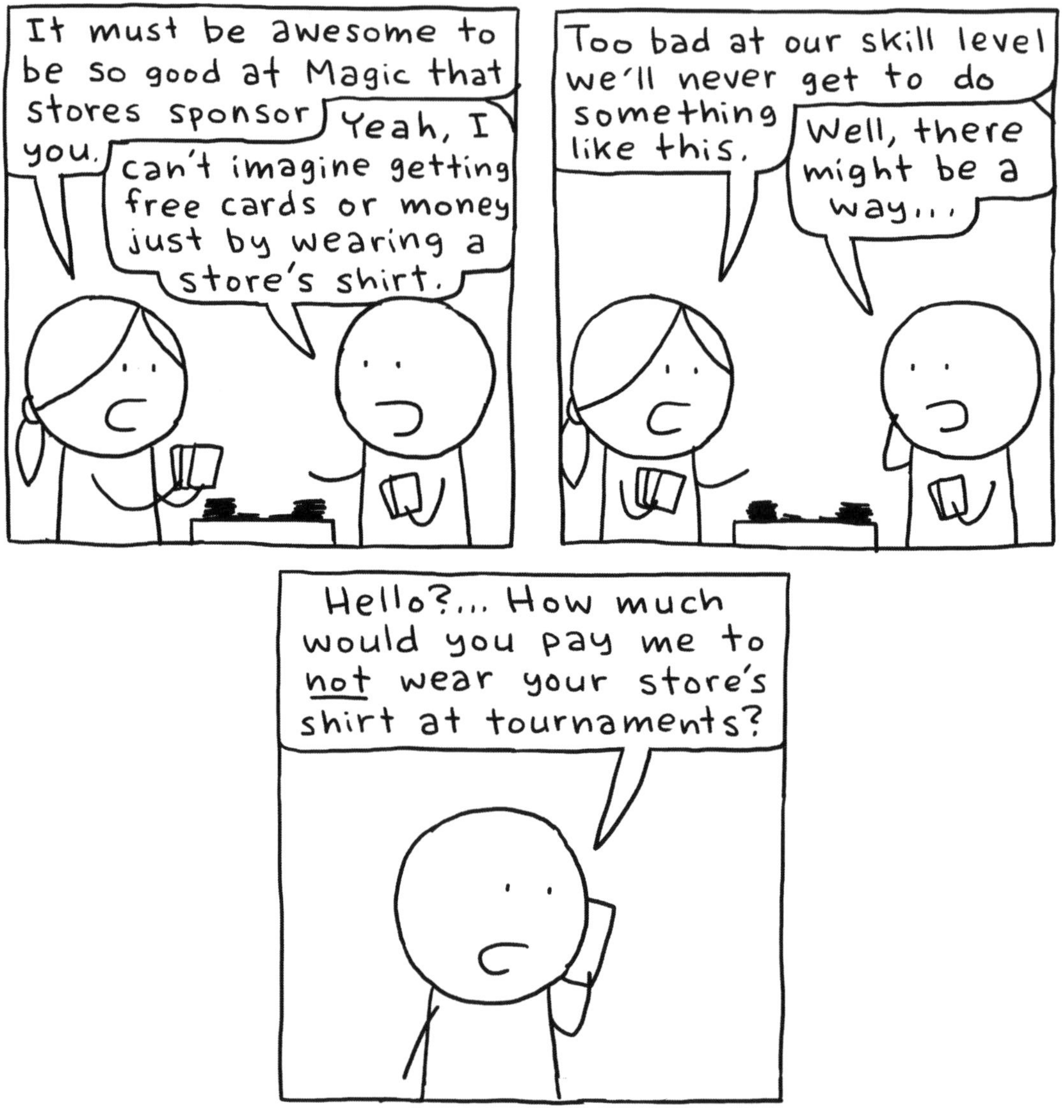
It must be awesome to be so good at Magic that stores sponsor you.
Yeah, I can't imagine getting free cards or money just by wearing a store's shirt.
Too bad at our skill level we'll never get to do something like this.
Well, there might be a way...
Hello?... How much would you pay me to not wear your store's shirt at tournaments?

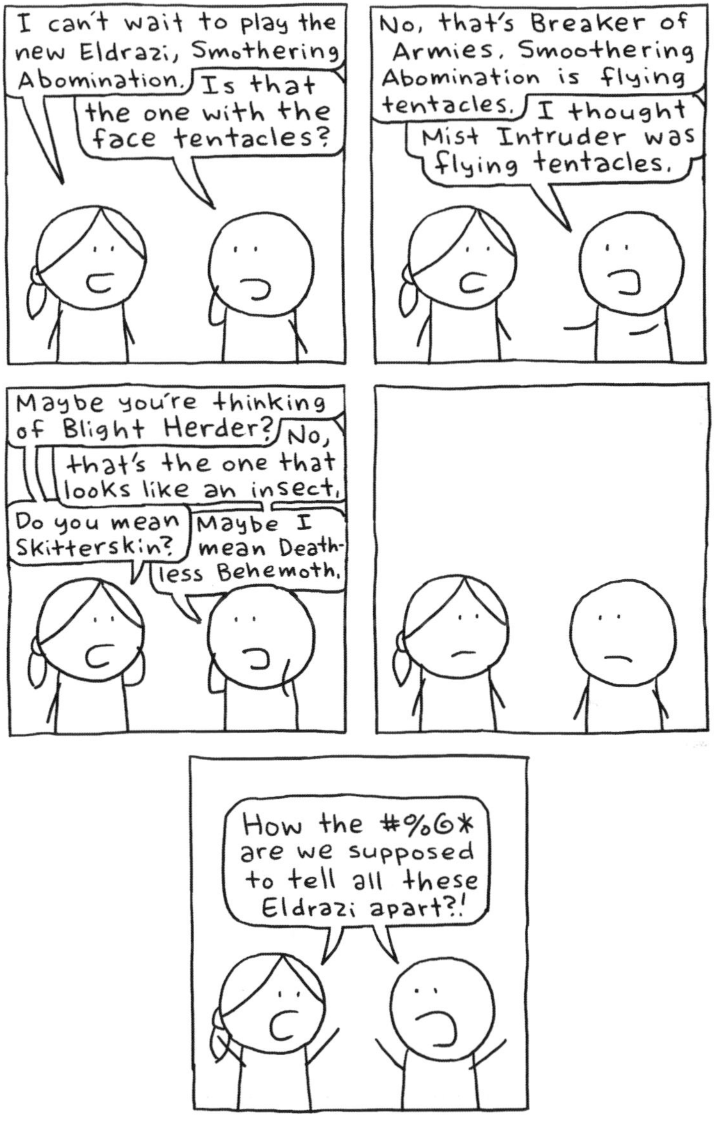
I can't wait to play the new Eldrazi, Smothering Abomination.
Is that the one with the face tentacles?
No, that's Breaker of Armies. Smoothering Abomination is flying tentacles.
I thought Mist Intruder was flying tentacles.
Maybe you're thinking of Blight Herder?
No, that's the one that looks like an insect.
Do you mean Skitterskin?
Maybe I mean Deathless Behemoth.
How the #%@* are we supposed to tell all these Eldrazi apart?!

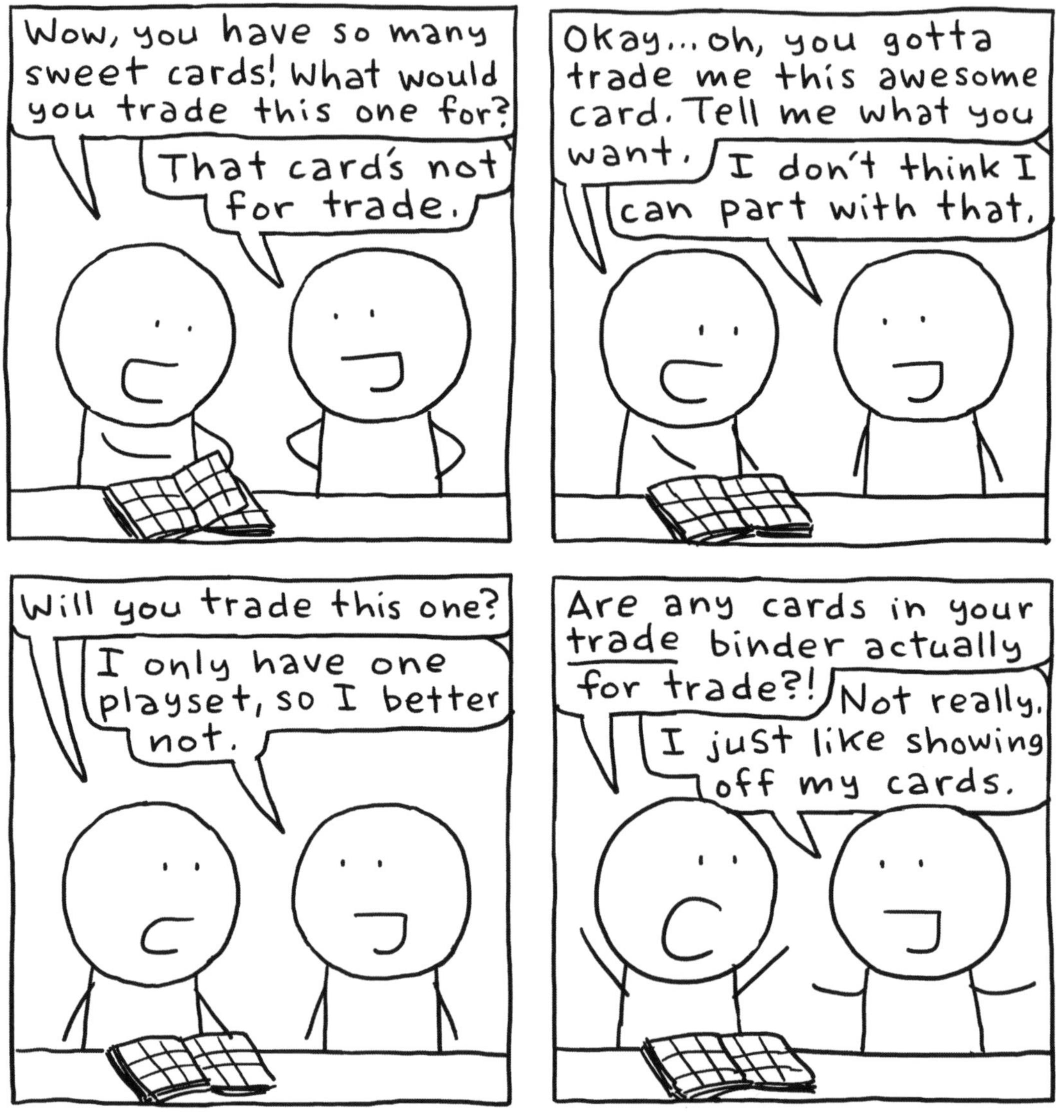
Wow, you have so many sweet cards! What would you trade this one for?
That card's not for trade.
Okay...oh, you gotta trade me this awesome card. Tell me what you want.
I don't think I can part with that.
Will you trade this one?
I only have one playset, so I better not.
Are any cards in your trade binder actually for trade?!
Not really. I just like showing off my cards.

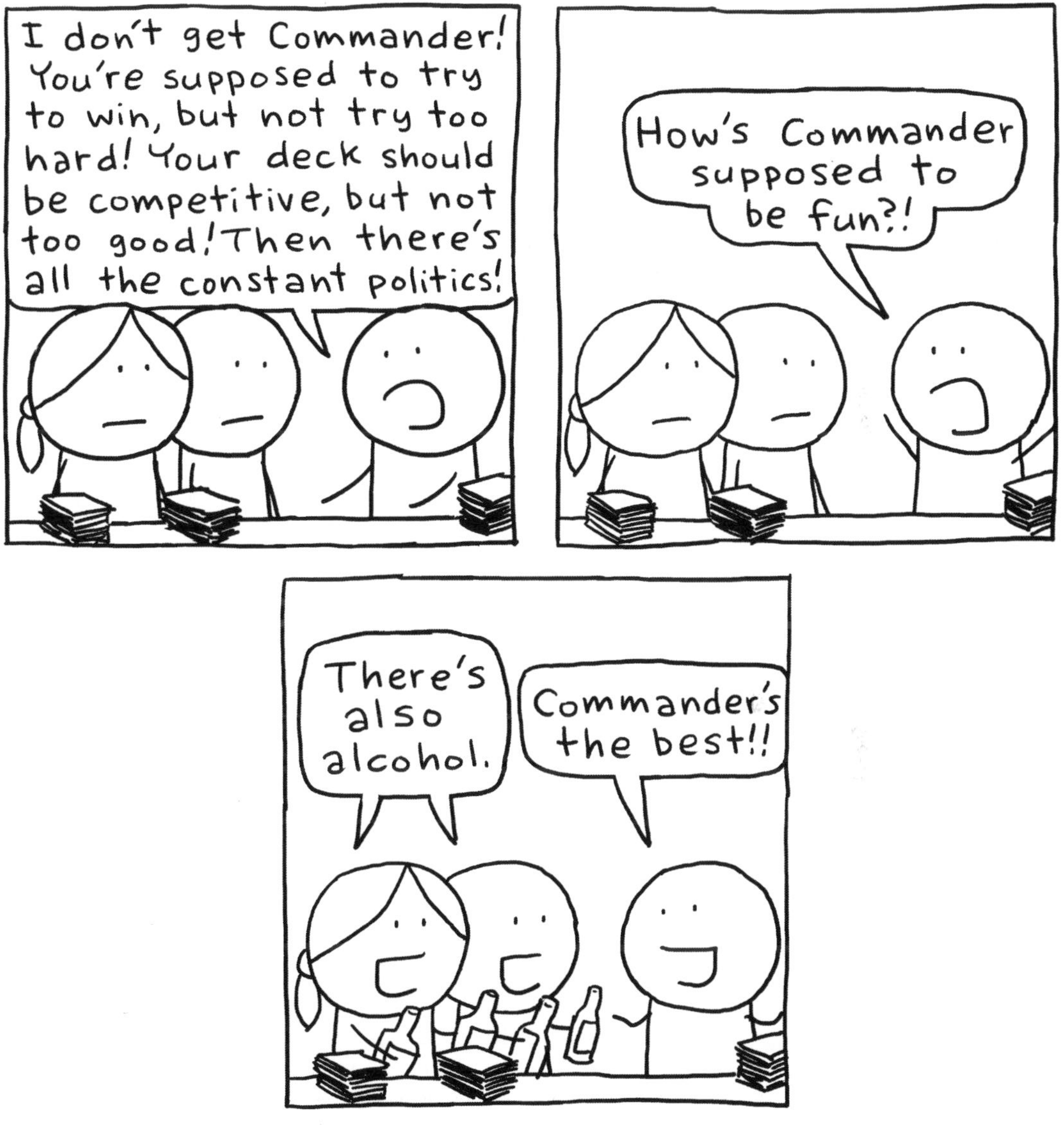
I don't get Commander! You're supposed to try to win, but not try too hard! Your deck should be competitive, but not too good! Then there's all the constant politics!
How's Commander supposed to be fun?!
There's also alcohol.
Commander's the best!!

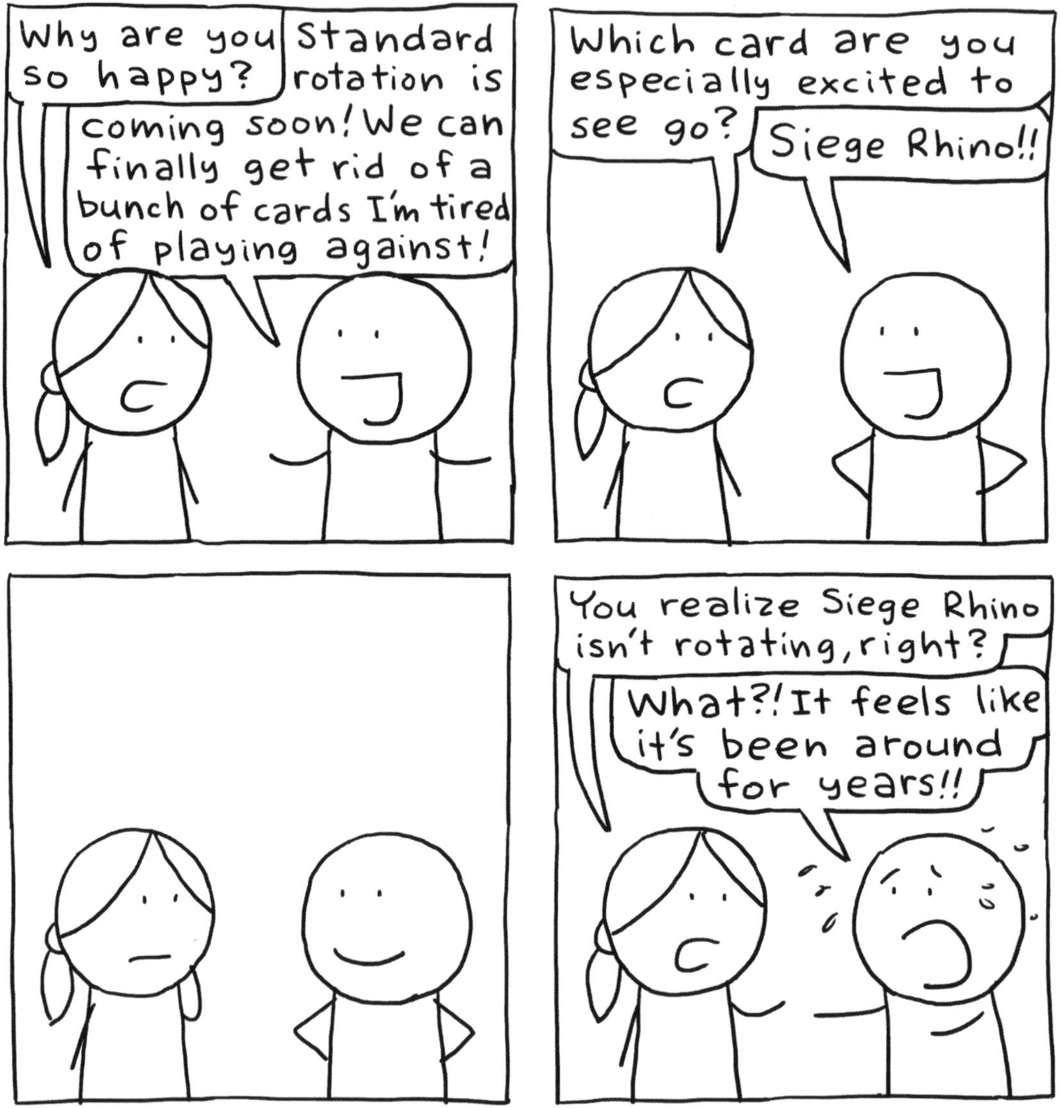

Why are you so happy?
Standard rotation is coming soon! We can finally get rid of a bunch of cards I'm tired of playing against!
Which card are you especially excited to see go?
Siege Rhino!!
You realize Siege Rhino isn't rotating, right?
What?! It feels like it's been around for years!!

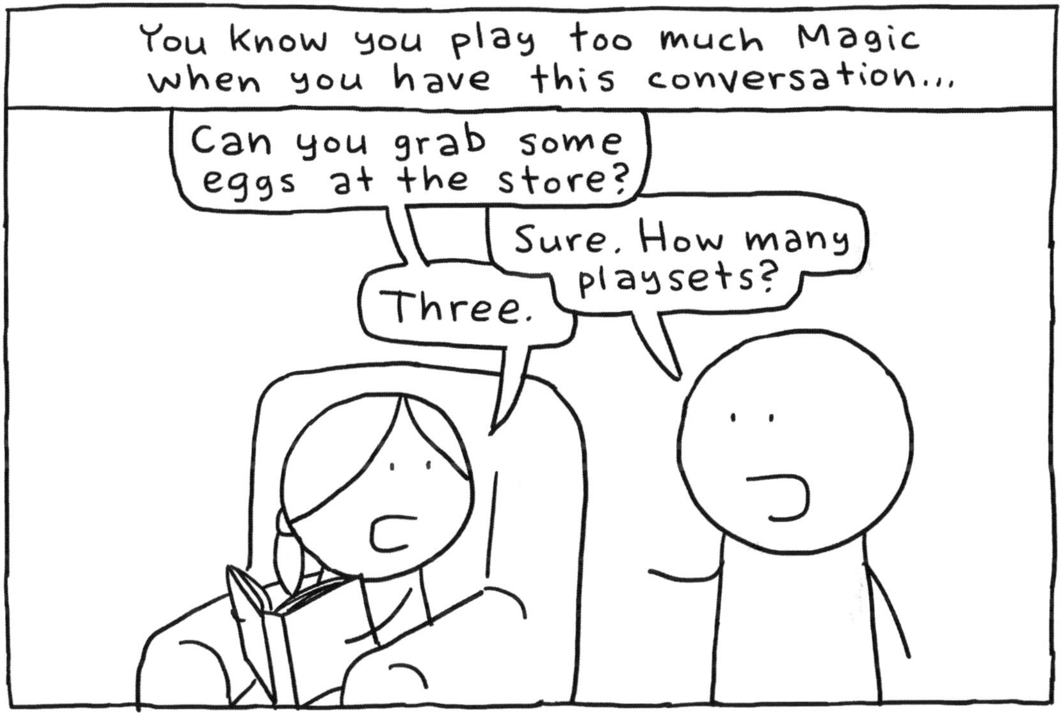
You know you play too much Magic when you have this conversation...
Can you grab some eggs at the store?
Sure. How many playsets?
Three.

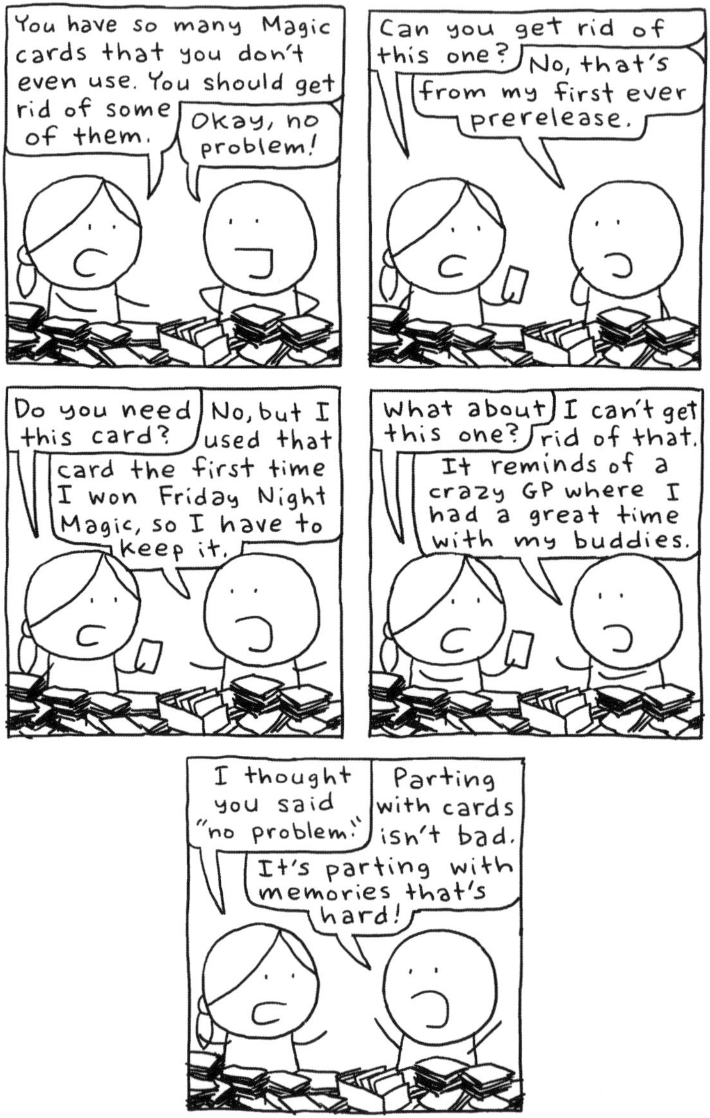
You have so many Magic cards that you don't even use. You should get rid of some of them.
Okay, no problem!
Can you get rid of this one?
No, that's from my first ever prerelease.
Do you need this card?
No, but I used that card the first time I won Friday Night Magic, so I have to keep it.
What about this one?
I can't get rid of that. It reminds of a crazy GP where I had a great time with my buddies.
I thought you said "no problem."
Parting with cards isn't bad.
It's parting with memories that's hard!

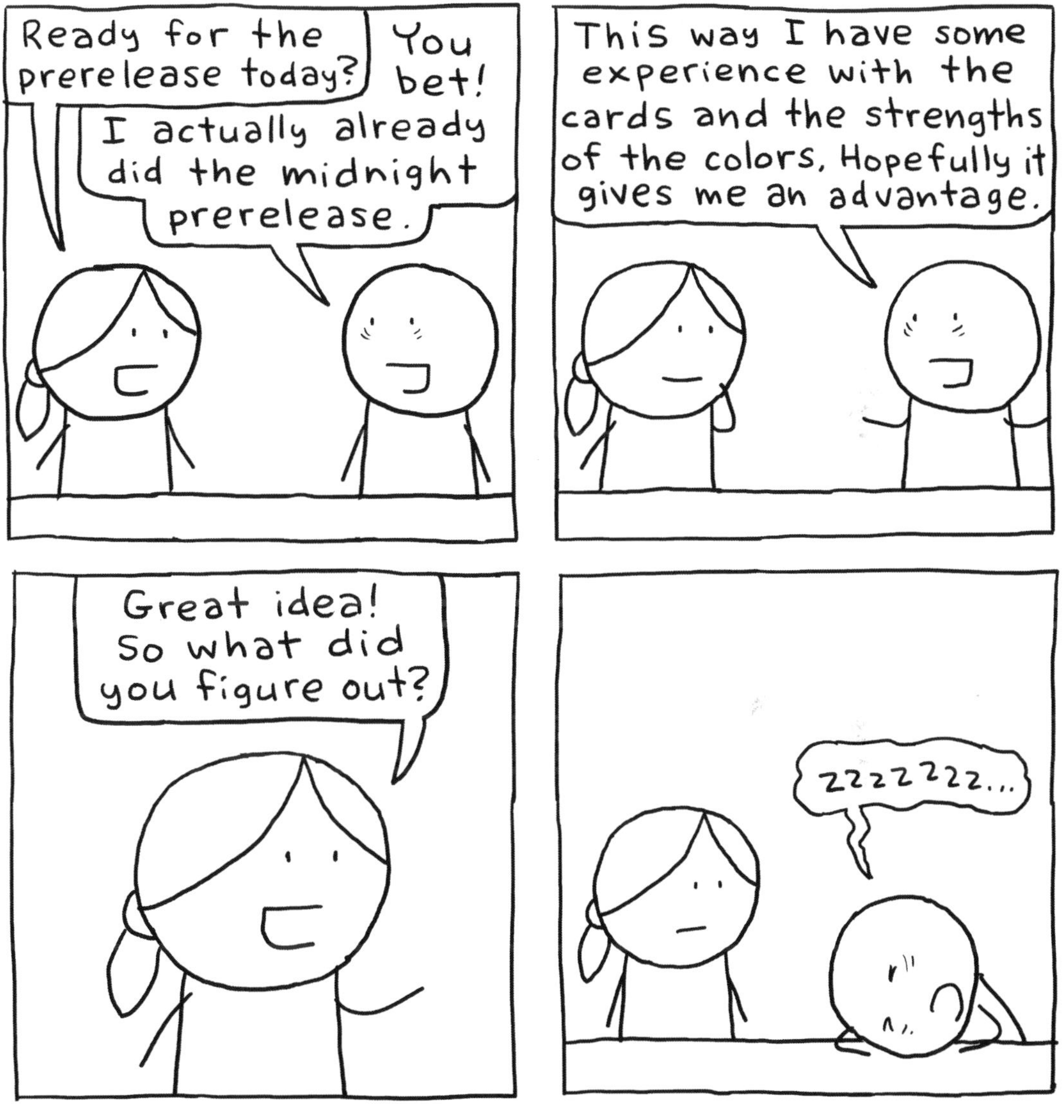
Ready for the prerelease today?
You bet!
I actually already did the midnight prerelease.
This way I have some experience with the cards and the strengths of the colors. Hopefully it gives me an advantage.
Great idea! So what did you figure out?
zzzzzzz...

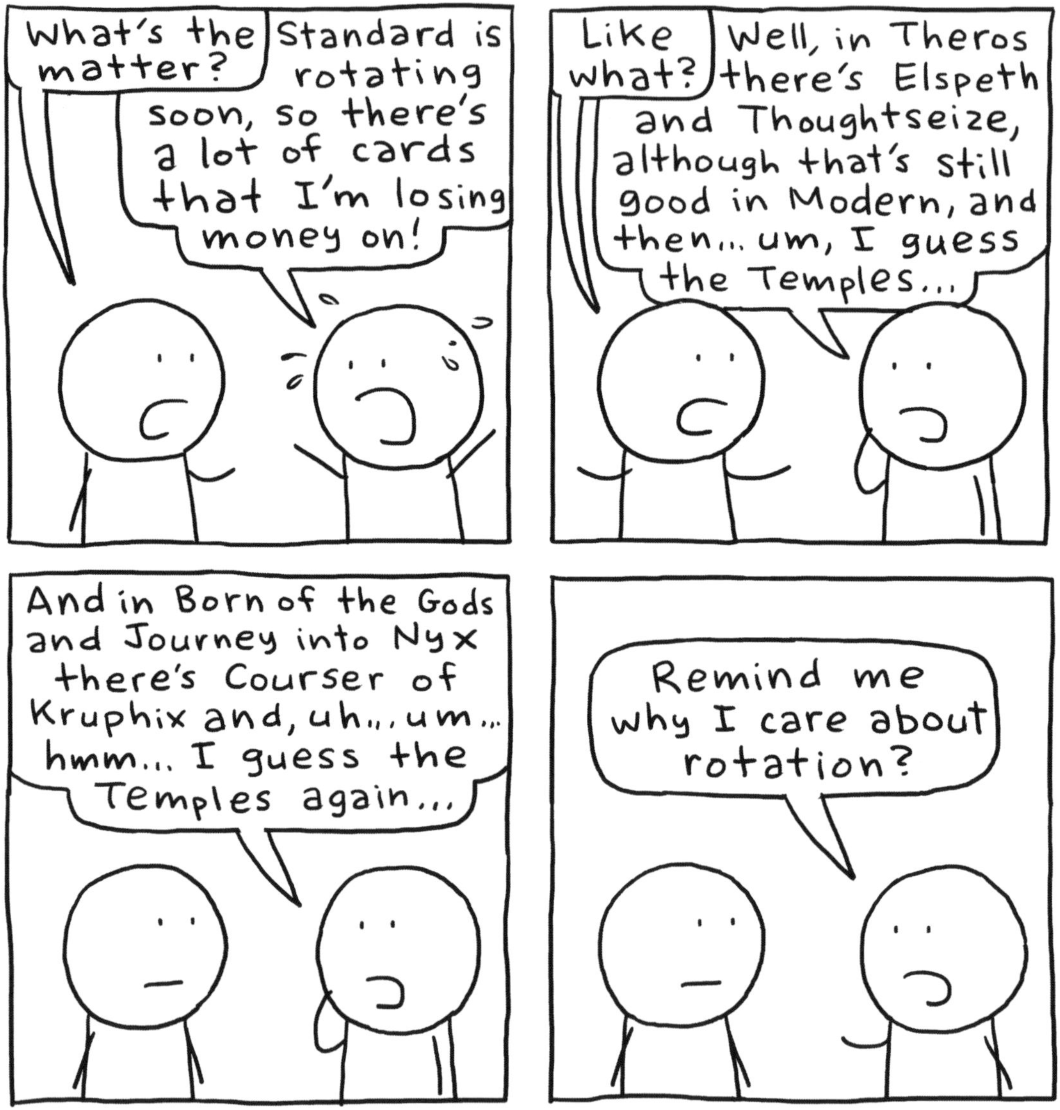
What's the matter?
Standard is rotating soon, so there's a lot of cards that I'm losing money on!
Like what?
Well, in Theros there's Elspeth and Thoughtseize, although that's still good in Modern, and then... um, I guess the Temples...
And in Born of the Gods and Journey into Nyx there's Courser of Kruphix and, uh... um... hmm... I guess the Temples again...
Remind me why I care about rotation?

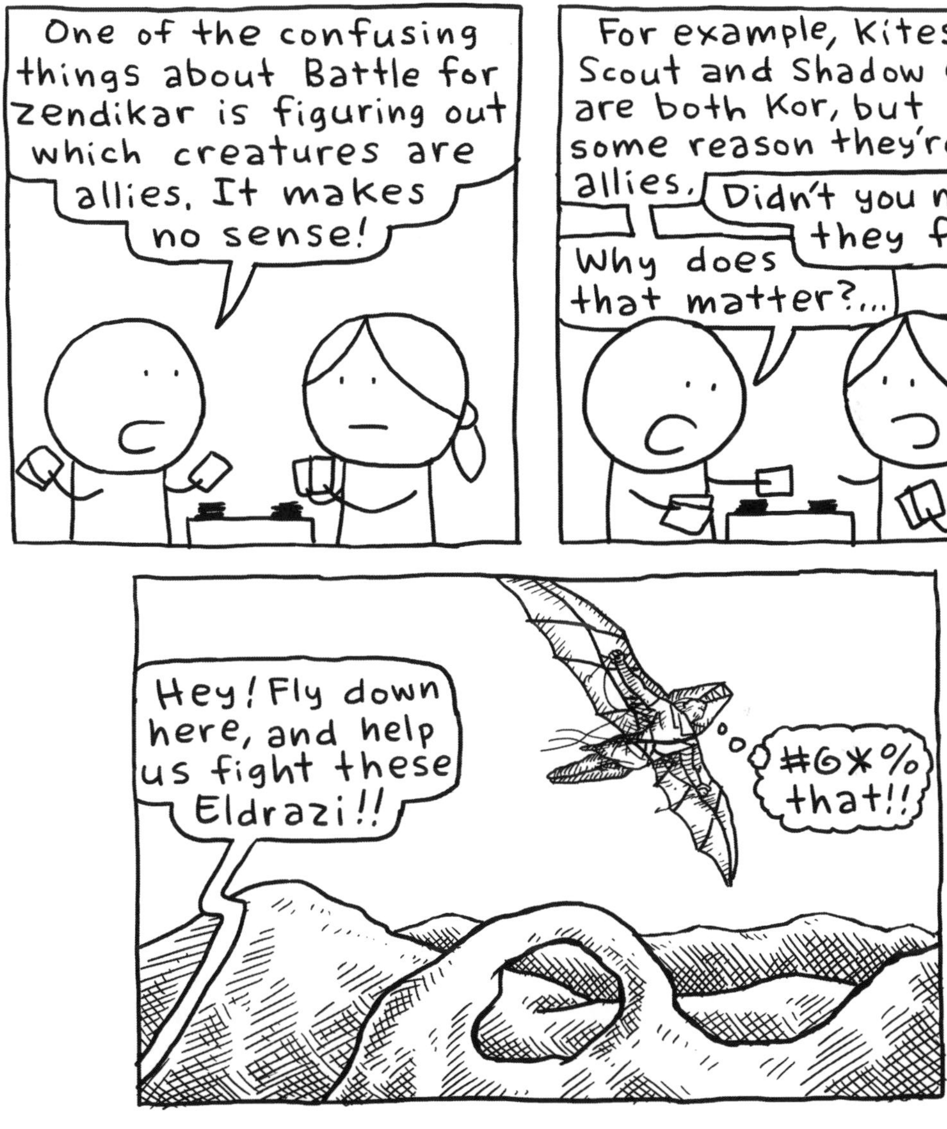
One of the confusing things about Battle for Zendikar is figuring out which creatures are allies. It makes no sense!
For example, Kitesail Scout and Shadow Glider are both Kor, but for some reason they're not allies.
Didn't you notice they fly?
Why does that matter?...
Hey! Fly down here, and help us fight these Eldrazi!!
#G*% that!!

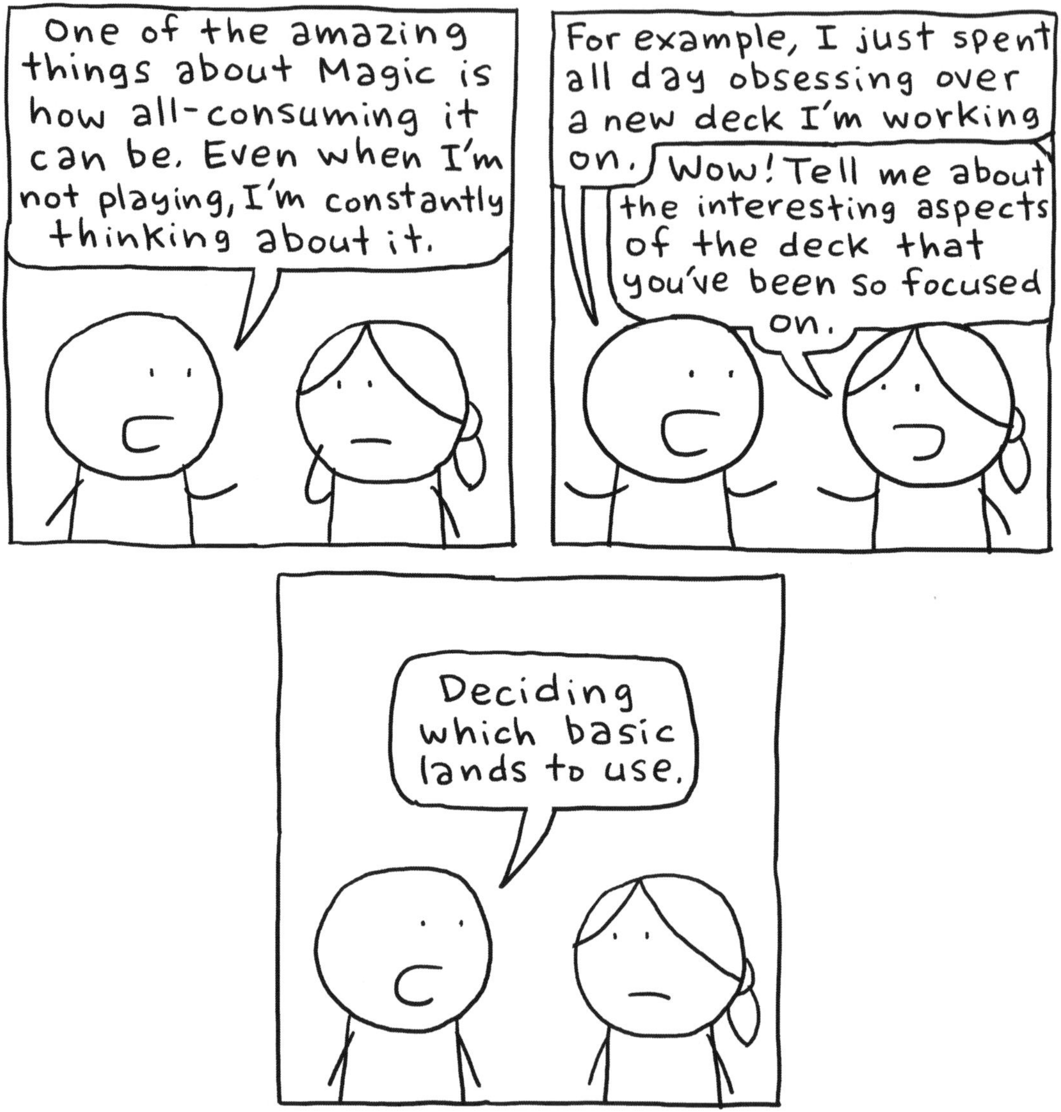
One of the amazing things about Magic is how all-consuming it can be. Even when I'm not playing, I'm constantly thinking about it.
For example, I just spent all day obsessing over a new deck I'm working on.
Wow! Tell me about the interesting aspects of the deck that you've been so focused on.
Deciding which basic lands to use.

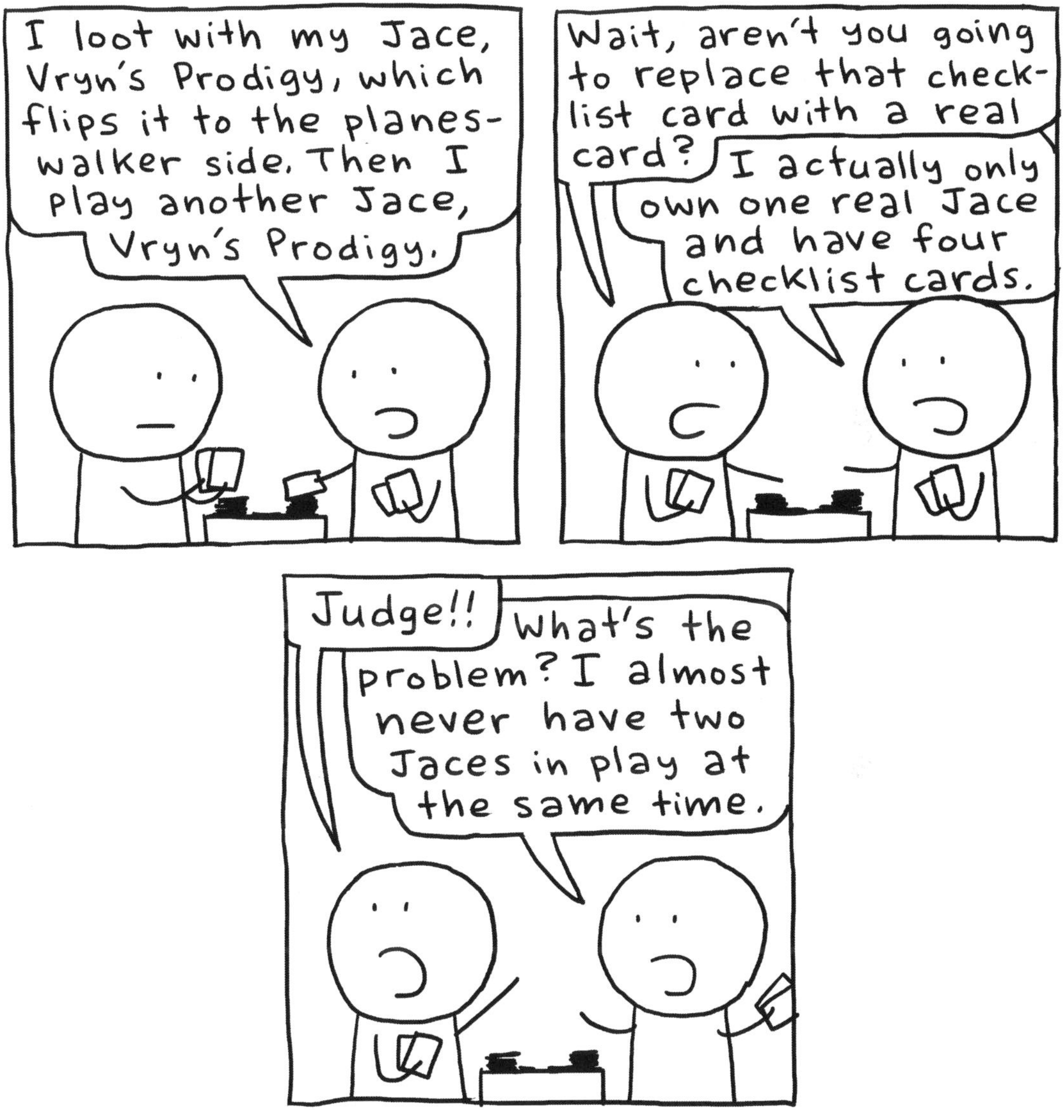
I loot with my Jace, Vryn's Prodigy, which flips it to the planes-walker side. Then I play another Jace, Vryn's Prodigy.
Wait, aren't you going to replace that check-list card with a real card?
I actually only own one real Jace and have four checklist cards.
Judge!!
What's the problem? I almost never have two Jaces in play at the same time.

Before...
Zendikar was such a great time for Magic. I can't wait to go back!
Now...
Well, we have an insanely priced Jace in Standard just like last time we were in Zendikar.
This isn't what I meant!!

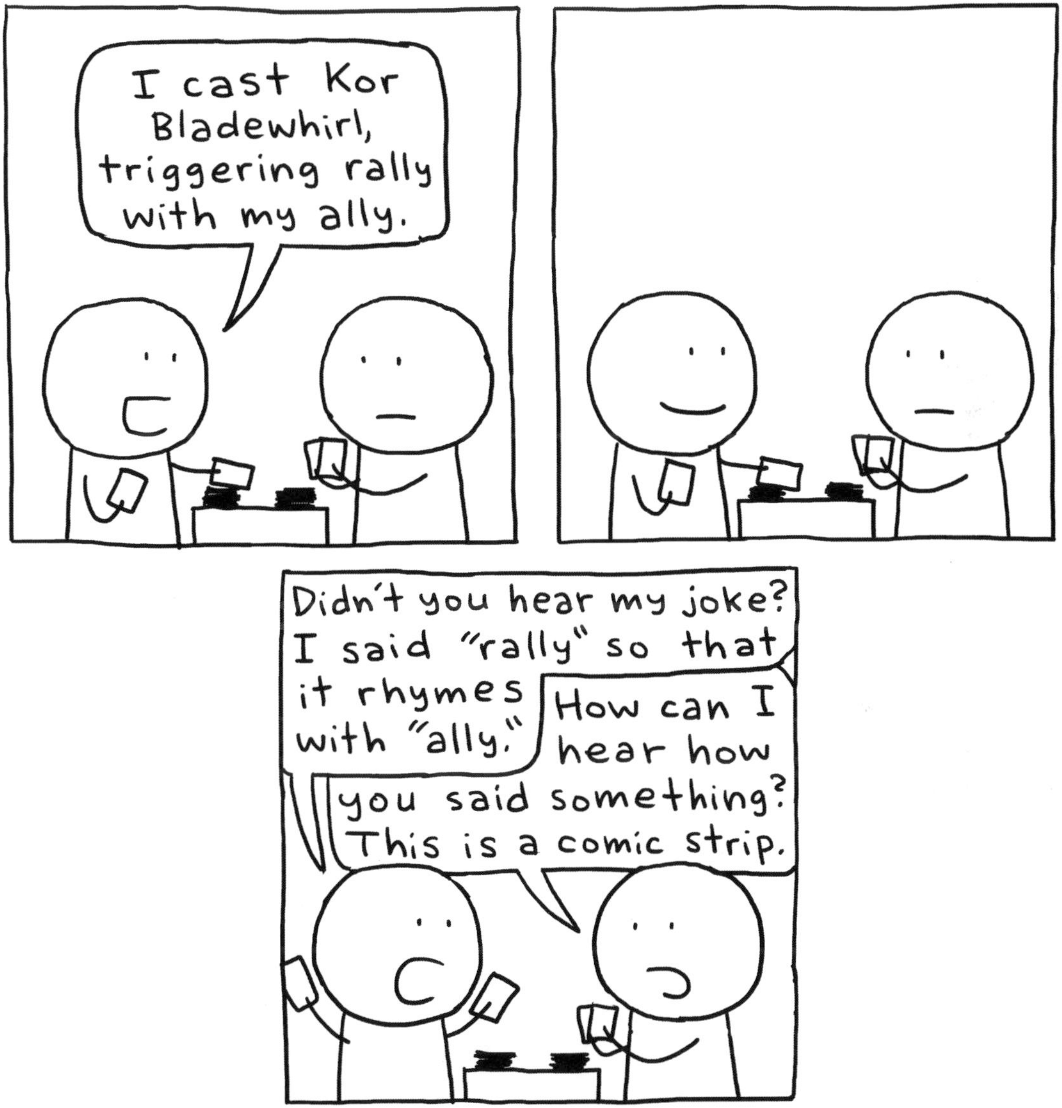
I cast Kor Bladewhirl, triggering rally with my ally.
Didn't you hear my joke? I said "rally" so that it rhymes with "ally."
How can I hear how you said something? This is a comic strip.

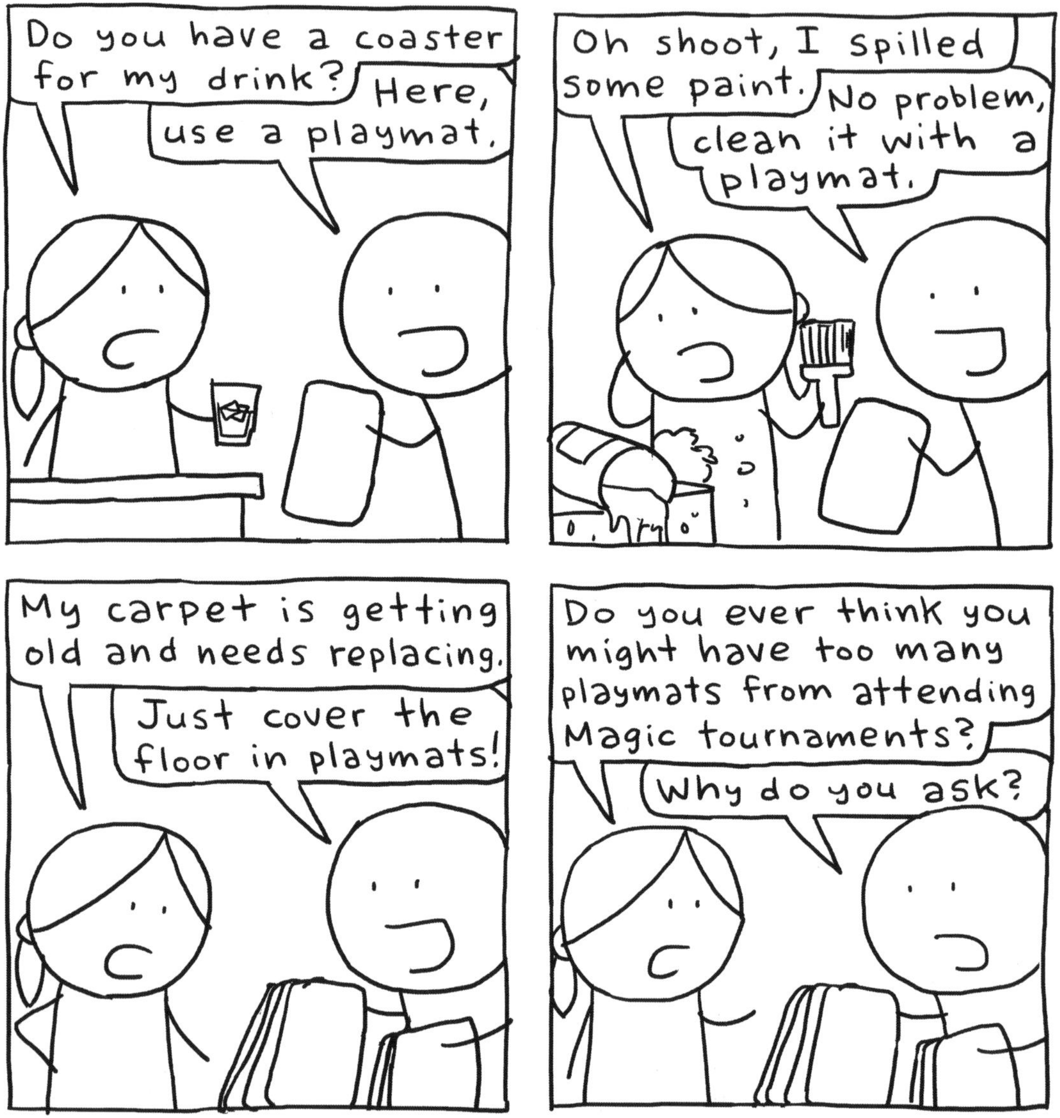
Do you have a coaster for my drink?
Here, use a playmat.
Oh shoot, I spilled some paint.
No problem, clean it with a playmat.
My carpet is getting old and needs replacing.
Just cover the floor in playmats!
Do you ever think you might have too many playmats from attending Magic tournaments?
Why do you ask?

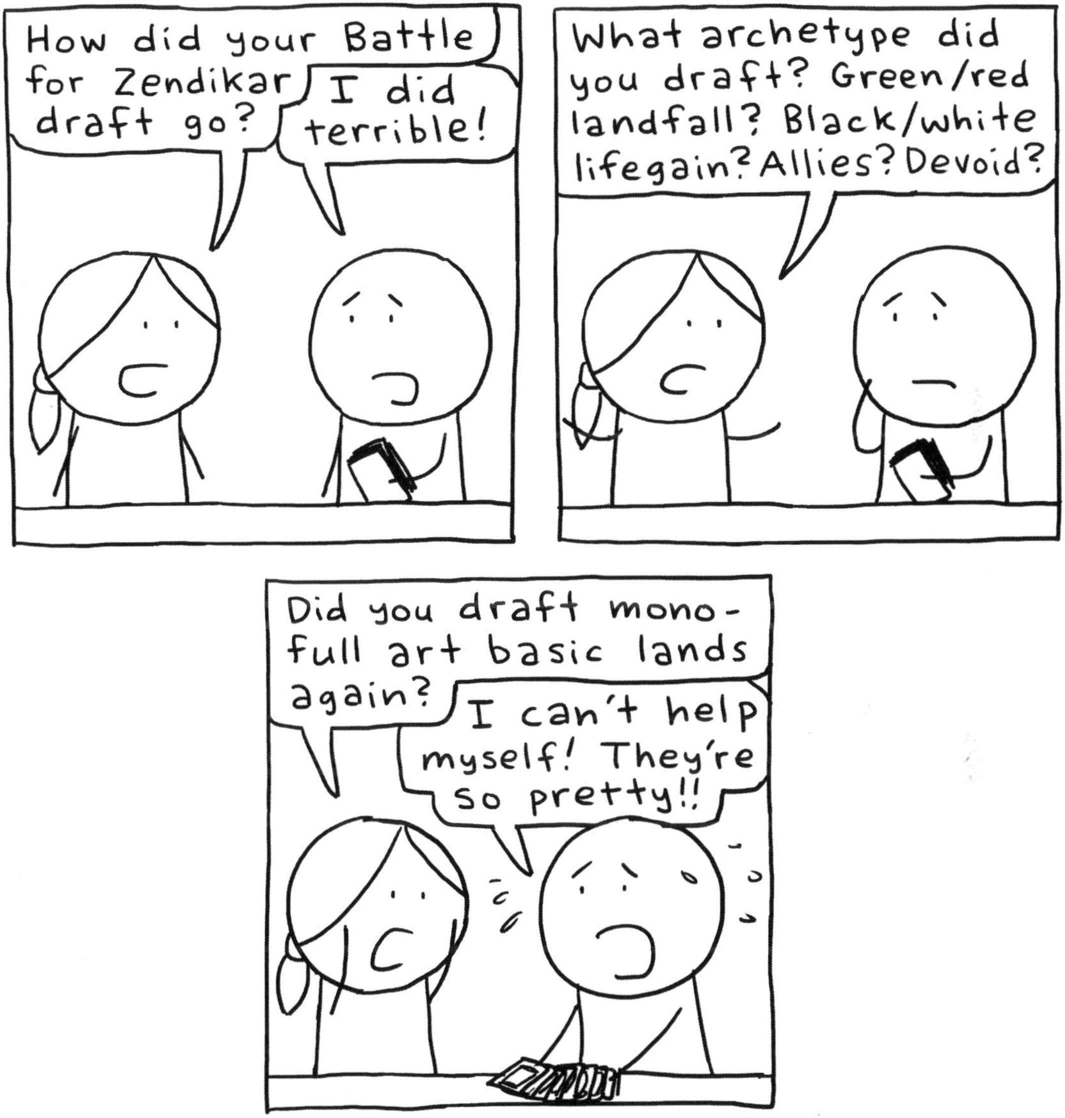
How did your Battle for Zendikar draft go?
I did terrible!
What archetype did you draft? Green/red landfall? Black/white lifegain? Allies? Devoid?
Did you draft mono-full art basic lands again?
I can't help myself! They're so pretty!!

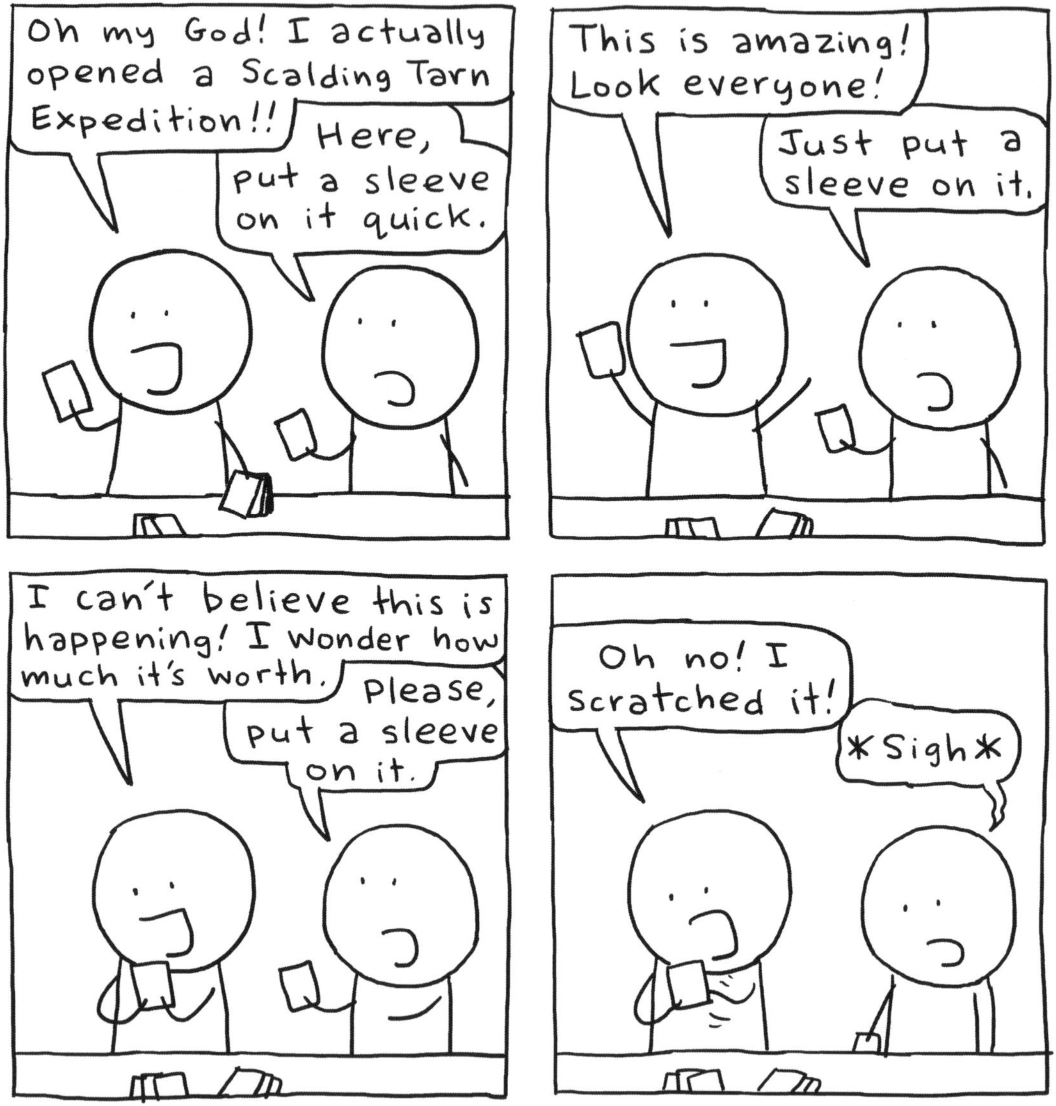
Oh my God! I actually opened a Scalding Tarn Expedition!!
Here, put a sleeve on it quick.
This is amazing! Look everyone!
Just put a sleeve on it.
I can't believe this is happening! I wonder how much it's worth.
Please, put a sleeve on it.
Oh no! I scratched it!
Sigh

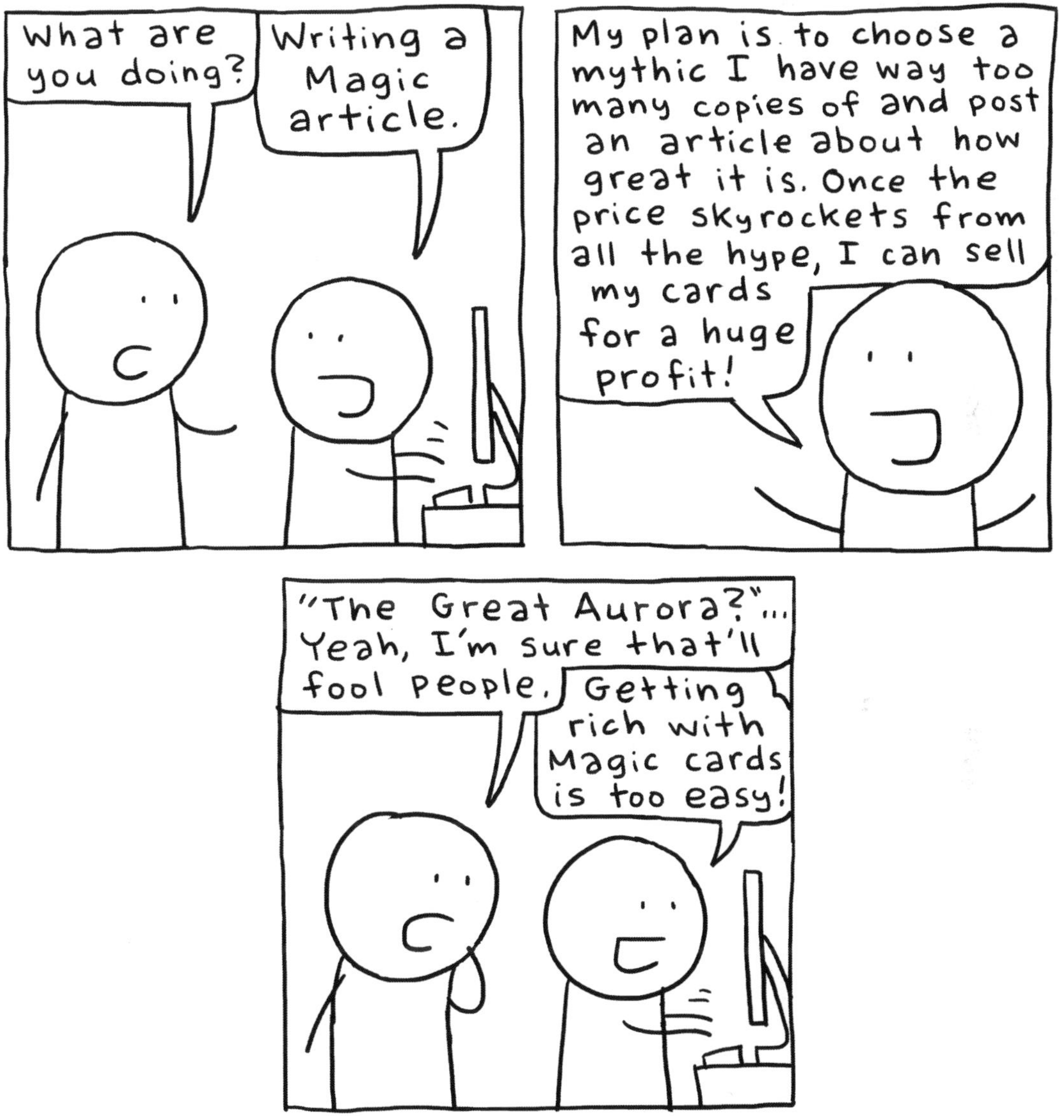
What are you doing?
Writing a Magic article.
My plan is to choose a mythic I have way too many copies of and post an article about how great it is. Once the price skyrockets from all the hype, I can sell my cards for a huge profit!
"The Great Aurora?"... Yeah, I'm sure that'll fool people.
Getting rich with Magic cards is too easy!

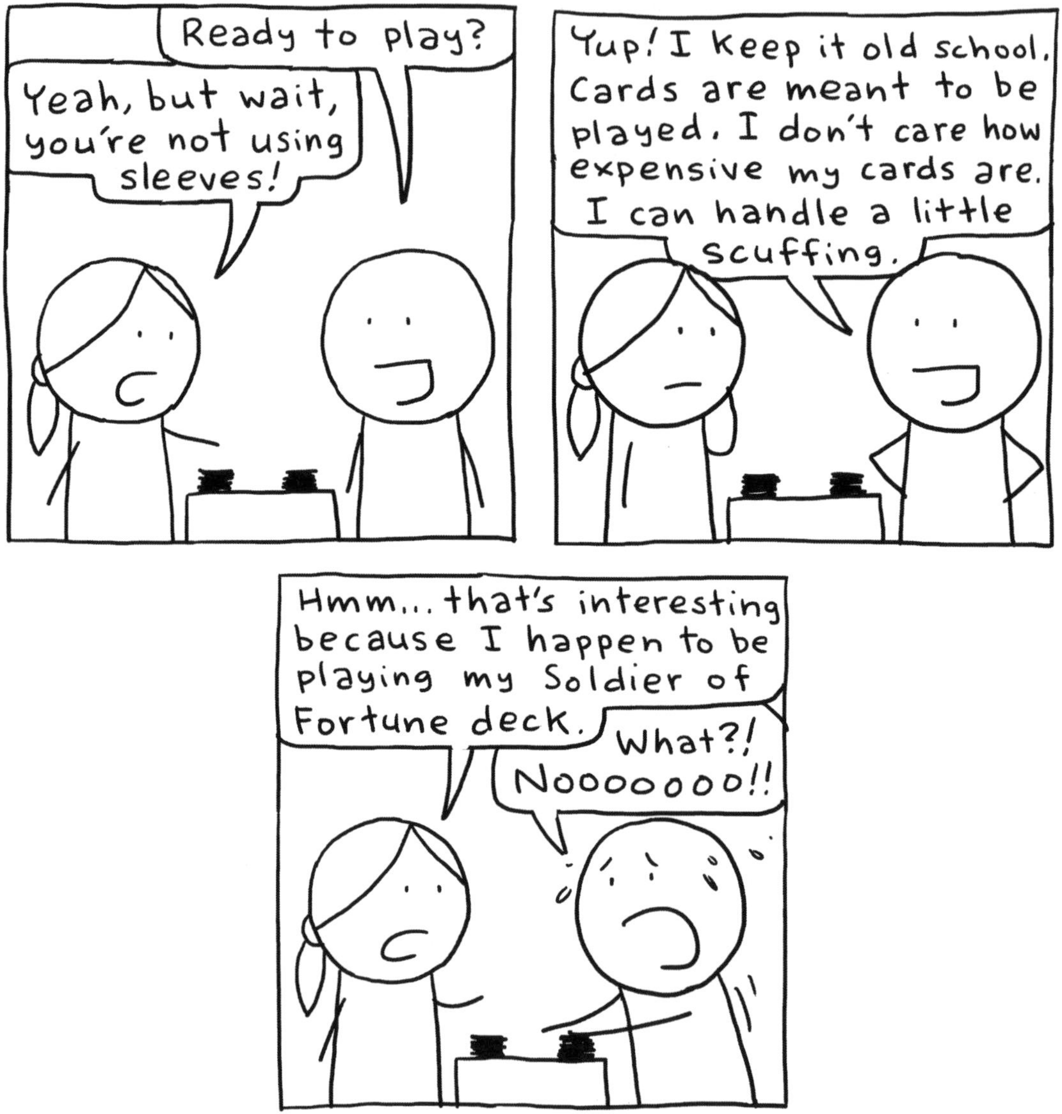
Ready to play?
Yeah, but wait, you're not using sleeves!
Yup! I keep it old school. Cards are meant to be played. I don't care how expensive my cards are. I can handle a little scuffing.
Hmm... that's interesting because I happen to be playing my Soldier of Fortune deck.
What?! Noooooooo!!

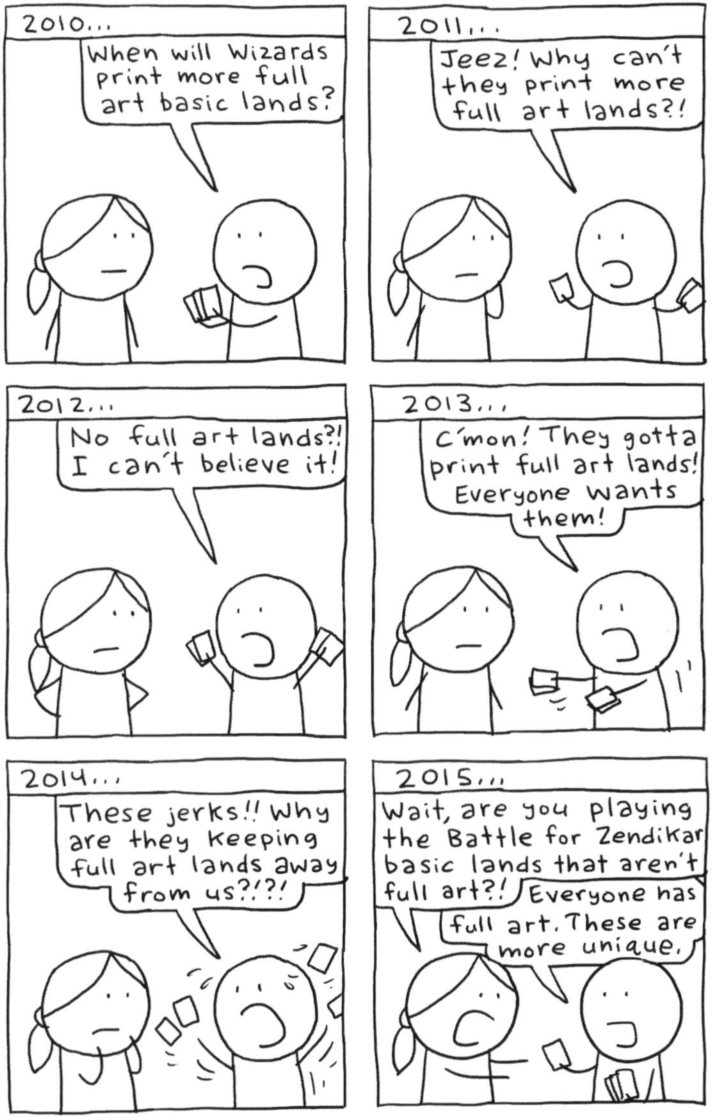
2010...
When will Wizards print more full art basic lands?
2011...
Jeez! Why can't they print more full art lands?!
2012...
No full art lands?! I can't believe it!
2013...
C'mon! They gotta print full art lands! Everyone wants them!
2014...
These jerks!! Why are they keeping full art lands away from us?!?!
2015...
Wait, are you playing the Battle for Zendikar basic lands that aren't full art?!
Everyone has full art. These are more unique.

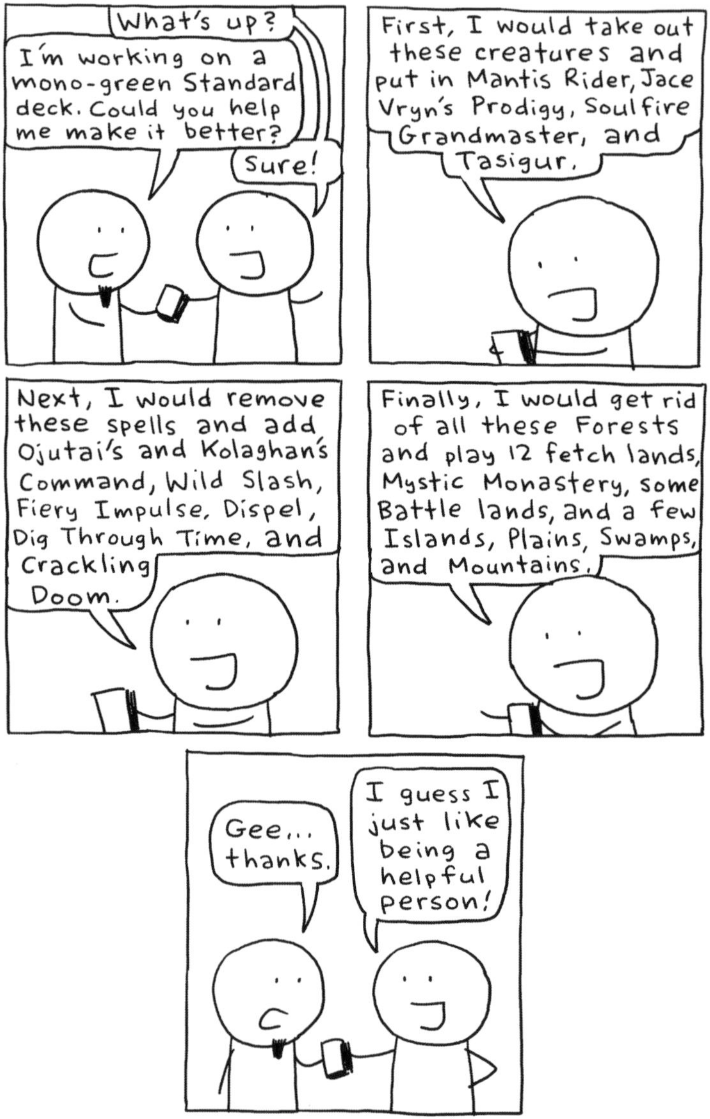
What's up?
I'm working on a mono-green Standard deck. Could you help me make it better?
Sure!
First, I would take out these creatures and put in Mantis Rider, Jace Vryn's Prodigy, Soulfire Grandmaster, and Tasigur.
Next, I would remove these spells and add Ojutai's and Kolaghan's Command, Wild Slash, Fiery Impulse, Dispel, Dig Through Time, and Crackling Doom.
Finally, I would get rid of all these Forests and play 12 fetch lands, Mystic Monastery, some Battle lands, and a few Islands, Plains, Swamps, and Mountains.
Gee... thanks.
I guess I just like being a helpful person!

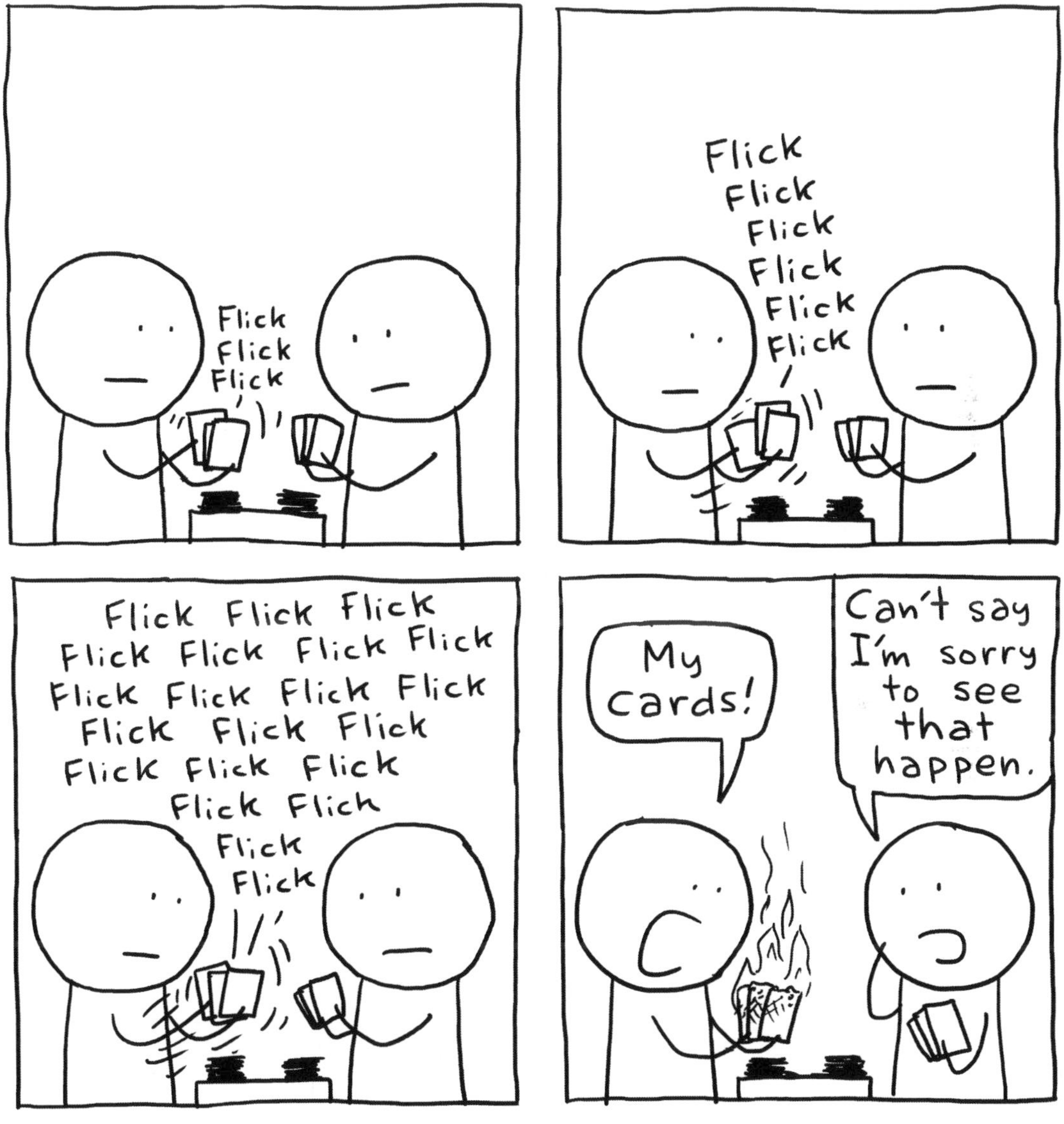
Flick
Flick
Flick
Flick
Flick
Flick
Flick
Flick
Flick
Flick Flick Flick
Flick Flick Flick Flick
Flick Flick Flick Flick
Flick Flick Flick
Flick Flick Flick
Flick Flich
Flick
Flick
My cards!
Can't say I'm sorry to see that happen.

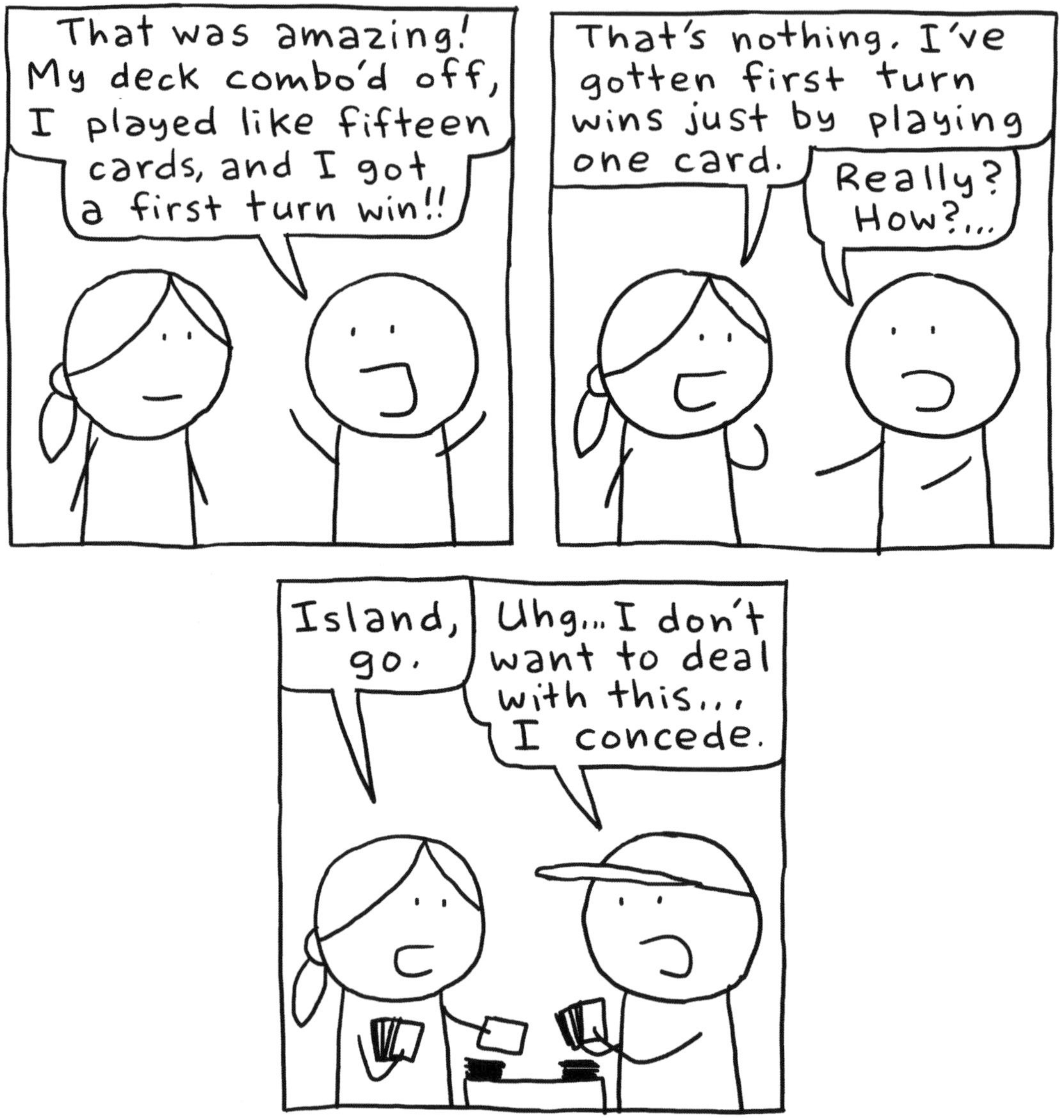
That was amazing! My deck combo'd off, I played like fifteen cards, and I got a first turn win!!
That's nothing. I've gotten first turn wins just by playing one card.
Really? How?...
Island, go.
Uhg... I don't want to deal with this... I concede.

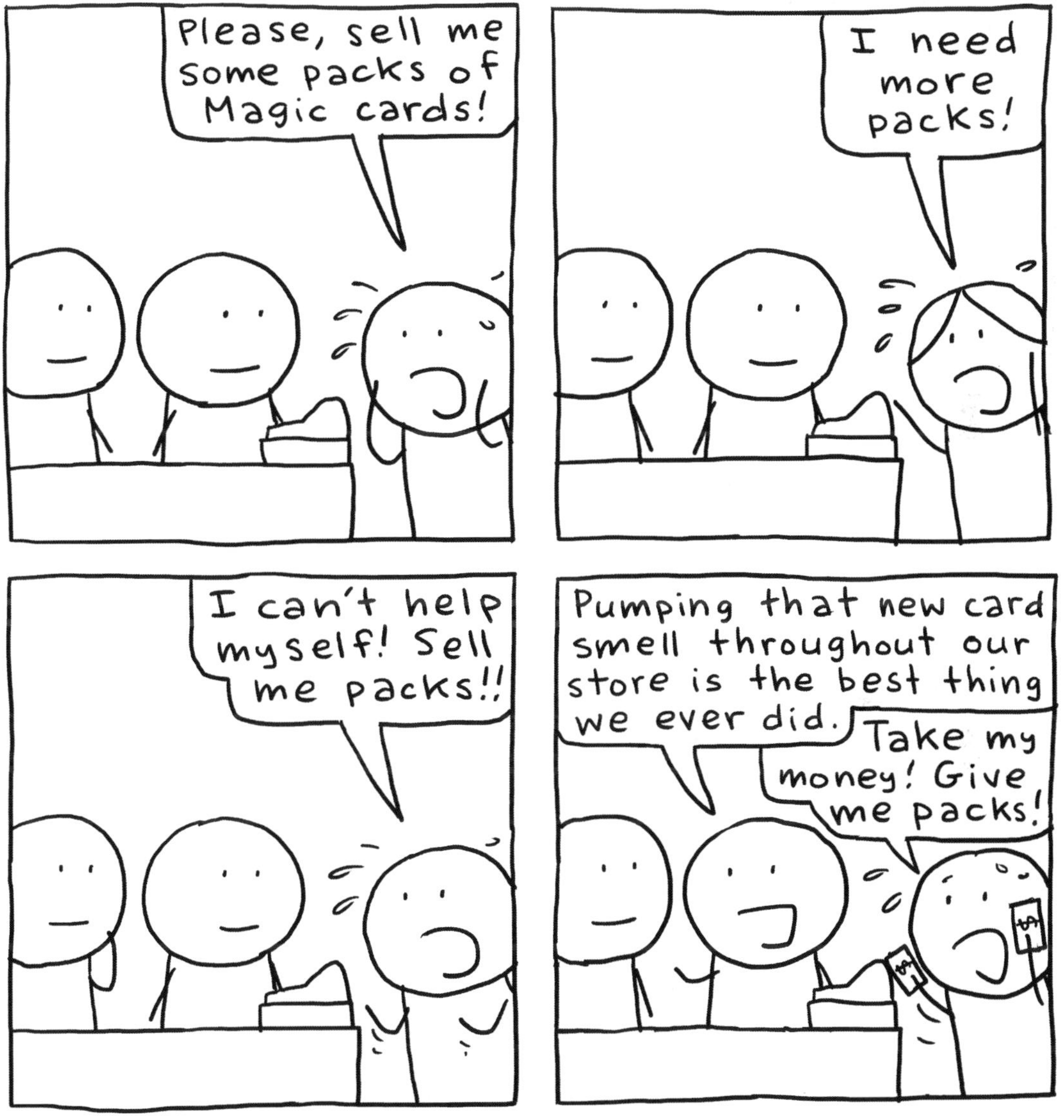
Please, sell me some packs of Magic cards!
I need more packs!
I can't help myself! Sell me packs!!
Pumping that new card smell throughout our store is the best thing we ever did.
Take my money! Give me packs!

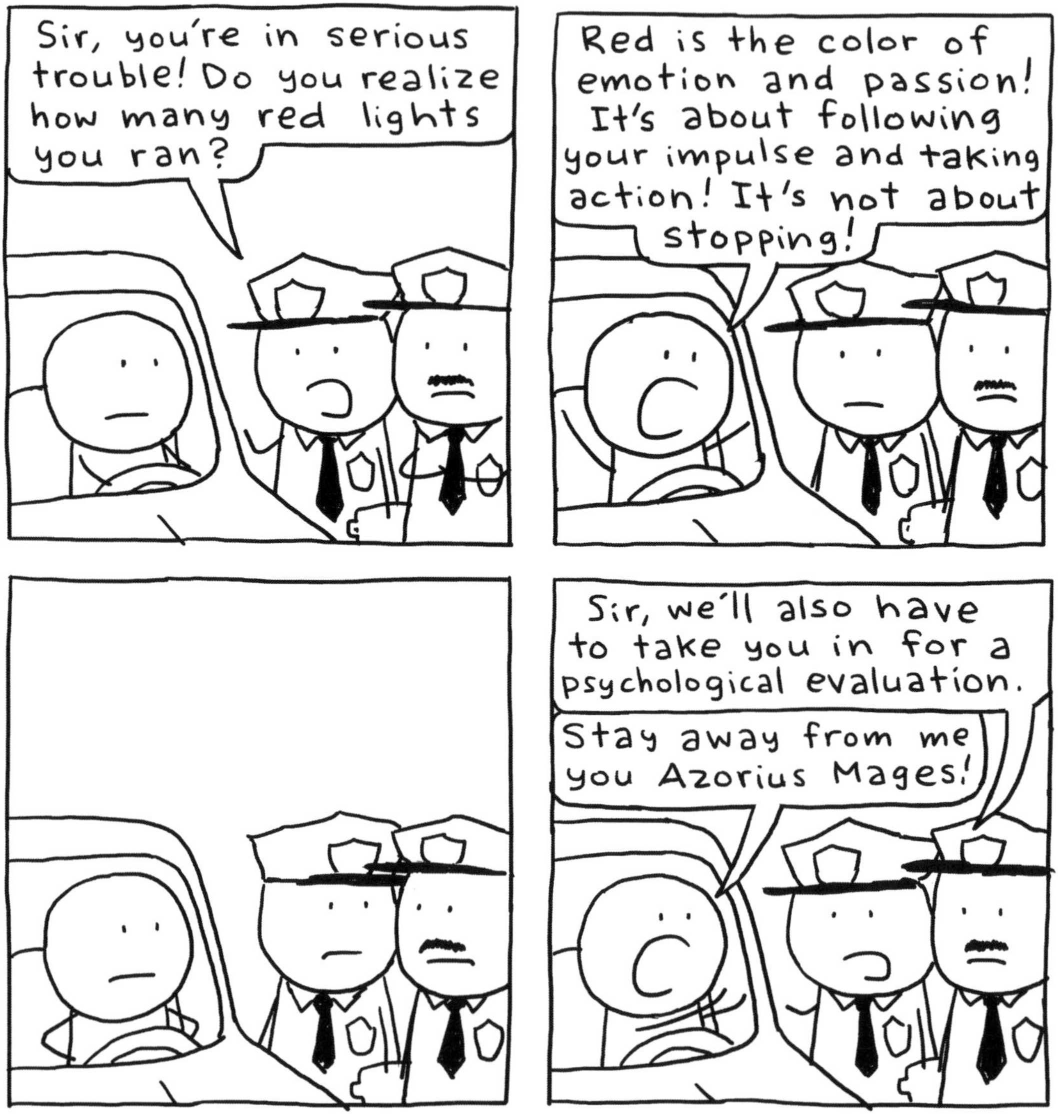
Sir, you're in serious trouble! Do you realize how many red lights you ran?
Red is the color of emotion and passion! It's about following your impulse and taking action! It's not about stopping!
Sir, we'll also have to take you in for a psychological evaluation.
Stay away from me you Azorius Mages!

Standard players...
Card prices in Standard are out of control! This is ridiculous! It has to stop!
Modern players...
Yes! Keep raising the price of Standard! Get more players to come to our side!

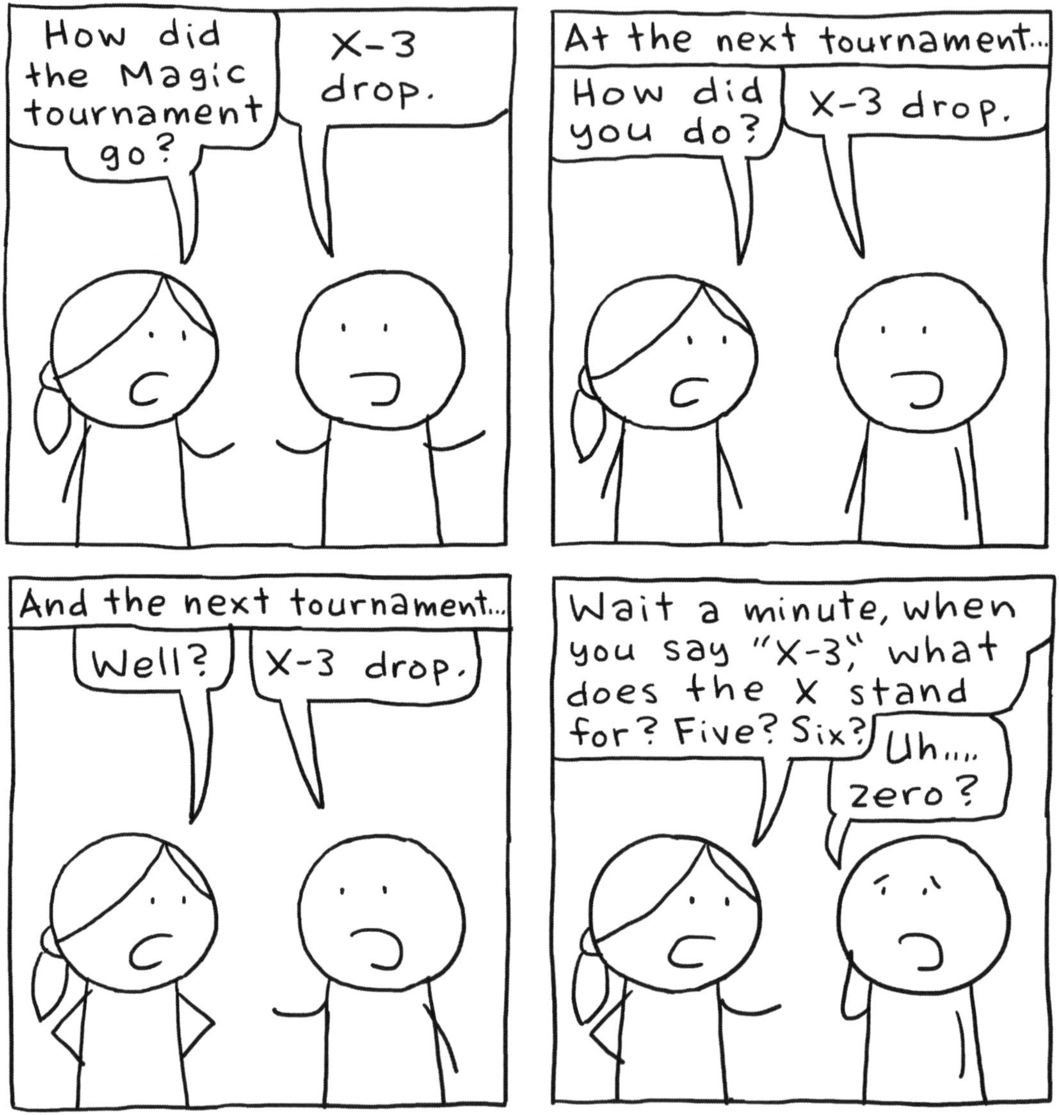
How did the Magic tournament go?
X-3 drop.
At the next tournament...
How did you do?
X-3 drop.
And the next tournament...
Well?
X-3 drop.
Wait a minute, when you say "X-3," what does the X stand for? Five? Six?
Uh.... zero?

You're watching reality shows? It's just a bunch of arguing, backstabbing, and drama. How can you enjoy this stuff?
Later...
Don't you dare attack me!
I'll attack who I want!
Do it!! Remember what he did last game!
This is so great!

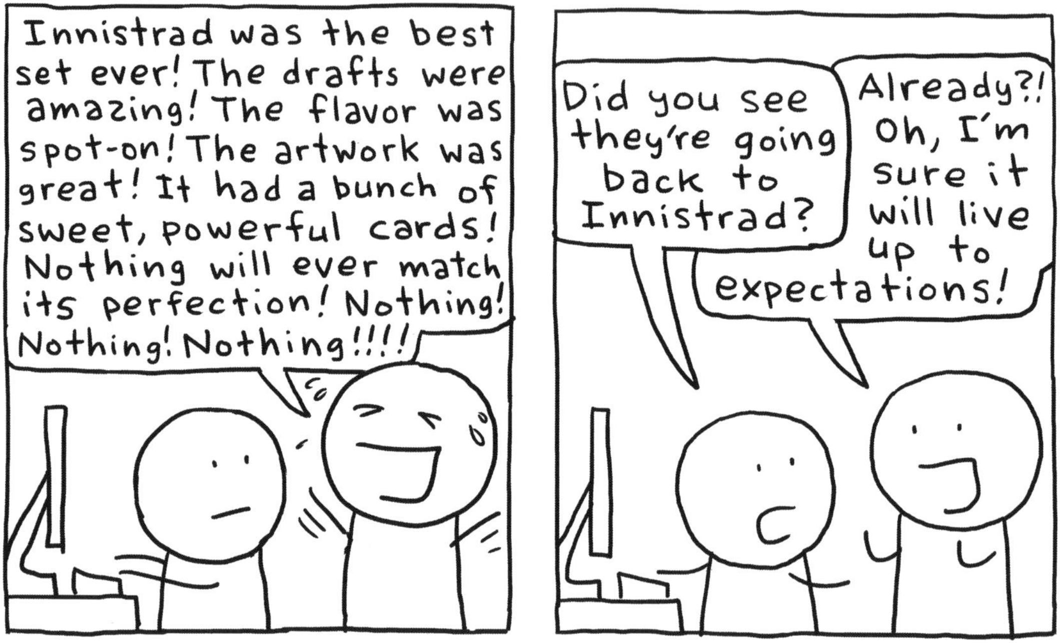
Innistrad was the best set ever! The drafts were amazing! The flavor was spot-on! The artwork was great! It had a bunch of sweet, powerful cards! Nothing will ever match its perfection! Nothing! Nothing! Nothing!!!!
Did you see they're going back to Innistrad?
Already?! Oh, I'm sure it will live up to expectations!

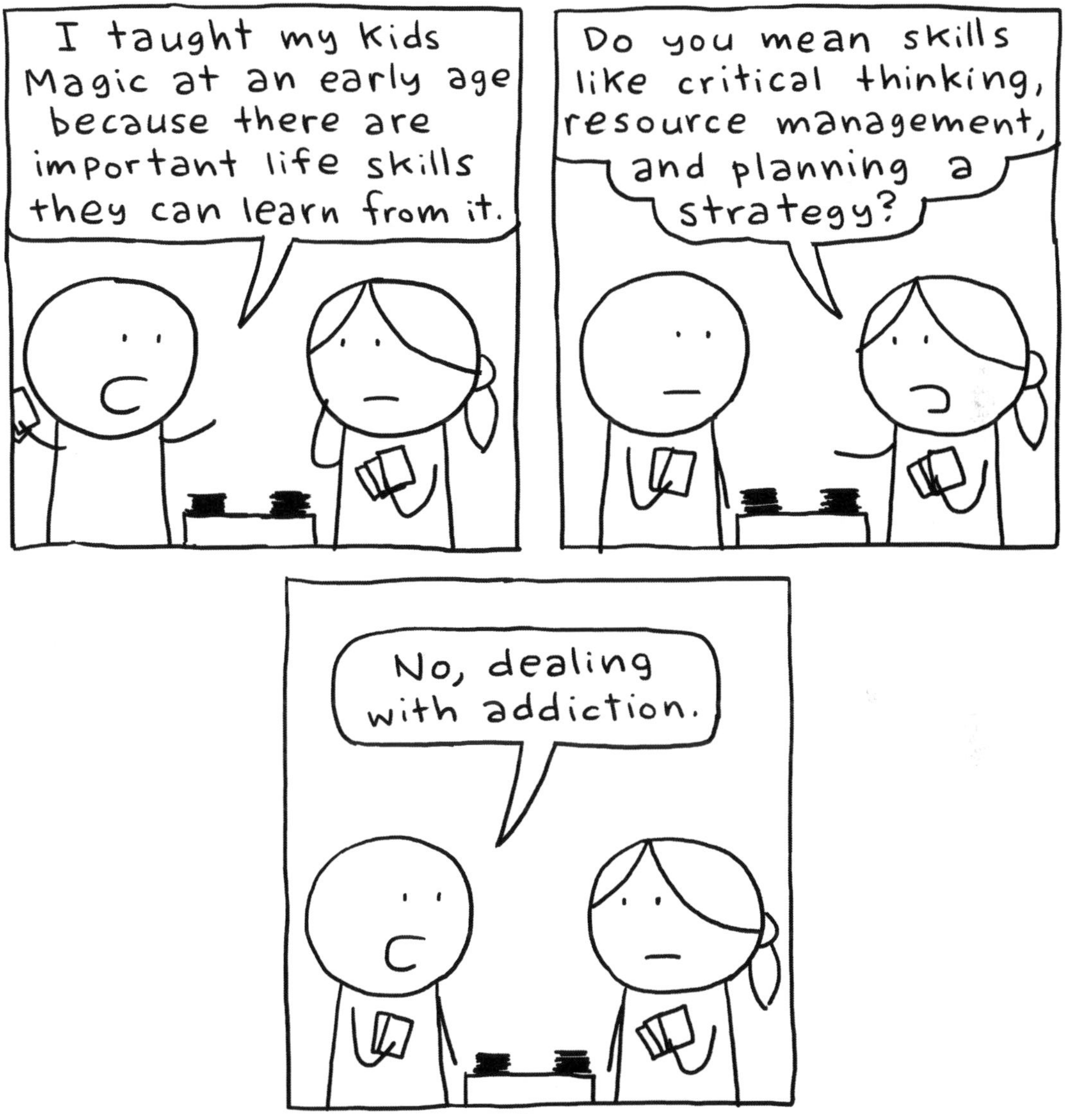
I taught my kids Magic at an early age because there are important life skills they can learn from it.
Do you mean skills like critical thinking, resource management, and planning a strategy?
No, dealing with addiction.

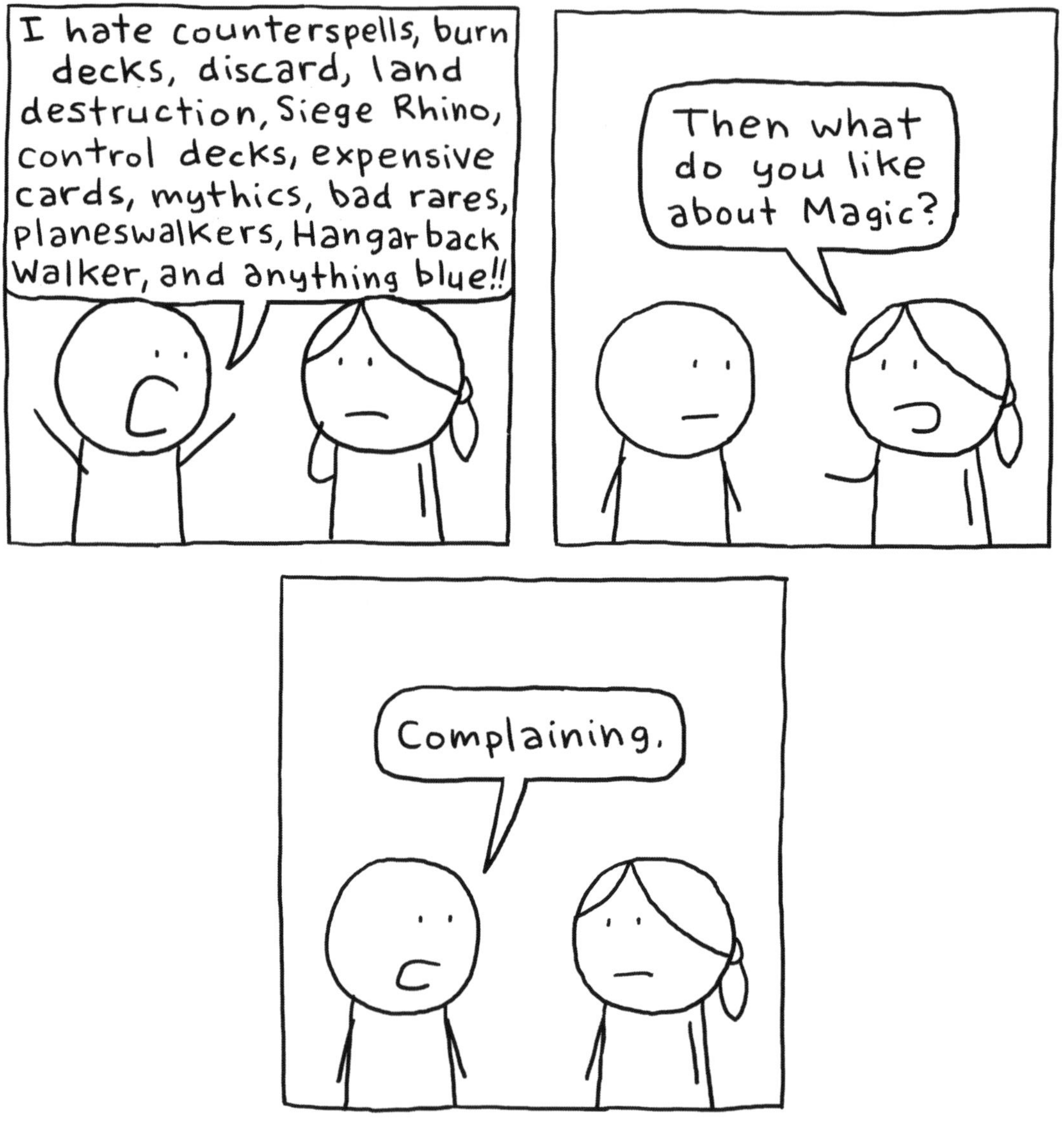
I hate counterspells, burn decks, discard, land destruction, Siege Rhino, control decks, expensive cards, mythics, bad rares, planeswalkers, Hangarback Walker, and anything blue!!
Then what do you like about Magic?
Complaining.

Ha! Ha! This comedian is really going blue!
Going blue? What does that mean?
I guess he's a controlling jerk.

When I win a draft...
My deck is amazing! I'm so good at draft!
When I lose a draft...
My opponent's deck is amazing! They're so lucky at draft!

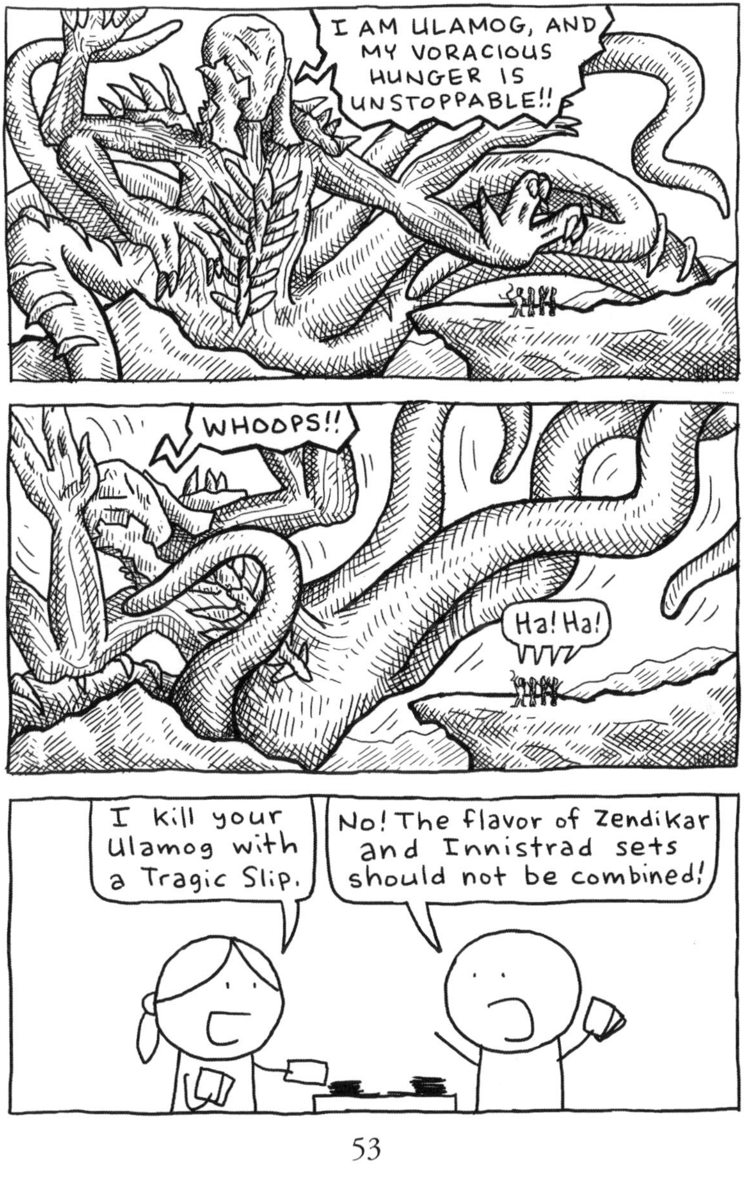
I AM ULAMOG, AND MY VORACIOUS HUNGER IS UNSTOPPABLE!!
WHOOPS!!
Ha! Ha!
I kill your Ulamog with a Tragic Slip.
No! The flavor of Zendikar and Innistrad sets should not be combined!

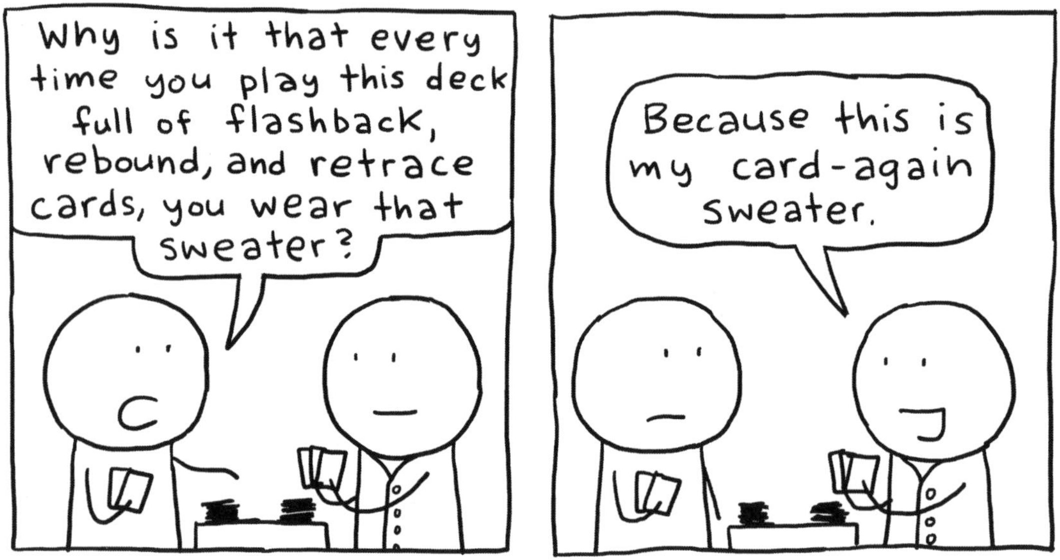
Why is it that every time you play this deck full of flashback, rebound, and retrace cards, you wear that sweater?
Because this is my card-again sweater.

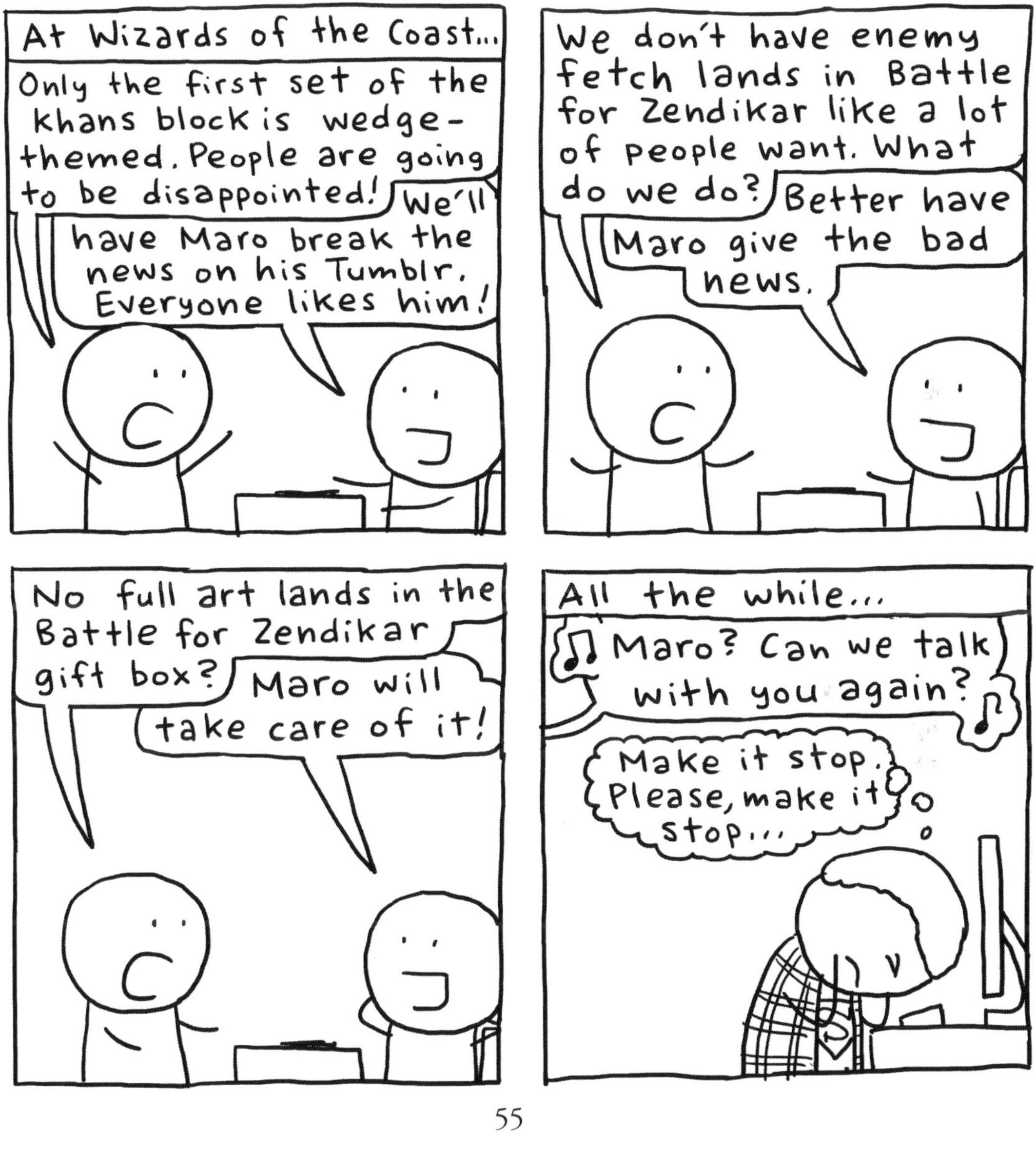
At Wizards of the Coast...
Only the first set of the khans block is wedge-themed. People are going to be disappointed!
We'll have Maro break the news on his Tumblr. Everyone likes him!
We don't have enemy fetch lands in Battle for Zendikar like a lot of people want. What do we do?
Better have Maro give the bad news.
No full art lands in the Battle for Zendikar gift box?
Maro will take care of it!
All the while...
Maro? Can we talk with you again?
Make it stop. Please, make it stop...

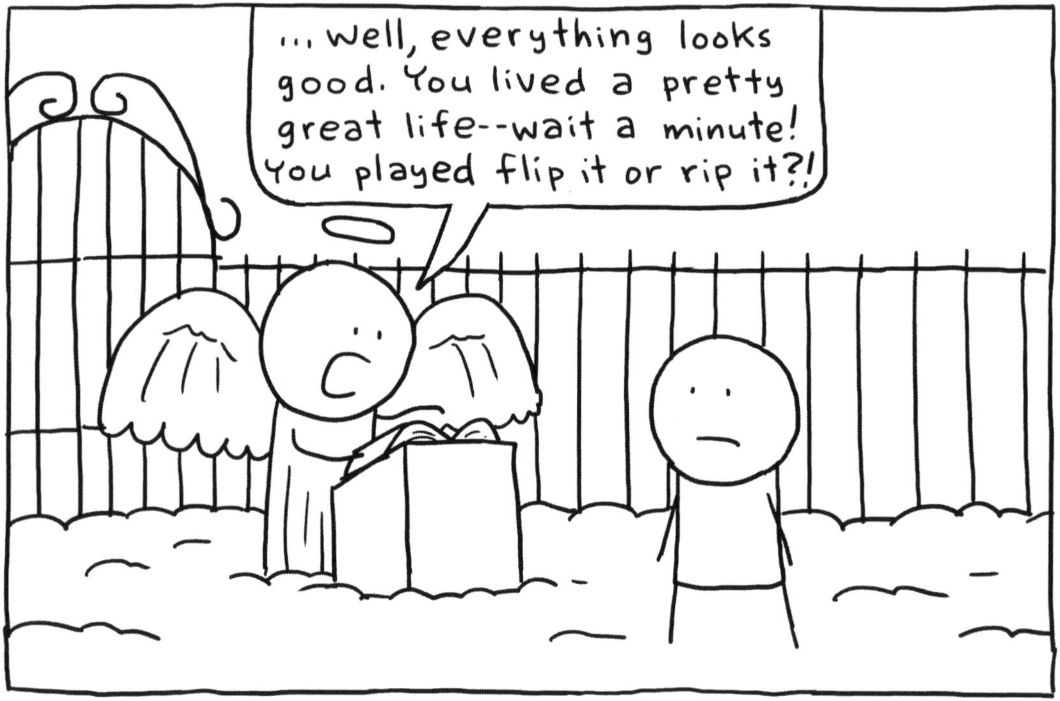
...well, everything looks good. You lived a pretty great life--wait a minute! You played flip it or rip it?!

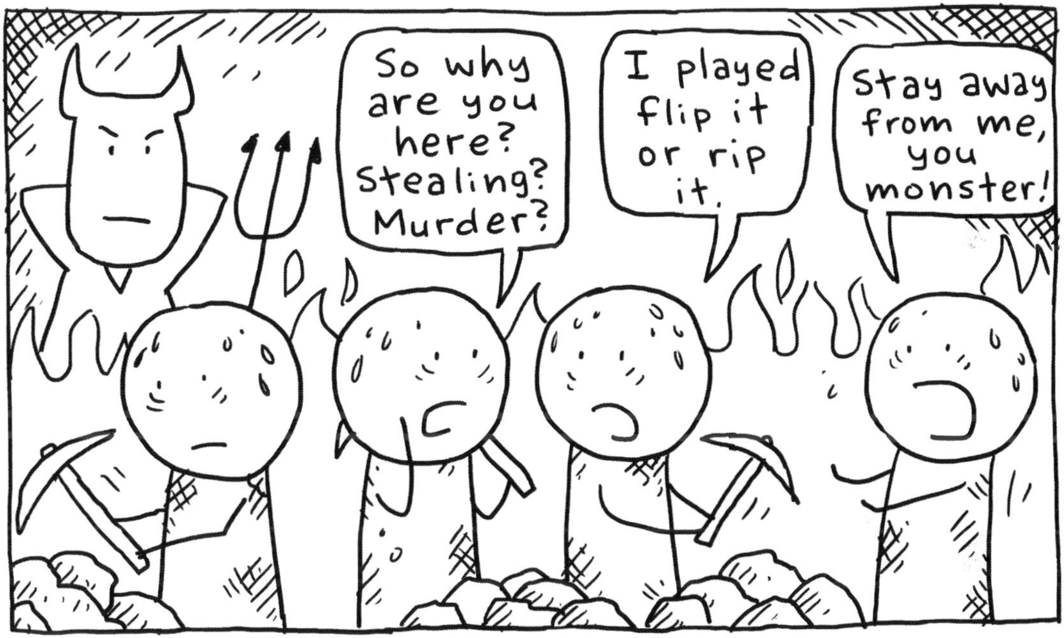
So why are you here? Stealing? Murder?
I played flip it or rip it.
Stay away from me, you monster!

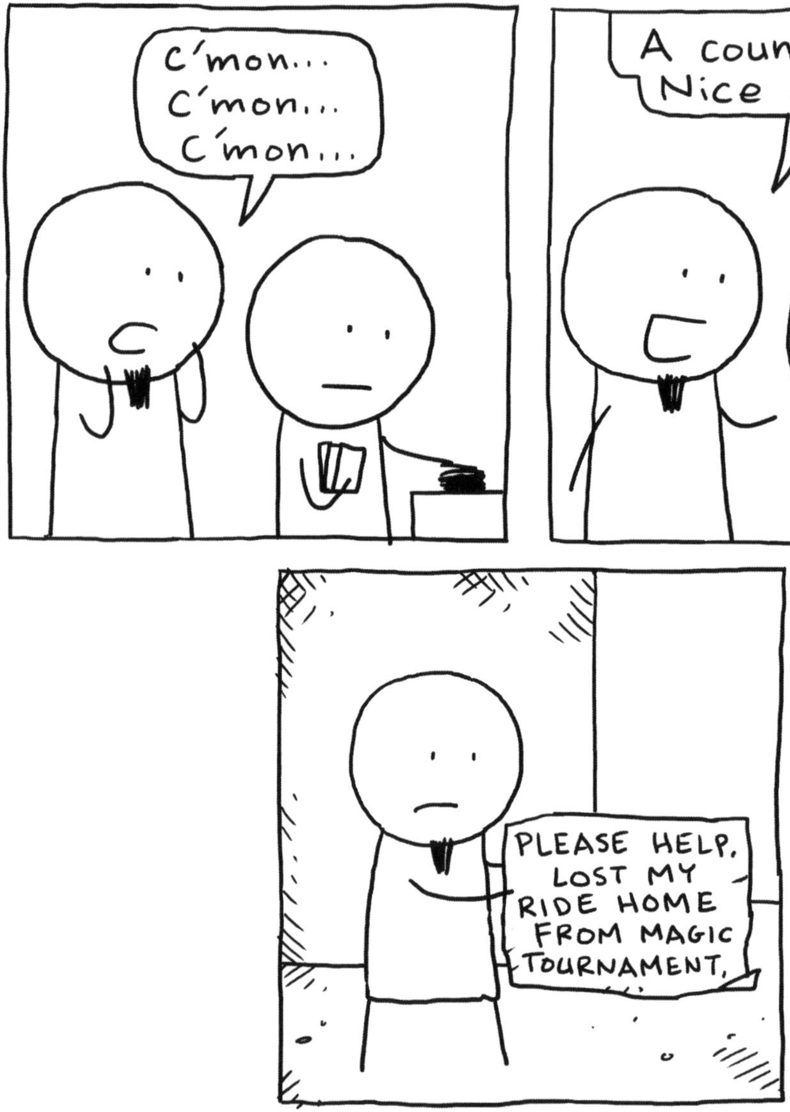
C'mon... C'mon... C'mon...
A counterspell? Nice draw!
PLEASE HELP, LOST MY RIDE HOME FROM MAGIC TOURNAMENT,

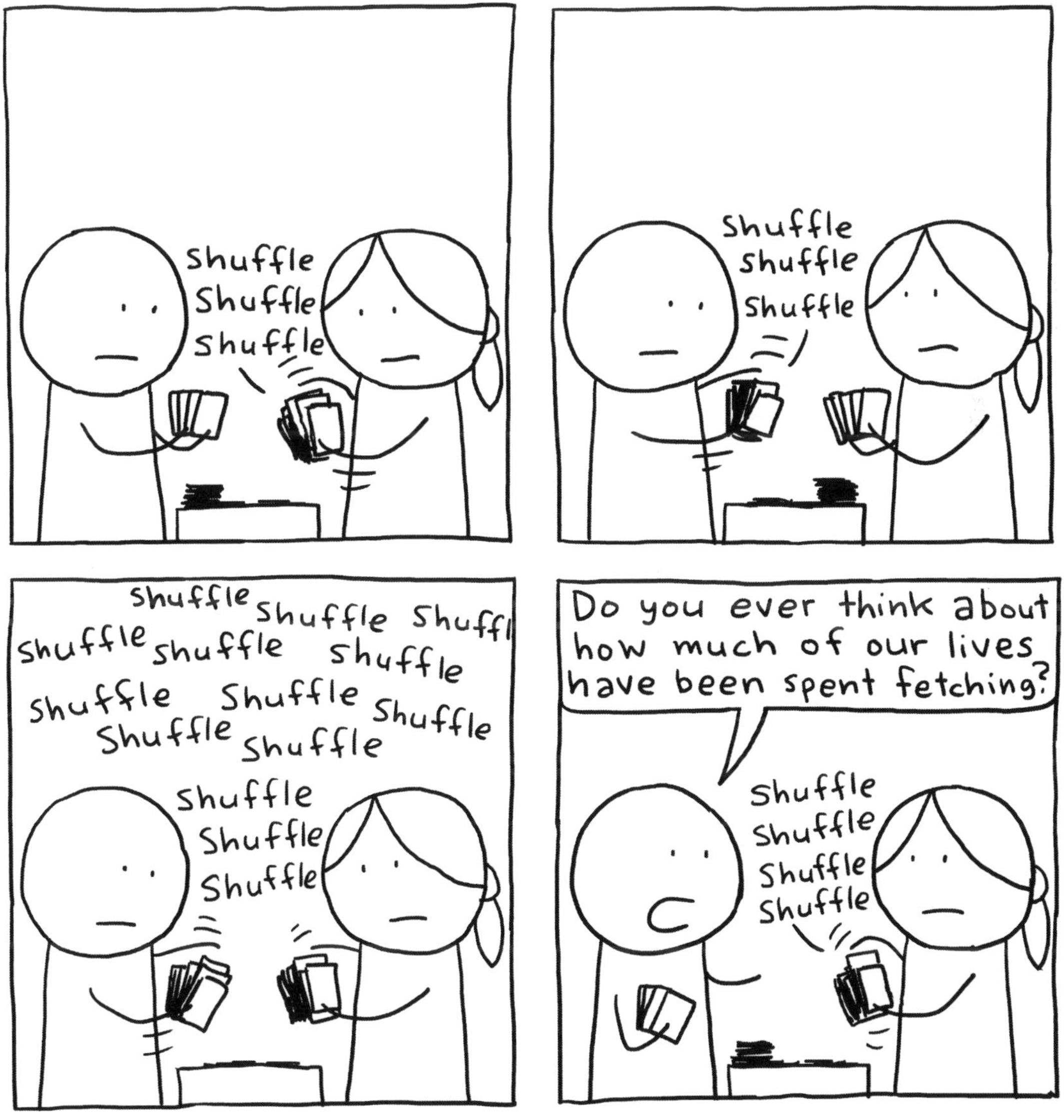
Shuffle
Shuffle
Shuffle
Shuffle
Shuffle
Shuffle
Shuffle Shuffle Shuffl
Shuffle Shuffle Shuffle
Shuffle Shuffle Shuffle
Shuffle Shuffle
Shuffle
Shuffle
Shuffle
Do you ever think about how much of our lives have been spent fetching?
Shuffle
Shuffle
Shuffle
Shuffle

When I was younger...
I can't wait until I have a real job, and then I'll buy all the Magic cards I want!
Now...
What the #@%*?! I have to pay rent?!

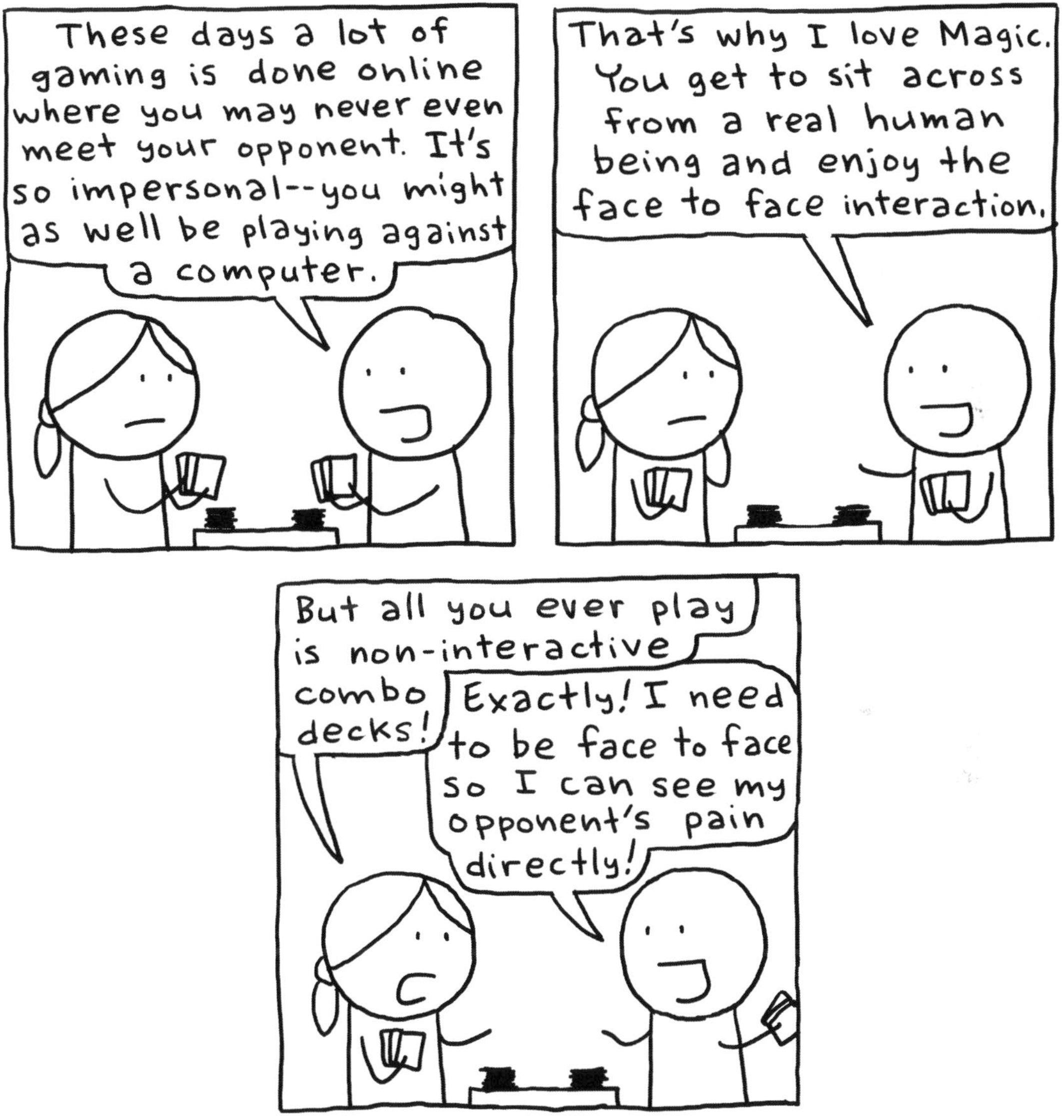
These days a lot of gaming is done online where you may never even meet your opponent. It's so impersonal--you might as well be playing against a computer.
That's why I love Magic. You get to sit across from a real human being and enjoy the face to face interaction.
But all you ever play is non-interactive combo decks!
Exactly! I need to be face to face so I can see my opponent's pain directly!

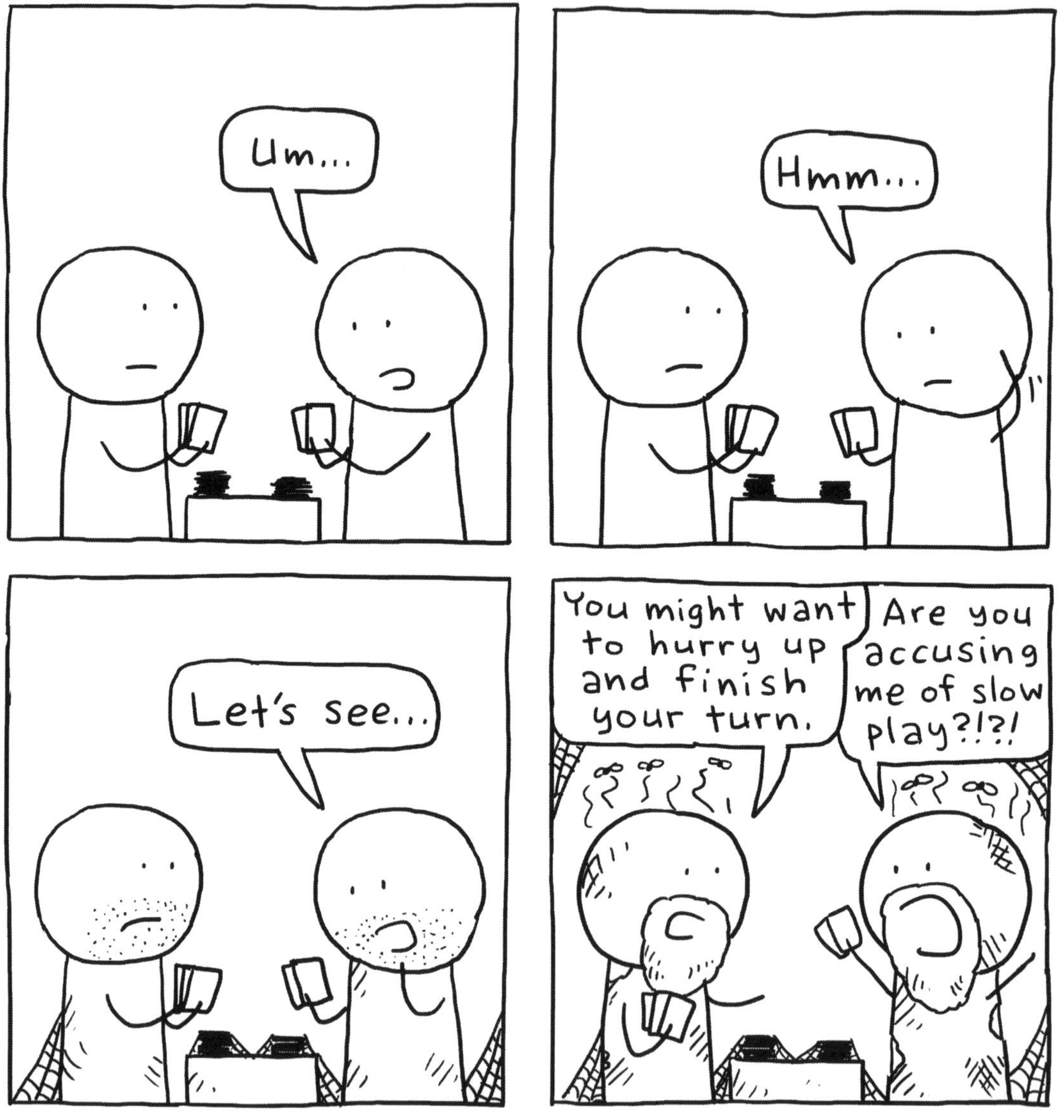
Um...
Hmm...
Let's see...
You might want to hurry up and finish your turn.
Are you accusing me of slow play?!?!

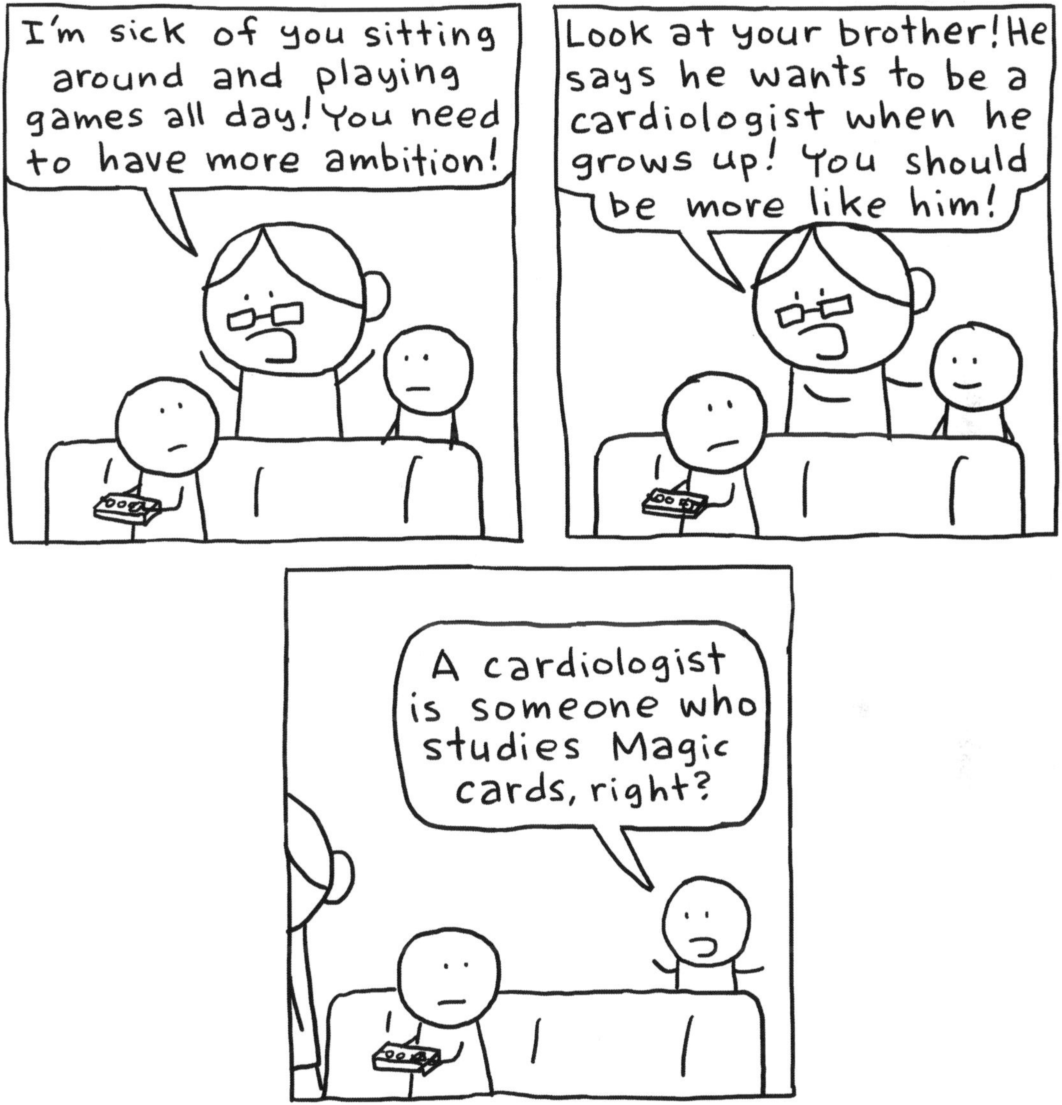
I'm sick of you sitting around and playing games all day! You need to have more ambition!
Look at your brother! He says he wants to be a cardiologist when he grows up! You should be more like him!
A cardiologist is someone who studies Magic cards, right?

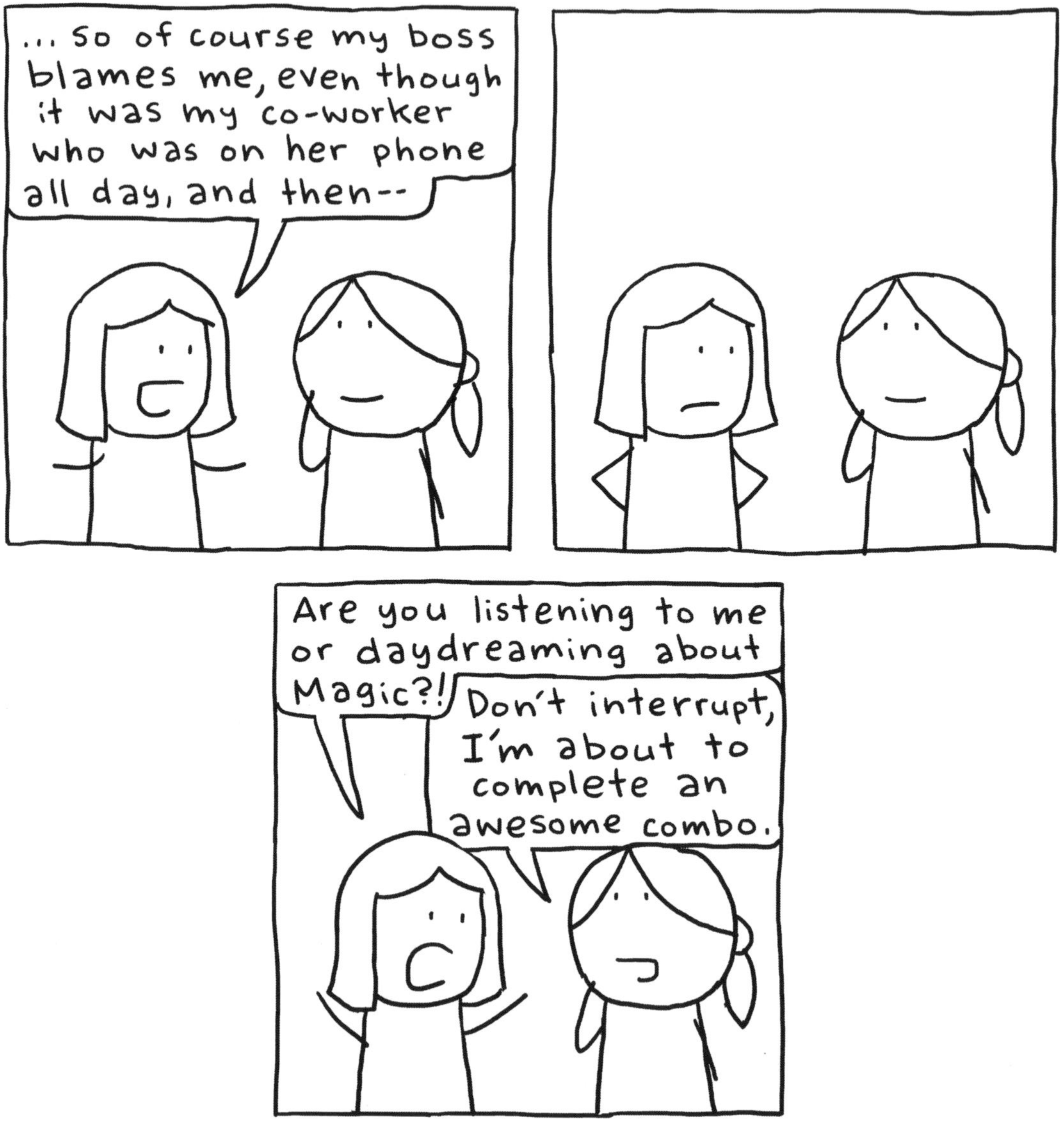
... so of course my boss blames me, even though it was my co-worker who was on her phone all day, and then--
Are you listening to me or daydreaming about Magic?!
Don't interrupt, I'm about to complete an awesome combo.

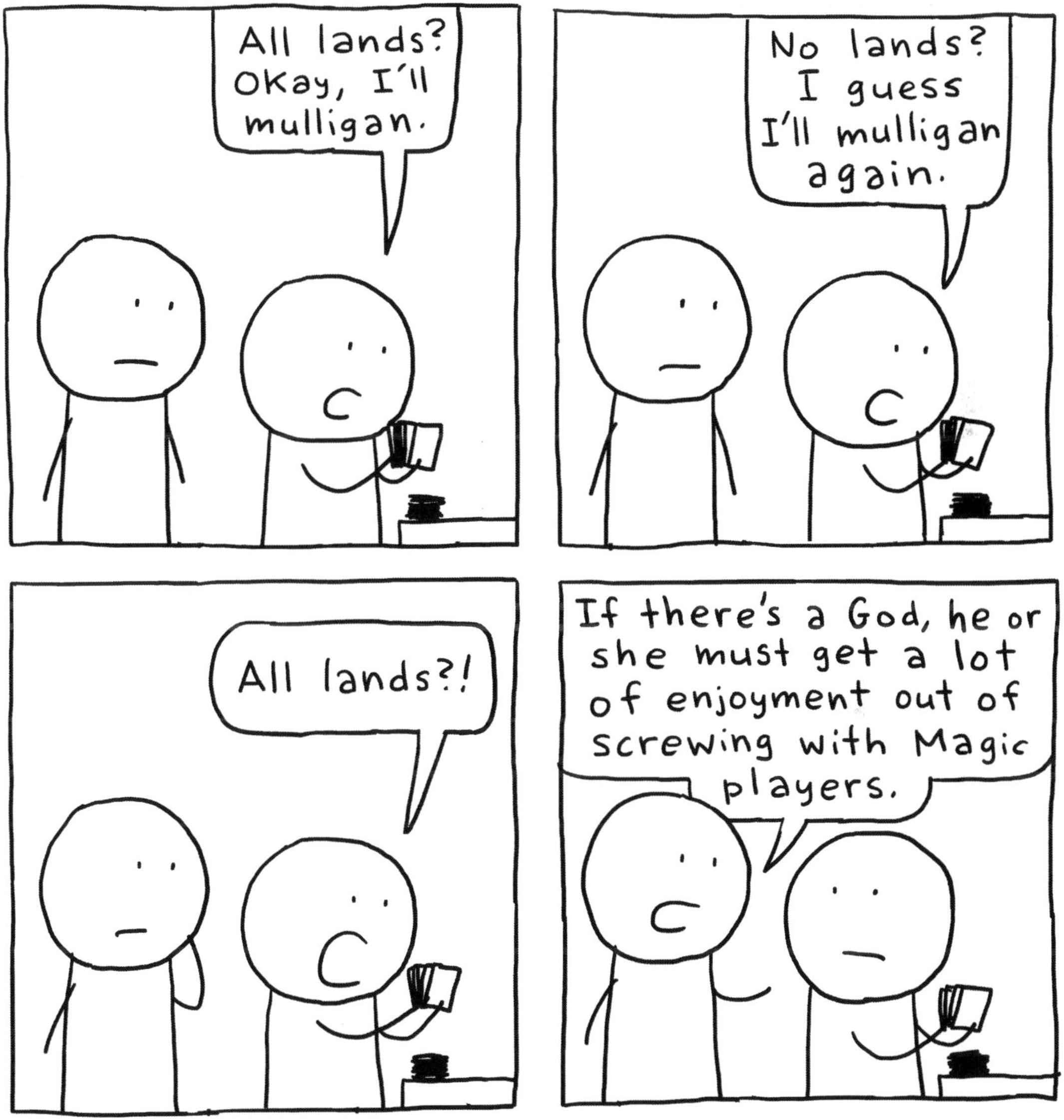
All lands? OKay, I'll mulligan.
No lands? I guess I'll mulligan again.
All lands?!
If there's a God, he or she must get a lot of enjoyment out of screwing with Magic players.

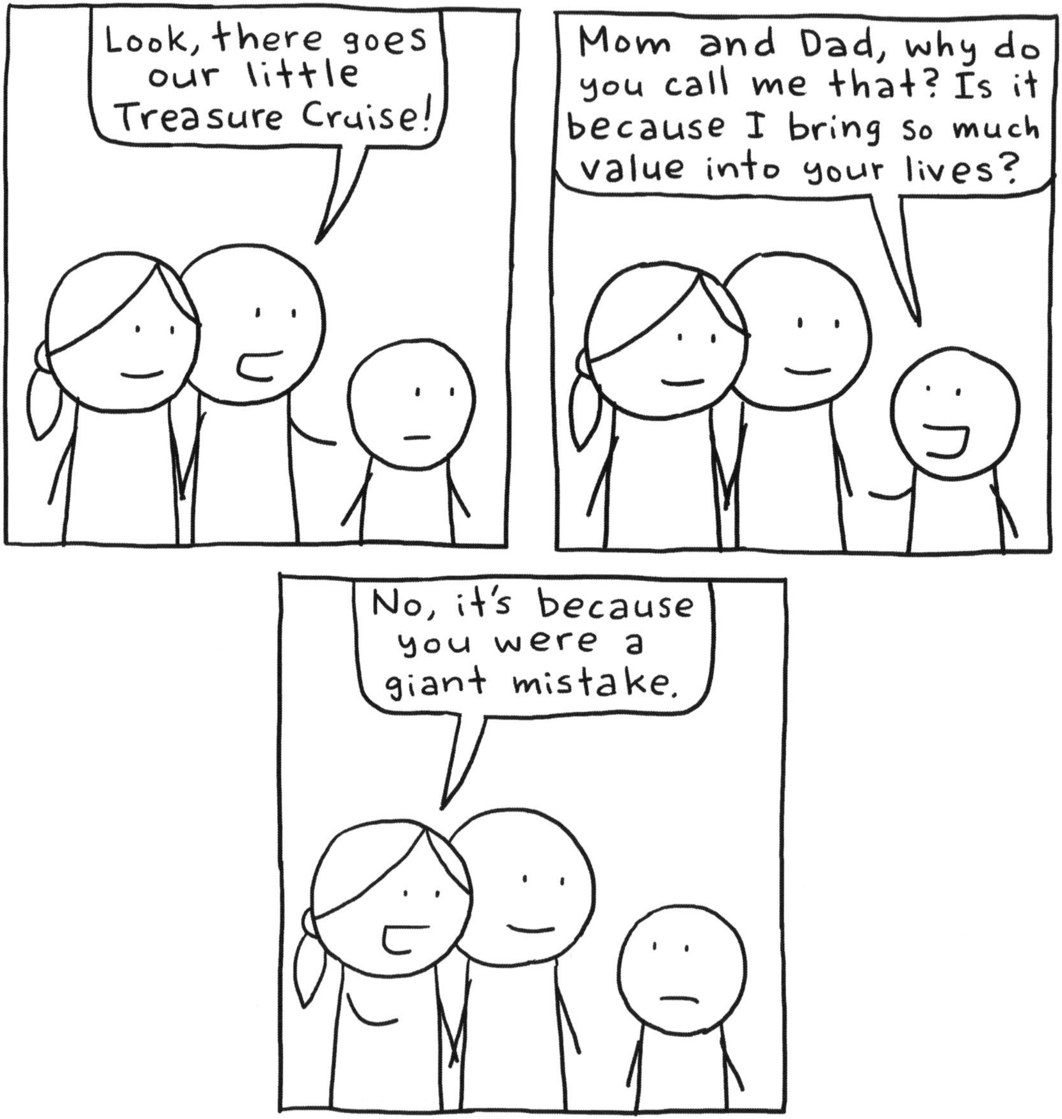
Look, there goes our little Treasure Cruise!
Mom and Dad, why do you call me that? Is it because I bring so much value into your lives?
No, it's because you were a giant mistake.

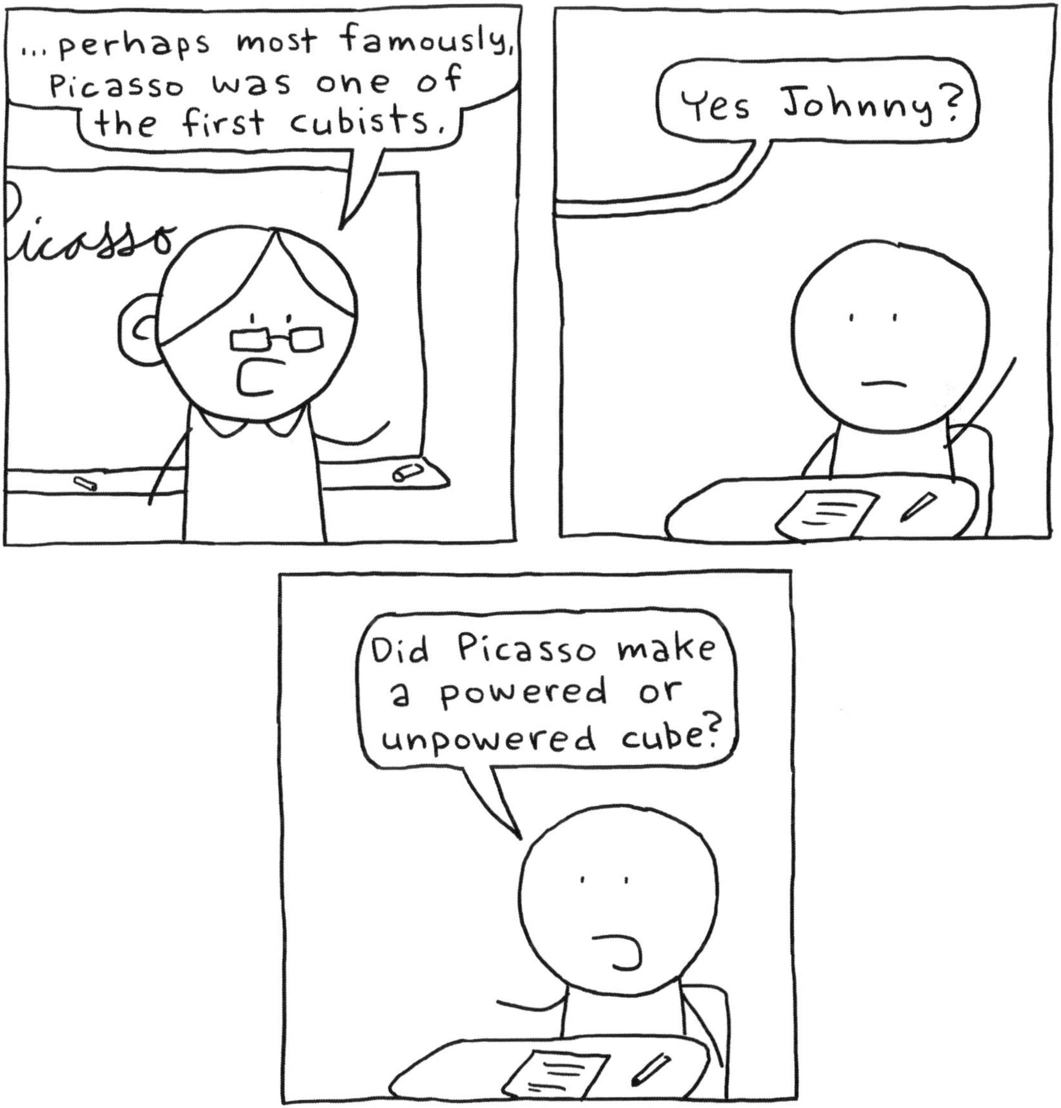
...perhaps most famously, Picasso was one of the first cubists.
Picasso
Yes Johnny?
Did Picasso make a powered or unpowered cube?

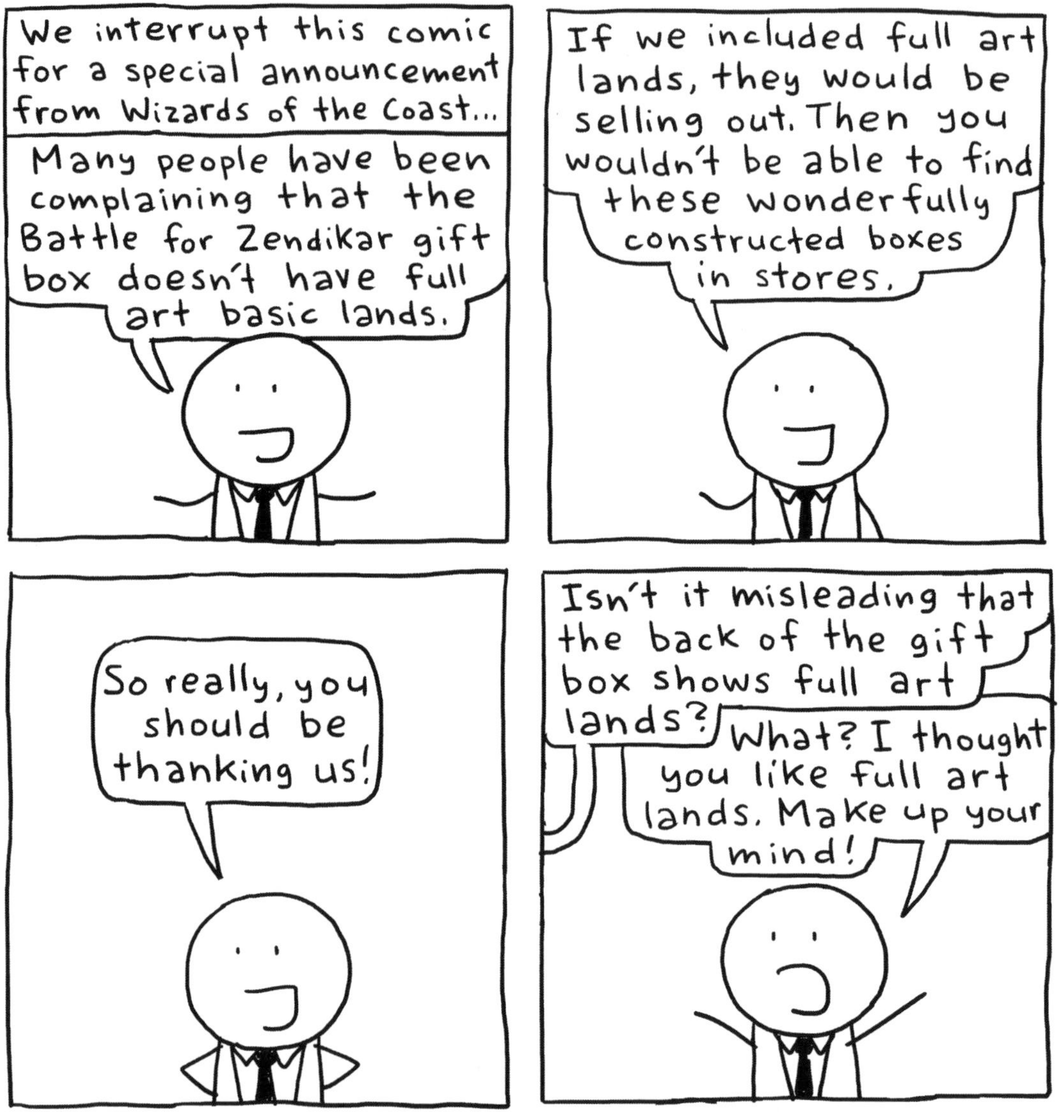
We interrupt this comic for a special announcement from Wizards of the Coast...
Many people have been complaining that the Battle for Zendikar gift box doesn't have full art basic lands.
If we included full art lands, they would be selling out. Then you wouldn't be able to find these wonderfully constructed boxes in stores.
So really, you should be thanking us!
Isn't it misleading that the back of the gift box shows full art lands?
What? I thought you like full art lands. Make up your mind!

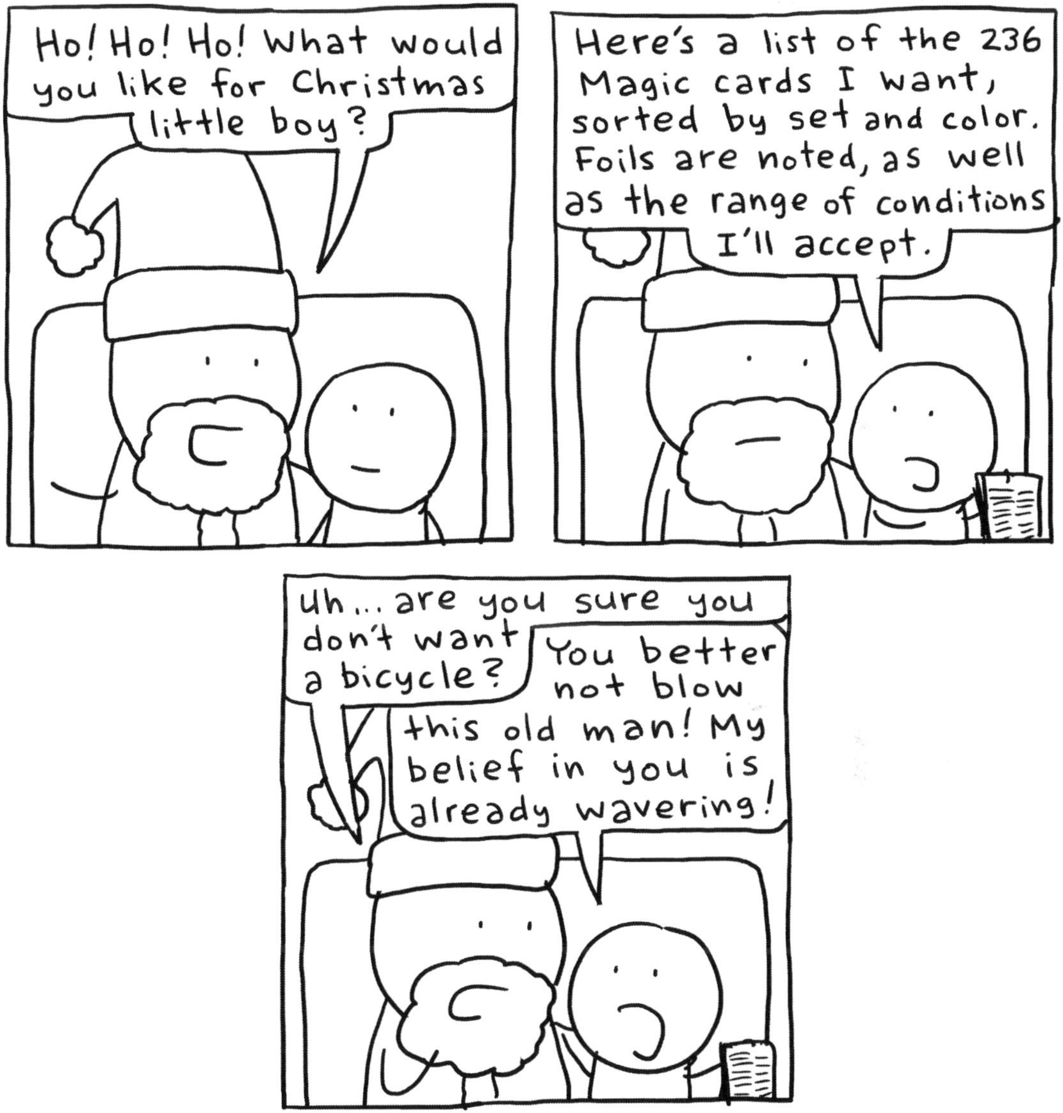
Ho! Ho! Ho! What would you like for Christmas little boy?
Here's a list of the 236 Magic cards I want, sorted by set and color. Foils are noted, as well as the range of conditions I'll accept.
Uh... are you sure you don't want a bicycle?
You better not blow this old man! My belief in you is already wavering!

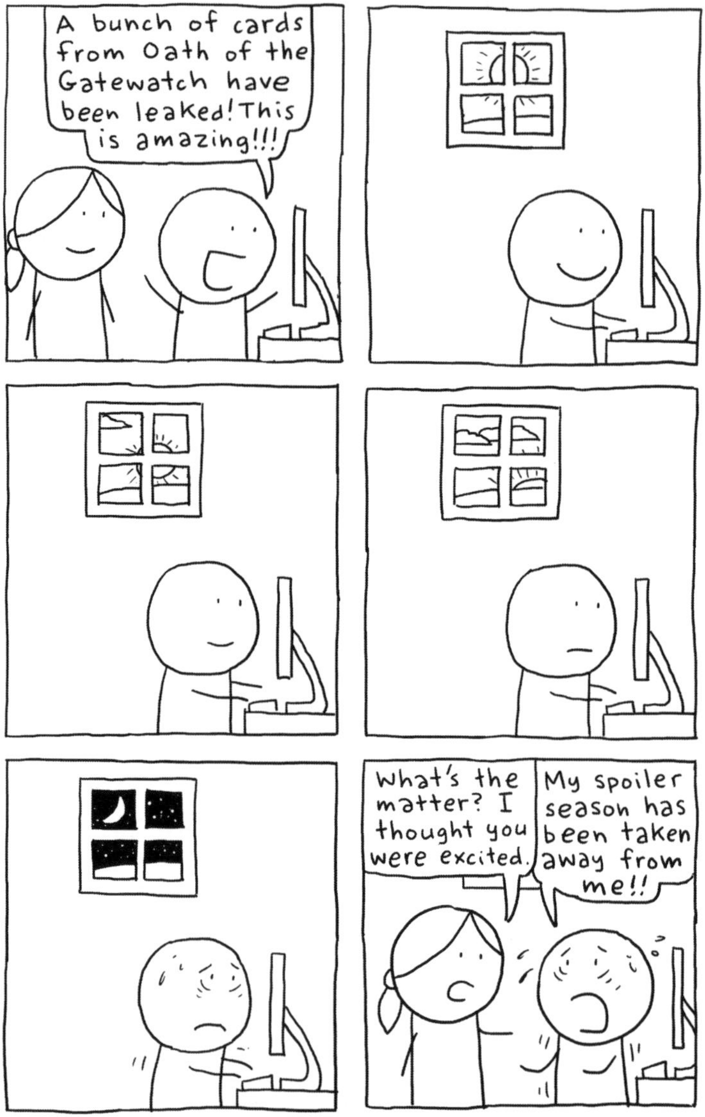
A bunch of cards from Oath of the Gatewatch have been leaked! This is amazing!!!
What's the matter? I thought you were excited.
My spoiler season has been taken away from me!!

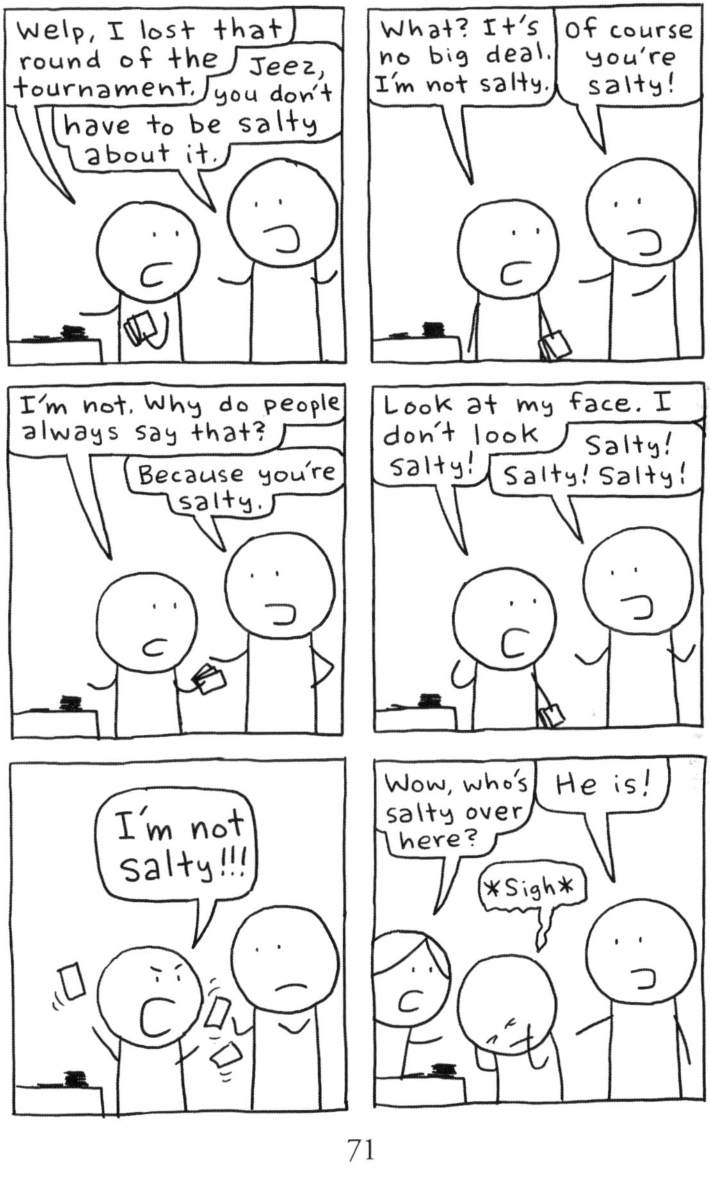
Welp, I lost that round of the tournament.
Jeez, you don't have to be salty about it.
What? It's no big deal. I'm not salty.
Of course you're salty!
I'm not. Why do people always say that?
Because you're salty.
Look at my face. I don't look salty!
Salty! Salty! Salty!
I'm not salty!!!
Wow, who's salty over here?
He is!
Sigh

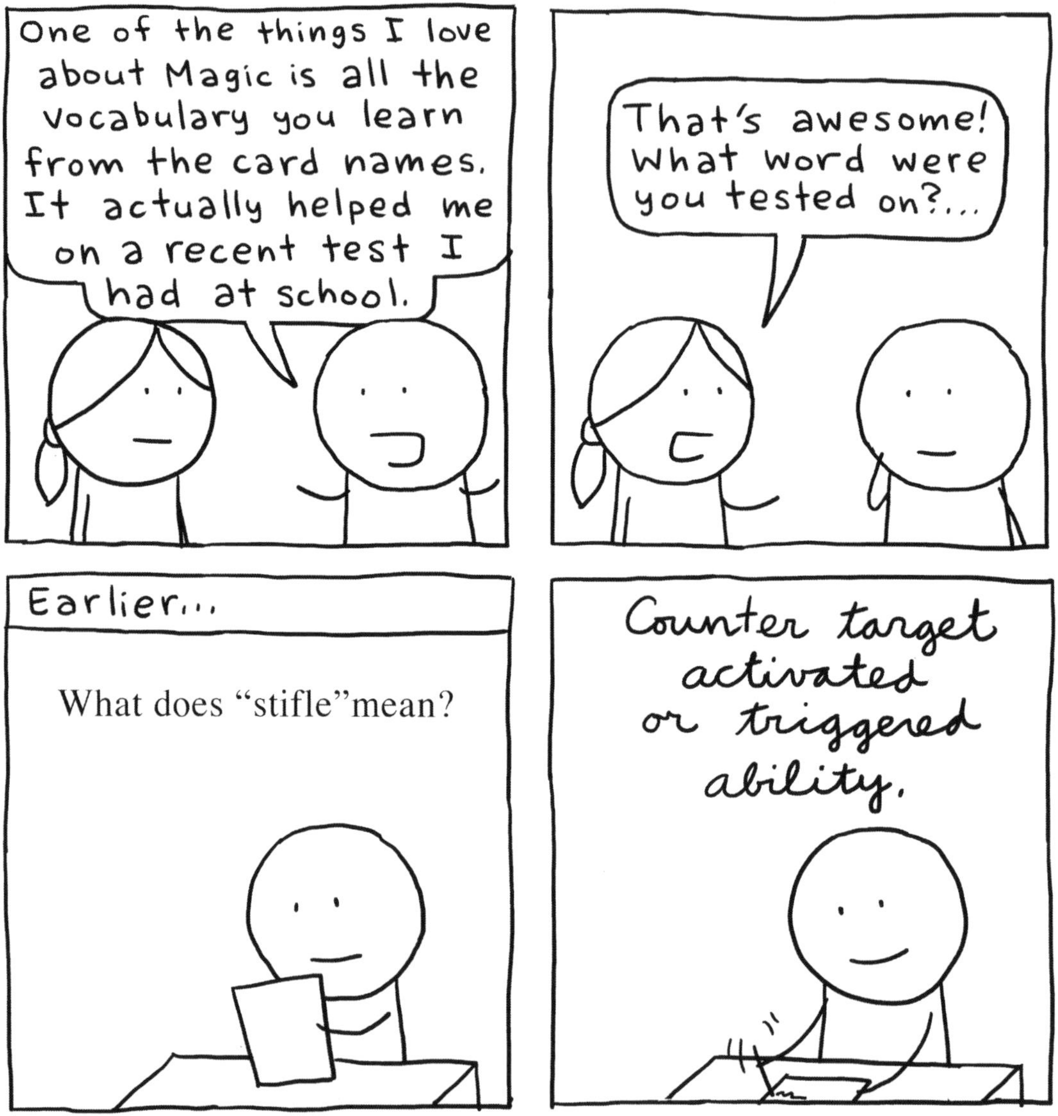
One of the things I love about Magic is all the vocabulary you learn from the card names. It actually helped me on a recent test I had at school.
That's awesome! What word were you tested on?...
Earlier...
What does "stifle" mean?
Counter target activated or triggered ability.

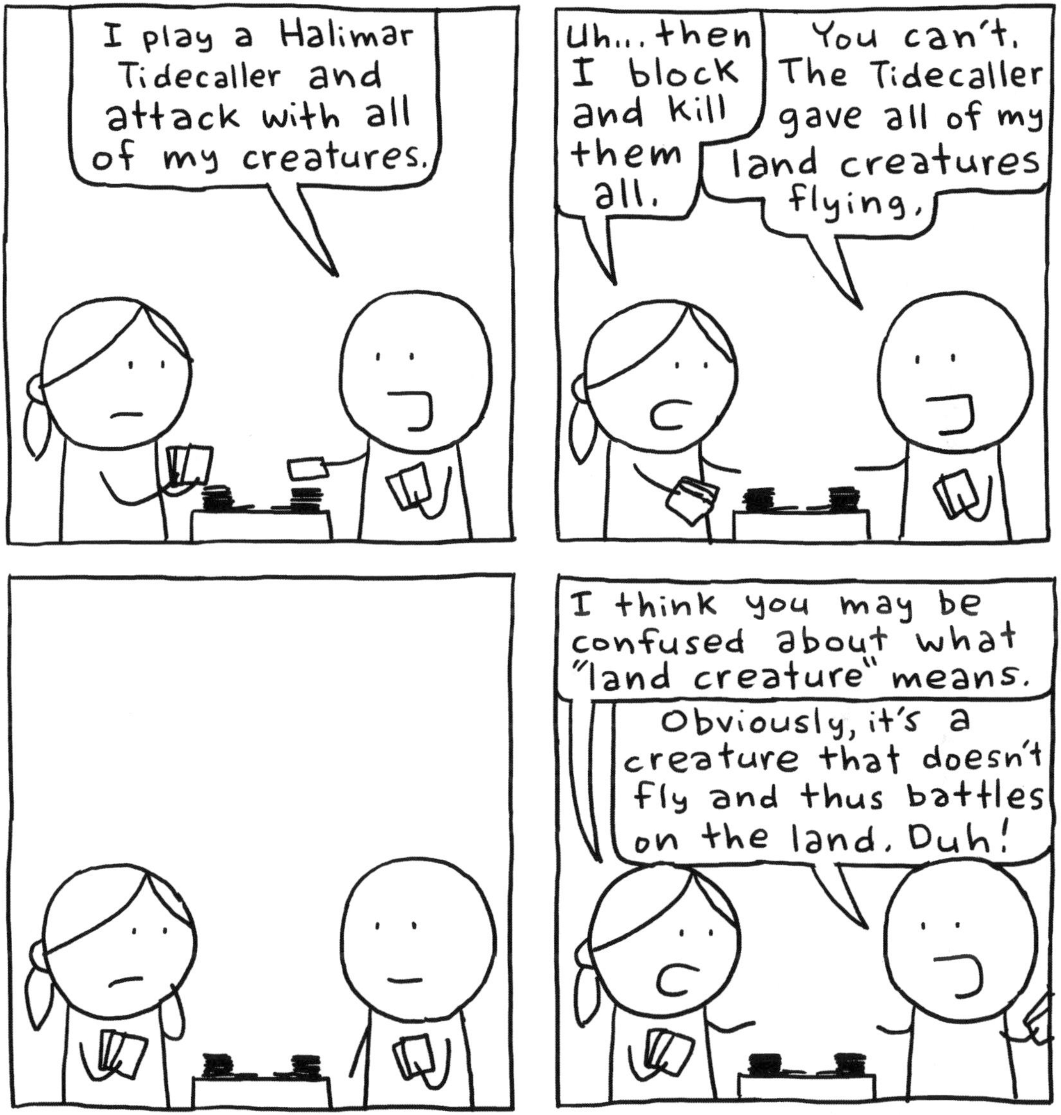

I play a Halimar Tidecaller and attack with all of my creatures.
Uh... then I block and kill them all.
You can't. The Tidecaller gave all of my land creatures flying.
I think you may be confused about what "land creature" means.
Obviously, it's a creature that doesn't fly and thus battles on the land. Duh!

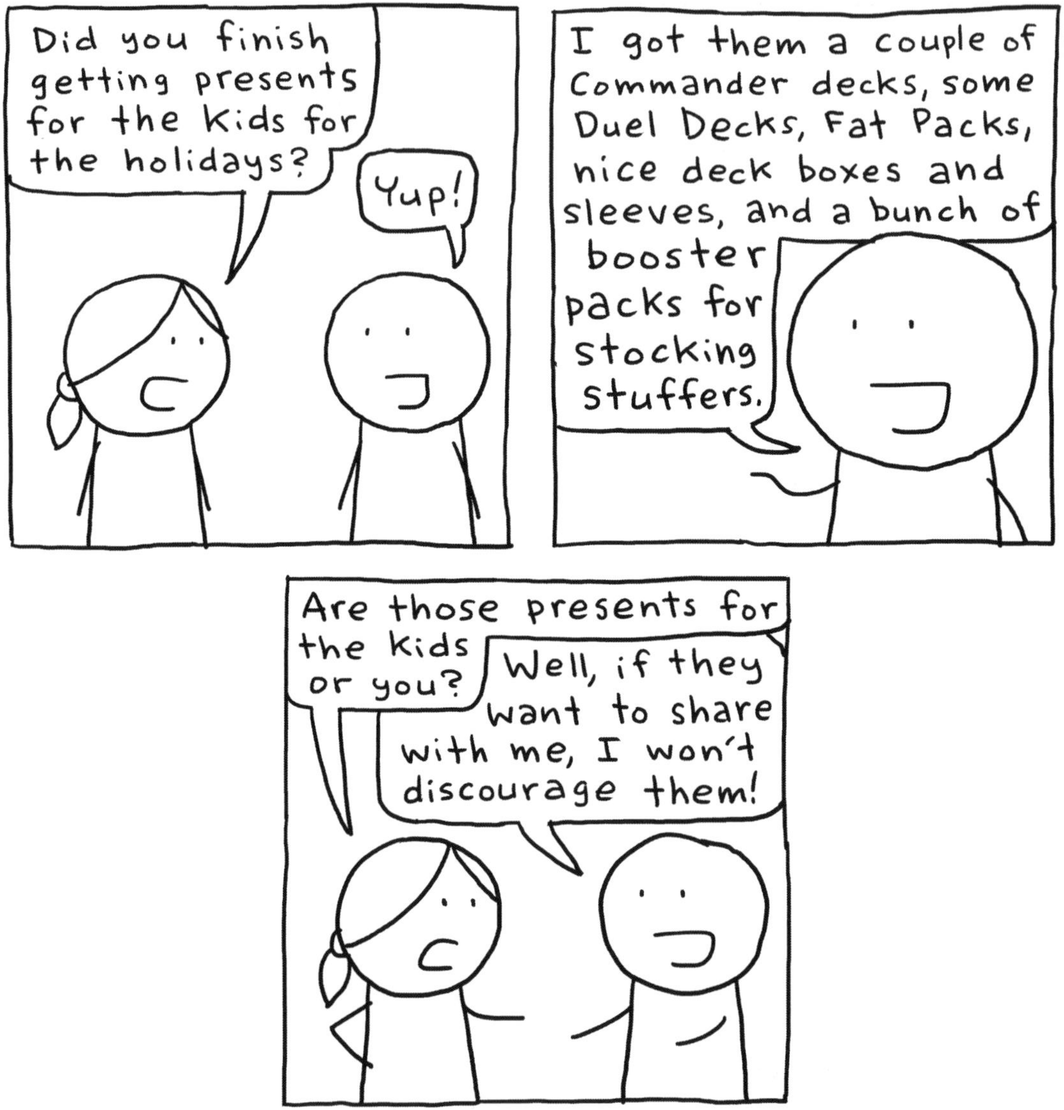
Did you finish getting presents for the Kids for the holidays?
Yup!
I got them a couple of Commander decks, some Duel Decks, Fat Packs, nice deck boxes and sleeves, and a bunch of booster packs for stocking stuffers.
Are those presents for the kids or you?
Well, if they want to share with me, I won't discourage them!

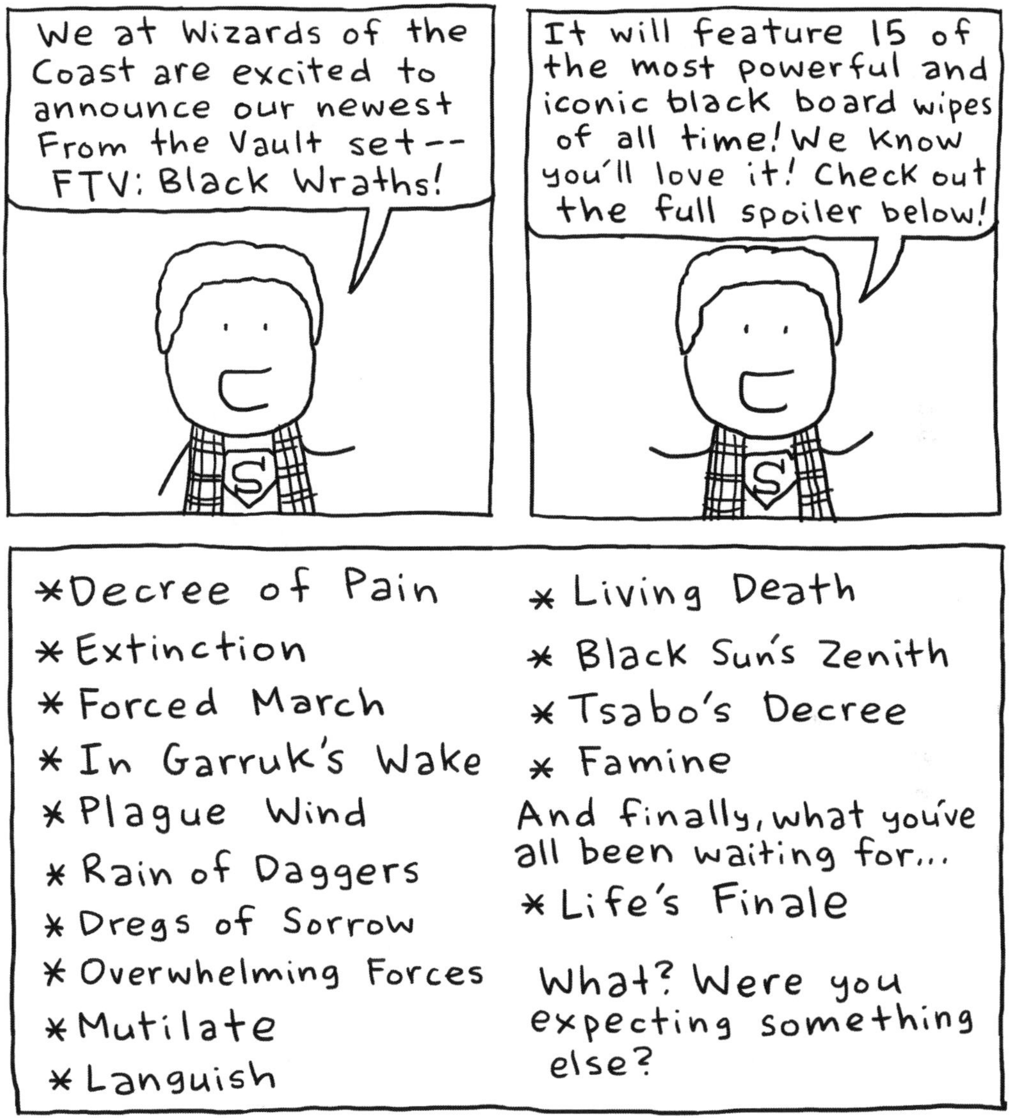
We at Wizards of the Coast are excited to announce our newest From the Vault set -- FTV: Black Wraths!
It will feature 15 of the most powerful and iconic black board wipes of all time! We know you'll love it! Check out the full spoiler below!
*Decree of Pain
*Extinction
*Forced March
*In Garruk's Wake
*Plague Wind
*Rain of Daggers
*Dregs of Sorrow
*Overwhelming Forces
*Mutilate
*Languish
*Living Death
*Black Sun's Zenith
*Tsabo's Decree
*Famine
And finally, what you've all been waiting for...
*Life's Finale
What? Were you expecting something else?

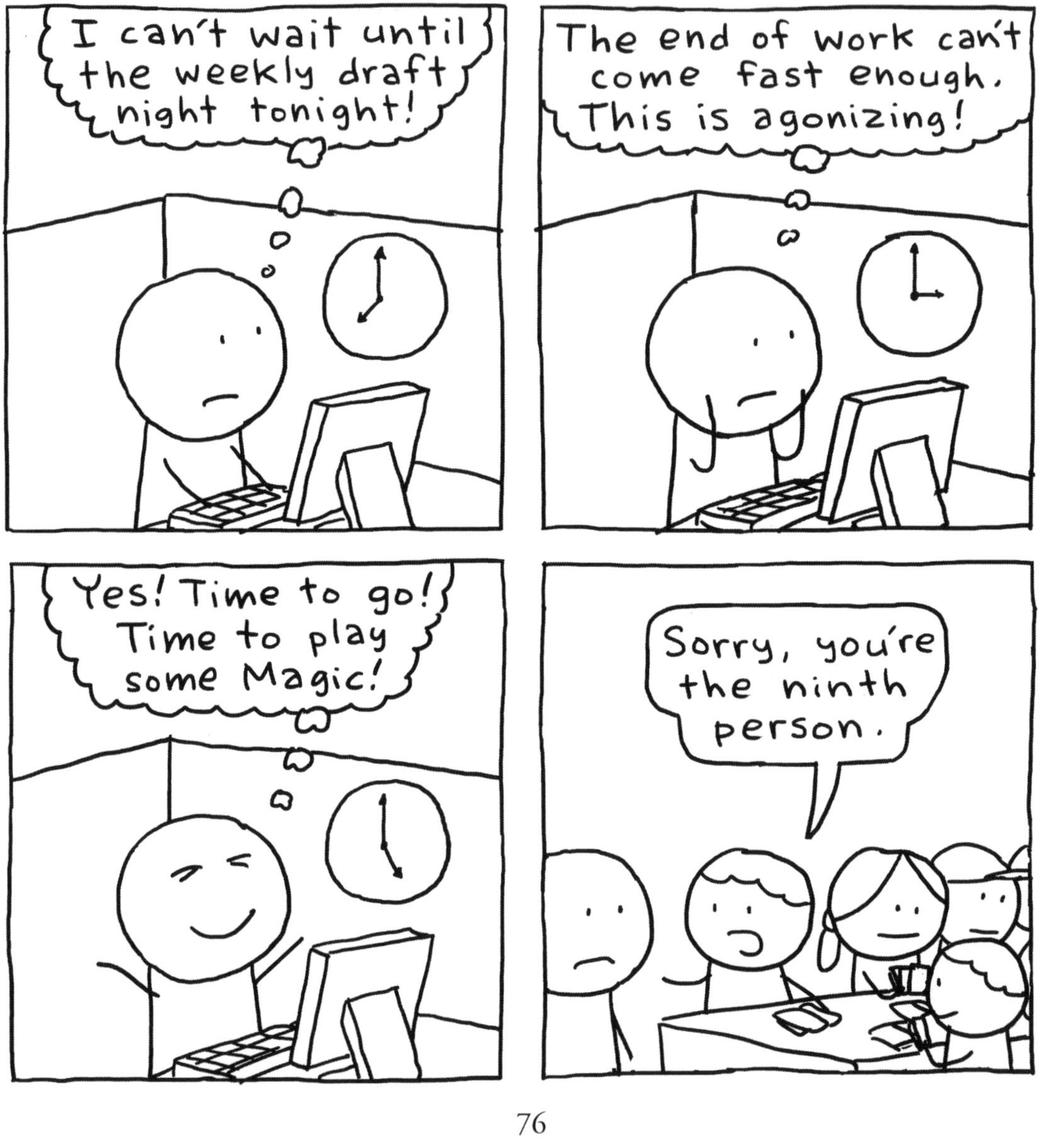
I can't wait until the weekly draft night tonight!
The end of work can't come fast enough. This is agonizing!
Yes! Time to go! Time to play some Magic!
Sorry, you're the ninth person.

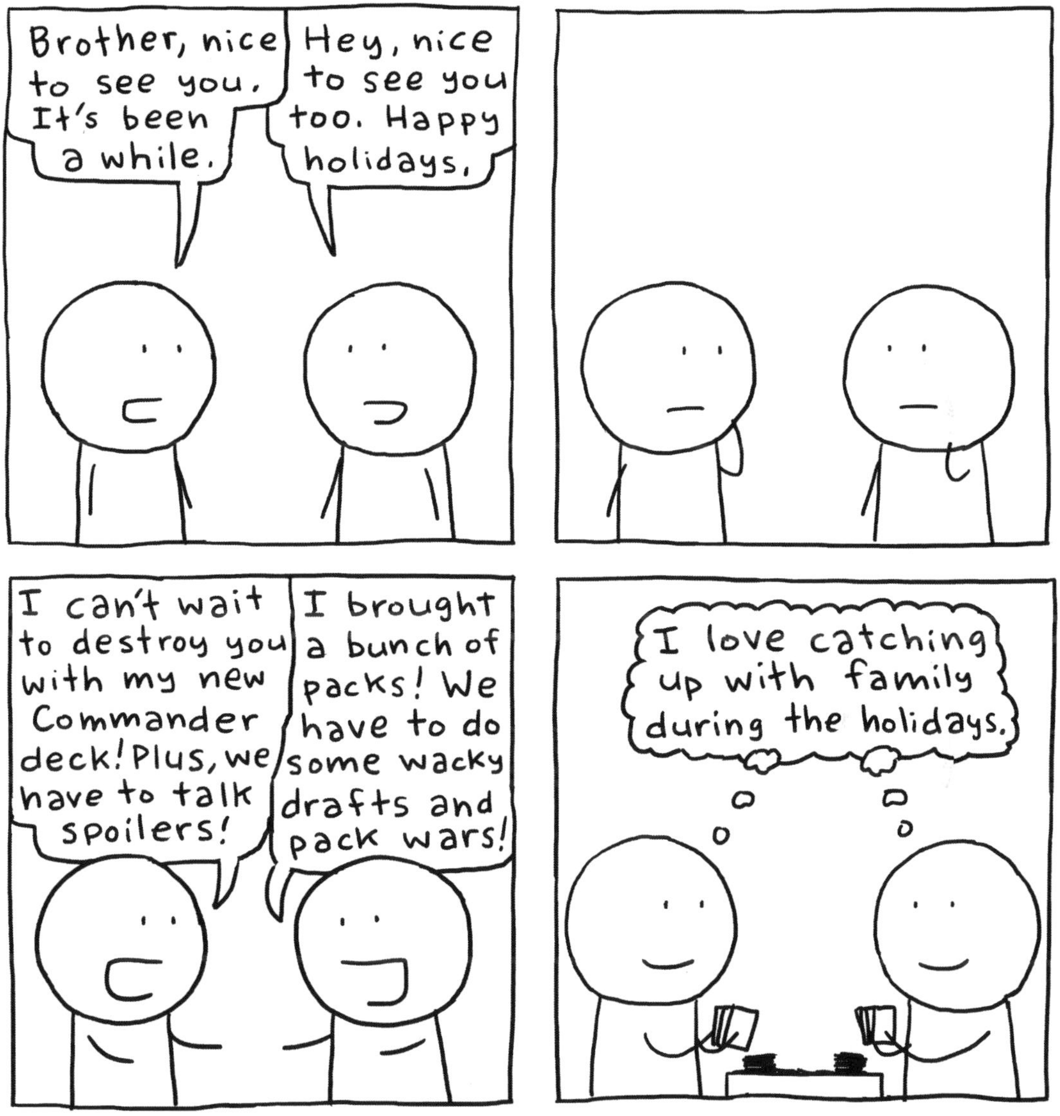
Brother, nice to see you. It's been a while.
Hey, nice to see you too. Happy holidays.
I can't wait to destroy you with my new Commander deck! Plus, we have to talk spoilers!
I brought a bunch of packs! We have to do some wacky drafts and pack wars!
I love catching up with family during the holidays.

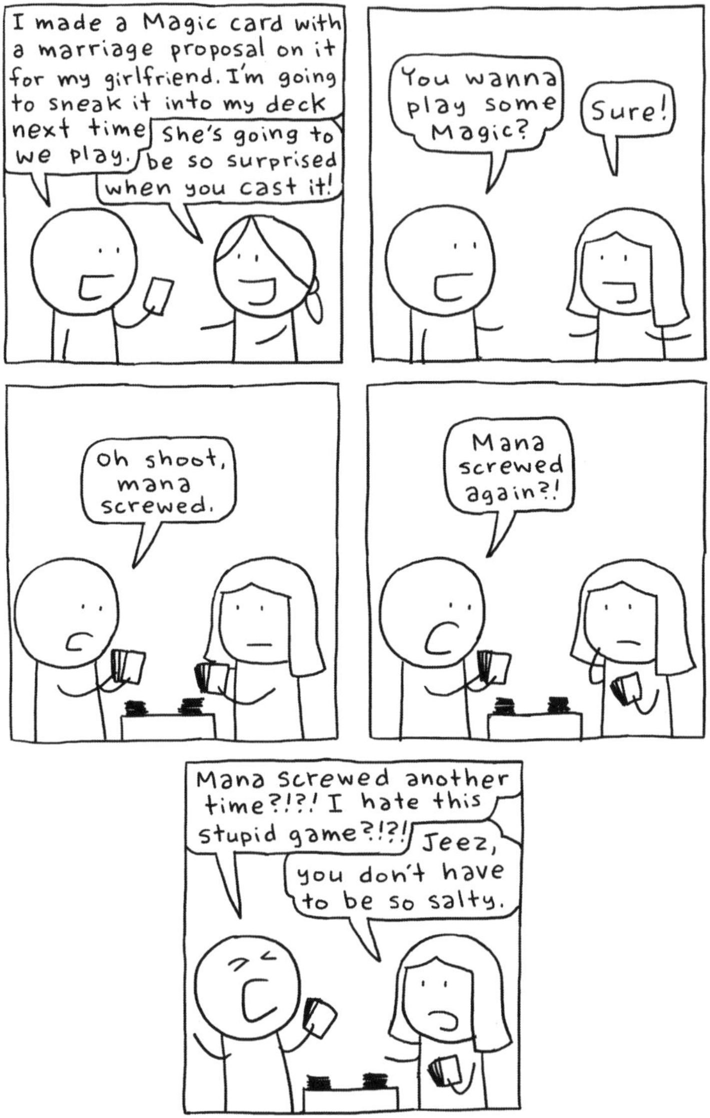
I made a Magic card with a marriage proposal on it for my girlfriend. I'm going to sneak it into my deck next time we play.
She's going to be so surprised when you cast it!
You wanna play some Magic?
Sure!
Oh shoot, mana screwed.
Mana screwed again?!
Mana screwed another time?!?! I hate this stupid game?!?!
Jeez, you don't have to be so salty.

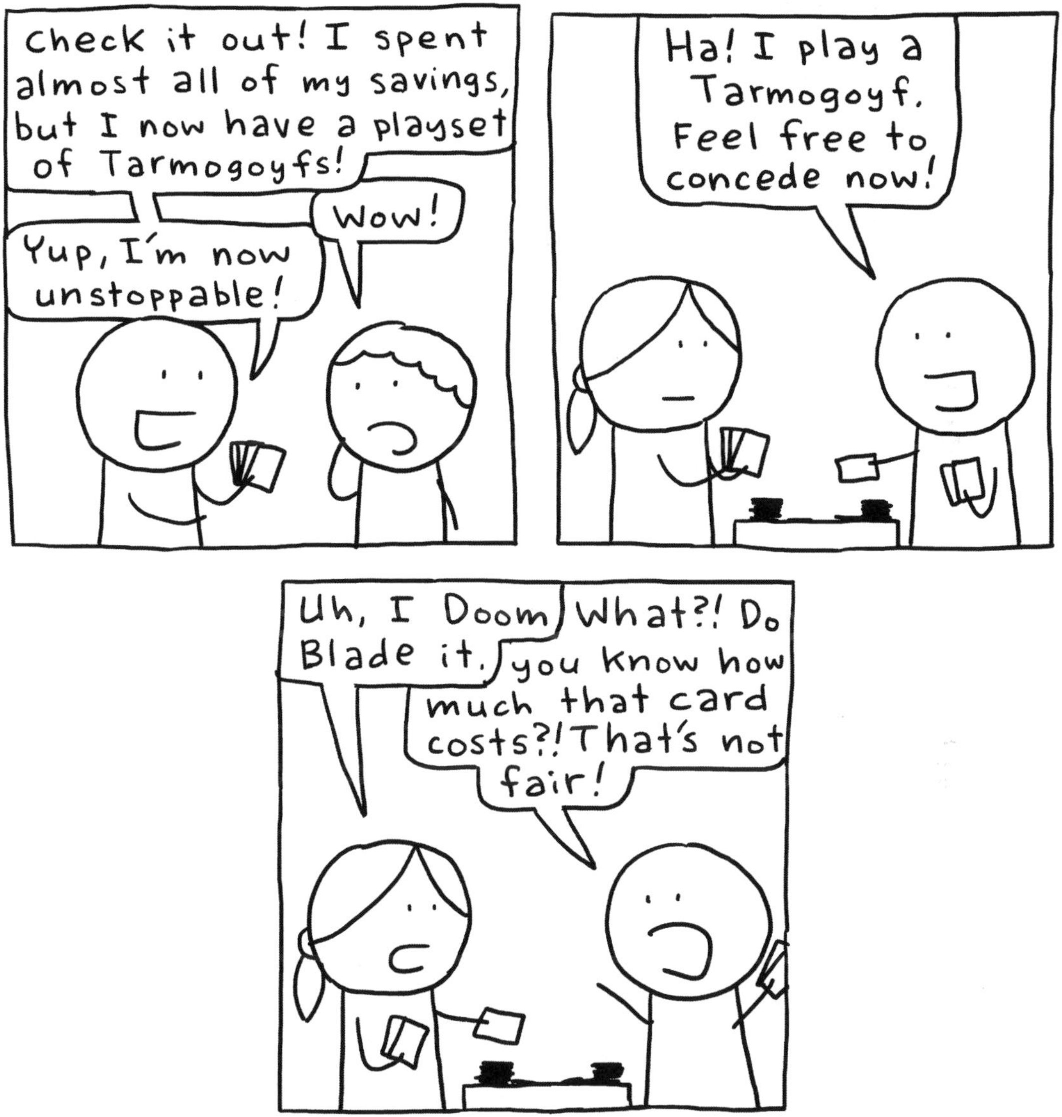
Check it out! I spent almost all of my savings, but I now have a playset of Tarmogoyfs!
Yup, I'm now unstoppable!
Wow!
Ha! I play a Tarmogoyf. Feel free to concede now!
Uh, I Doom Blade it.
What?! Do you know how much that card costs?! That's not fair!

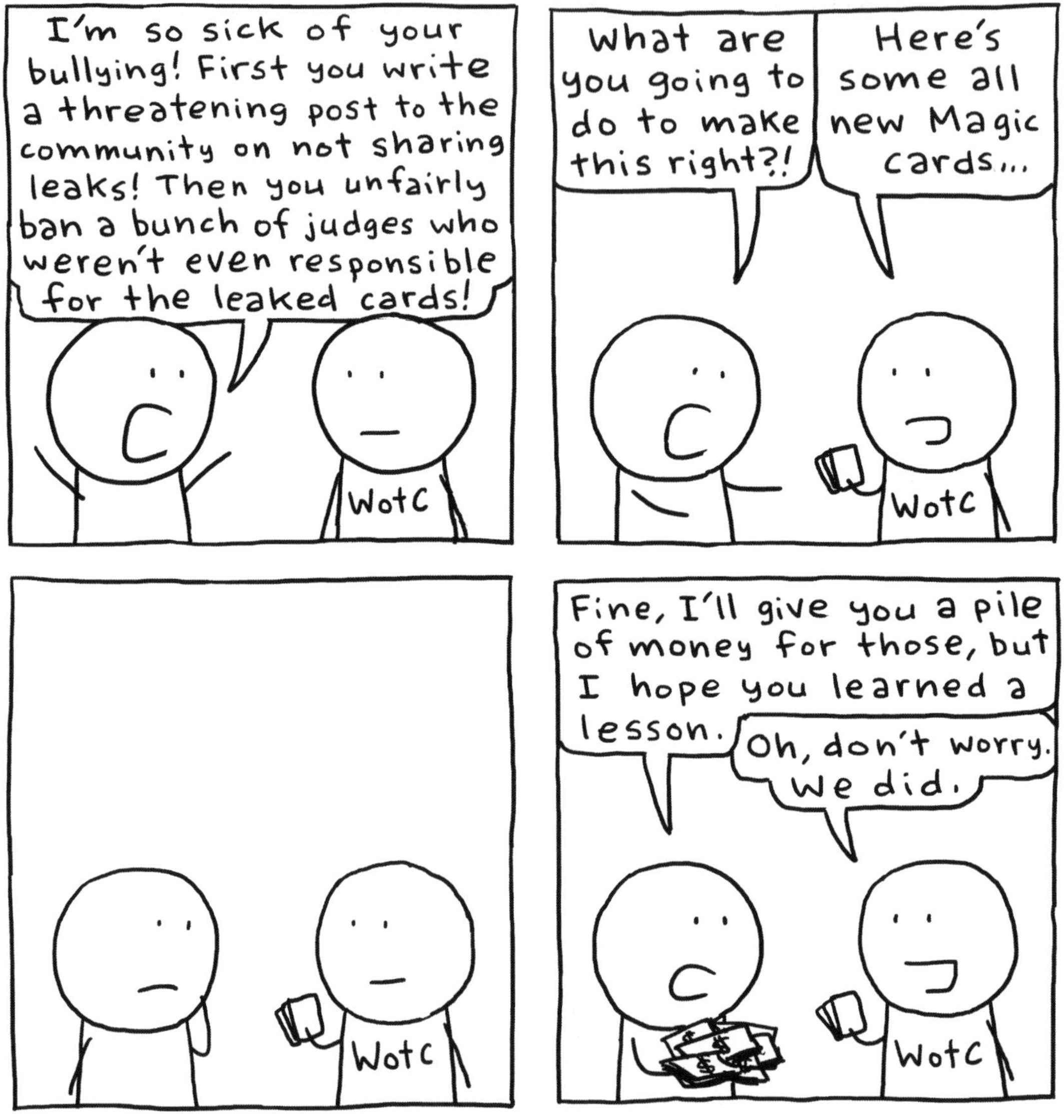
I'm so sick of your bullying! First you write a threatening post to the community on not sharing leaks! Then you unfairly ban a bunch of judges who weren't even responsible for the leaked cards!
WotC
What are you going to do to make this right?!
Here's some all new Magic cards...
WotC
WotC
Fine, I'll give you a pile of money for those, but I hope you learned a lesson.
Oh, don't worry. We did.
WotC

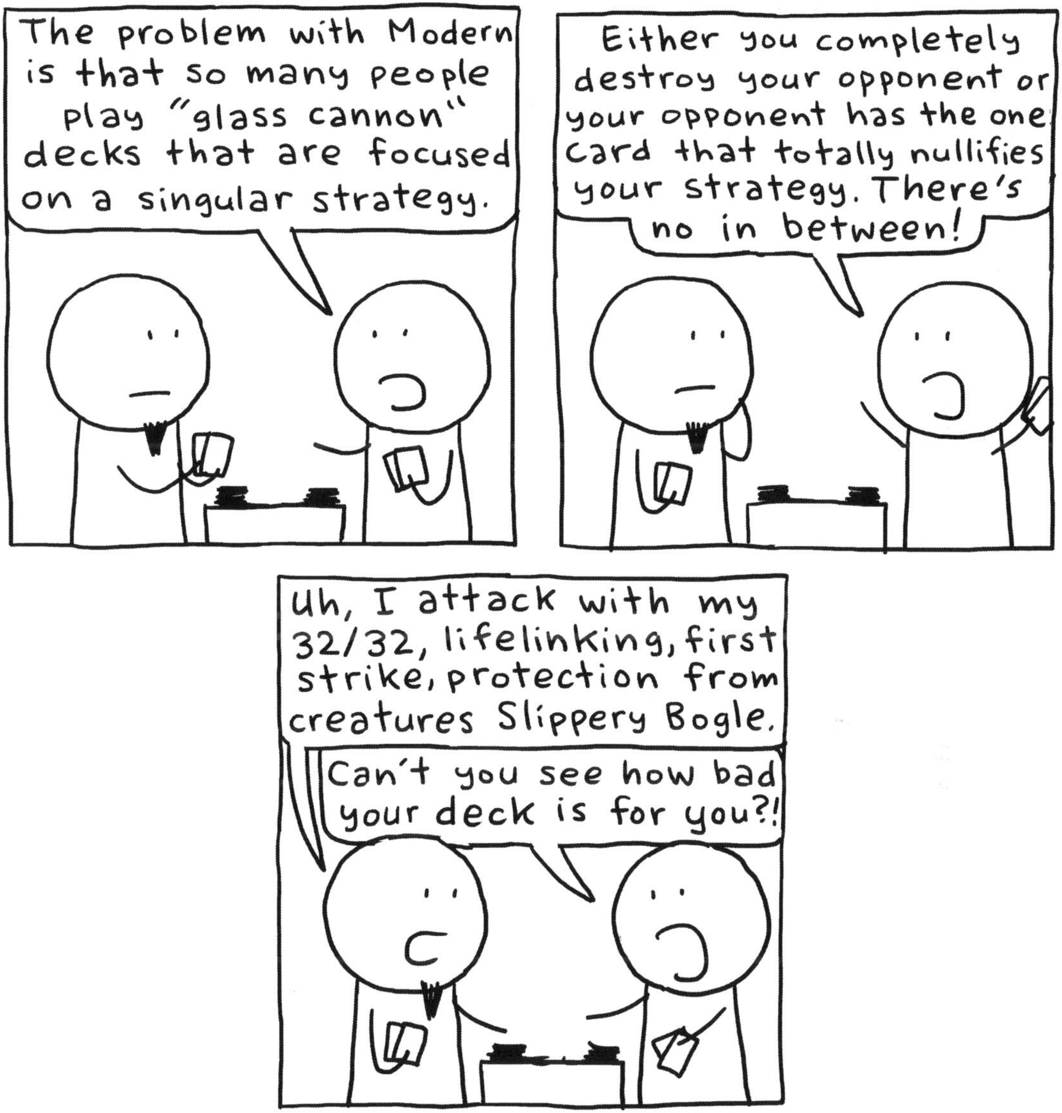
The problem with Modern is that so many people play "glass cannon" decks that are focused on a singular strategy.
Either you completely destroy your opponent or your opponent has the one card that totally nullifies your strategy. There's no in between!
Uh, I attack with my 32/32, lifelinking, first strike, protection from creatures Slippery Bogle.
Can't you see how bad your deck is for you?!

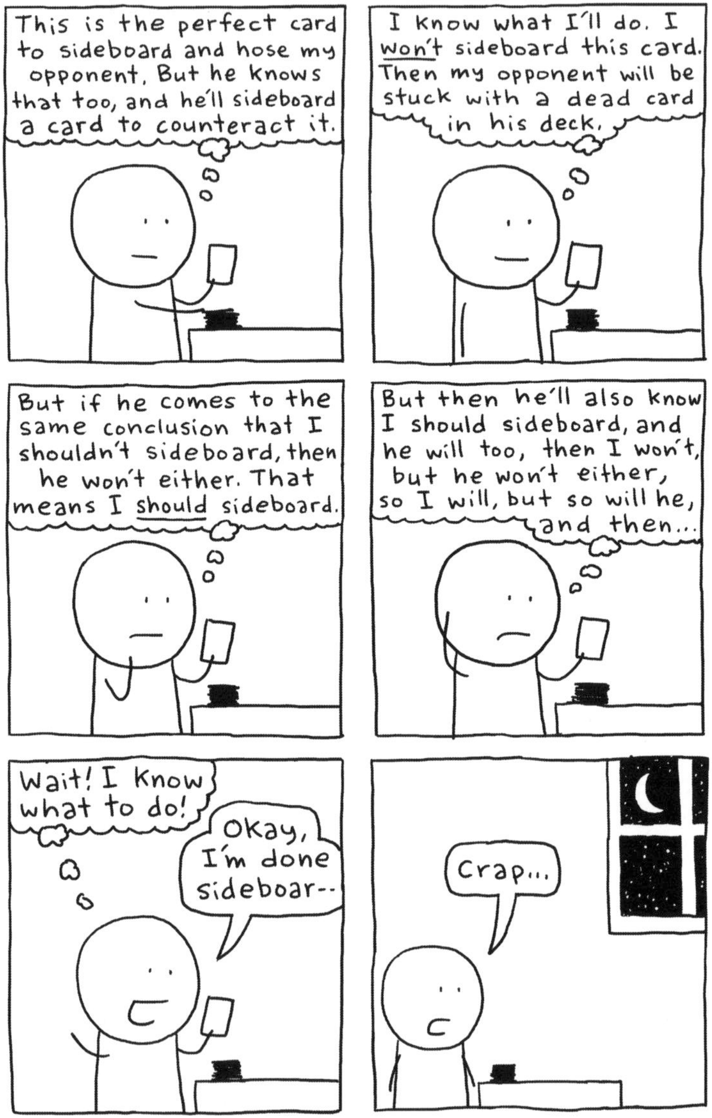
This is the perfect card to sideboard and hose my opponent. But he knows that too, and he'll sideboard a card to counteract it.
I know what I'll do. I won't sideboard this card. Then my opponent will be stuck with a dead card in his deck.
But if he comes to the same conclusion that I shouldn't sideboard, then he won't either. That means I should sideboard.
But then he'll also know I should sideboard, and he will too, then I won't, but he won't either, so I will, but so will he, and then...
Wait! I know what to do!
Okay, I'm done sideboar--
Crap...

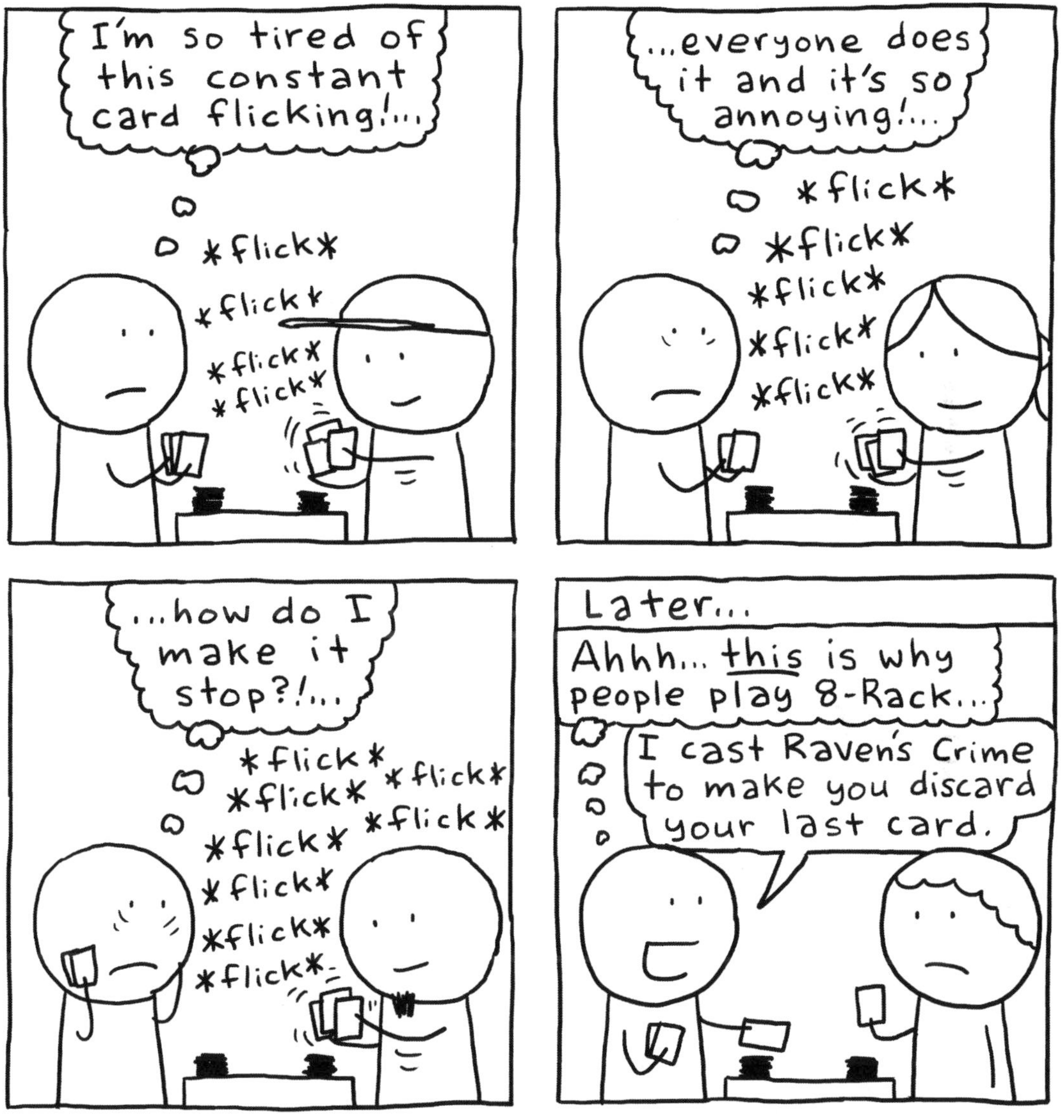
I'm so tired of this constant card flicking!...
flick
flick
flick
flick
...everyone does it and it's so annoying!...
flick
flick
flick
flick
flick
...how do I make it stop?!...
flick
flick
flick
flick
flick
flick
flick
flick
Later...
Ahhh... this is why people play 8-Rack...
I cast Raven's Crime to make you discard your last card.

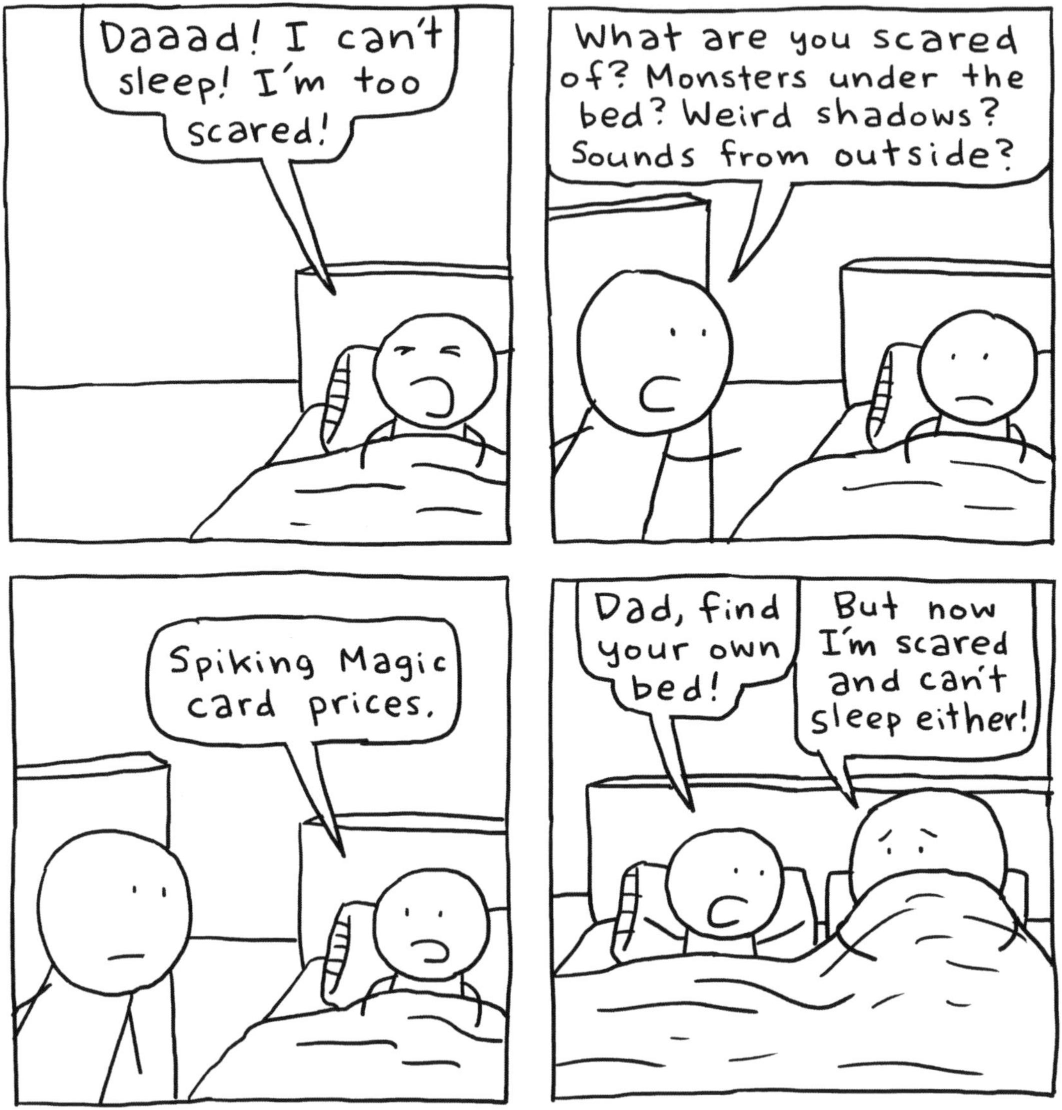
Daaad! I can't sleep! I'm too scared!
What are you scared of? Monsters under the bed? Weird shadows? Sounds from outside?
Spiking Magic card prices.
Dad, find your own bed!
But now I'm scared and can't sleep either!

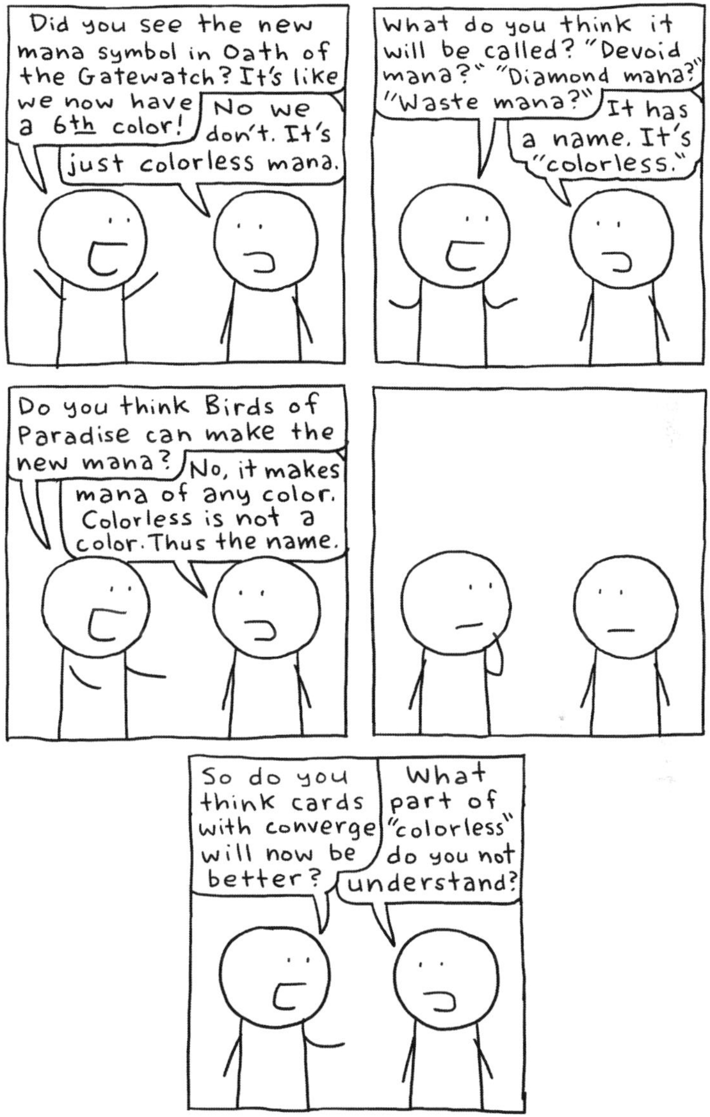
Did you see the new mana symbol in Oath of the Gatewatch? It's like we now have a 6th color!
No we don't. It's just colorless mana.
What do you think it will be called? "Devoid mana?" "Diamond mana?" "Waste mana?"
It has a name. It's "colorless."
Do you think Birds of Paradise can make the new mana?
No, it makes mana of any color. Colorless is not a color. Thus the name.
So do you think cards with converge will now be better?
What part of "colorless" do you not understand?

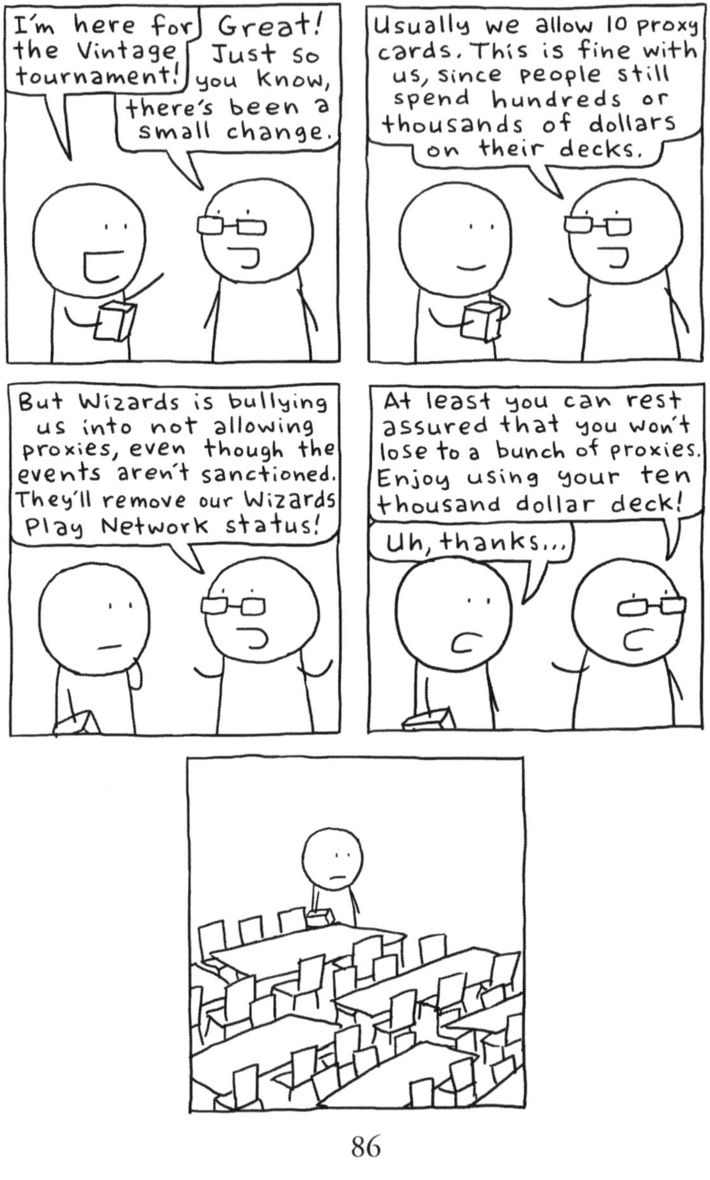
I'm here for the Vintage tournament!
Great! Just so you know, there's been a small change.
Usually we allow 10 proxy cards. This is fine with us, since people still spend hundreds or thousands of dollars on their decks.
But Wizards is bullying us into not allowing proxies, even though the events aren't sanctioned. They'll remove our Wizards Play Network status!
At least you can rest assured that you won't lose to a bunch of proxies. Enjoy using your ten thousand dollar deck!
Uh, thanks...

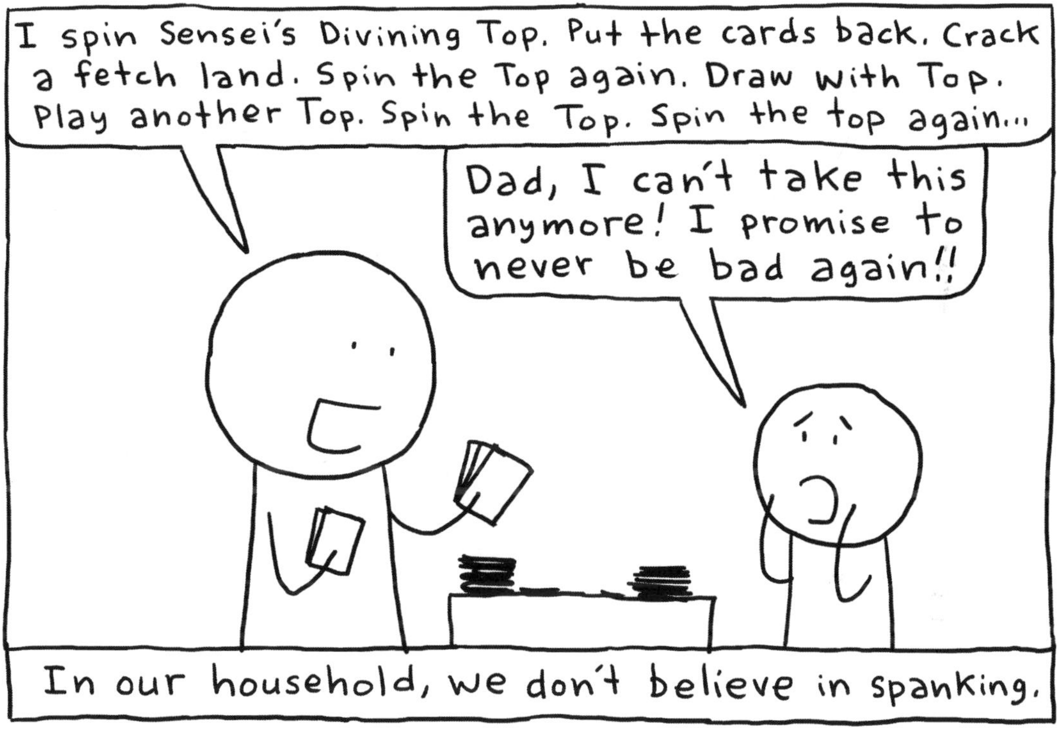
I spin Sensei's Divining Top. Put the cards back. Crack a fetch land. Spin the Top again. Draw with Top. Play another Top. Spin the Top. Spin the top again...
Dad, I can't take this anymore! I promise to never be bad again!!
In our household, we don't believe in spanking.

If you want a Modern Pro Tour, we have no choice but to ban cards every year to make sure it is a diverse and interesting format.
WotC
Meanwhile, in Standard...
I play a Siege Rhino.
I play a Siege Rhino.
I play a Siege Rhino.
I play a Siege Rhino.

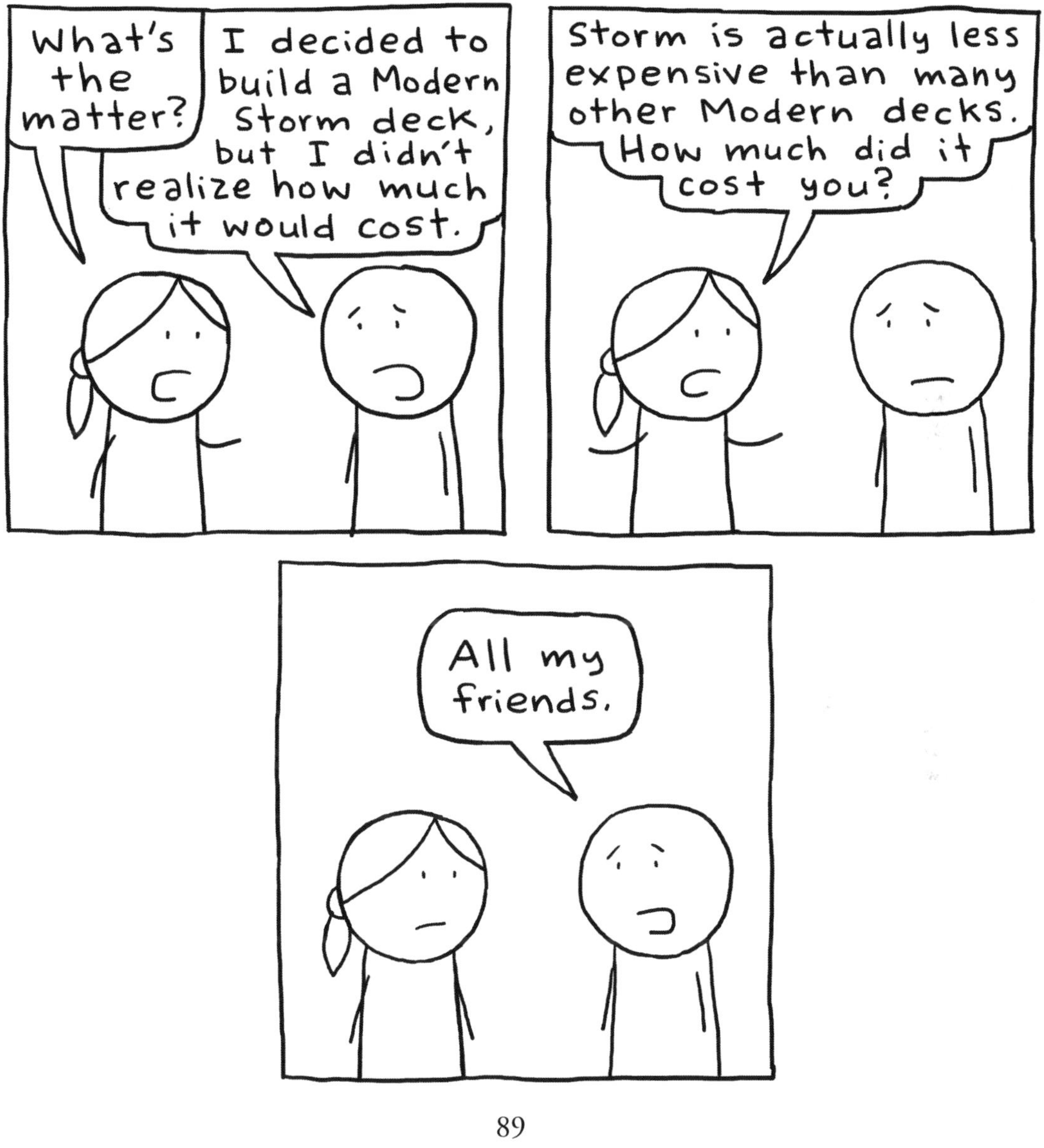
What's the matter?
I decided to build a Modern Storm deck, but I didn't realize how much it would cost.
Storm is actually less expensive than many other Modern decks. How much did it cost you?
All my friends.

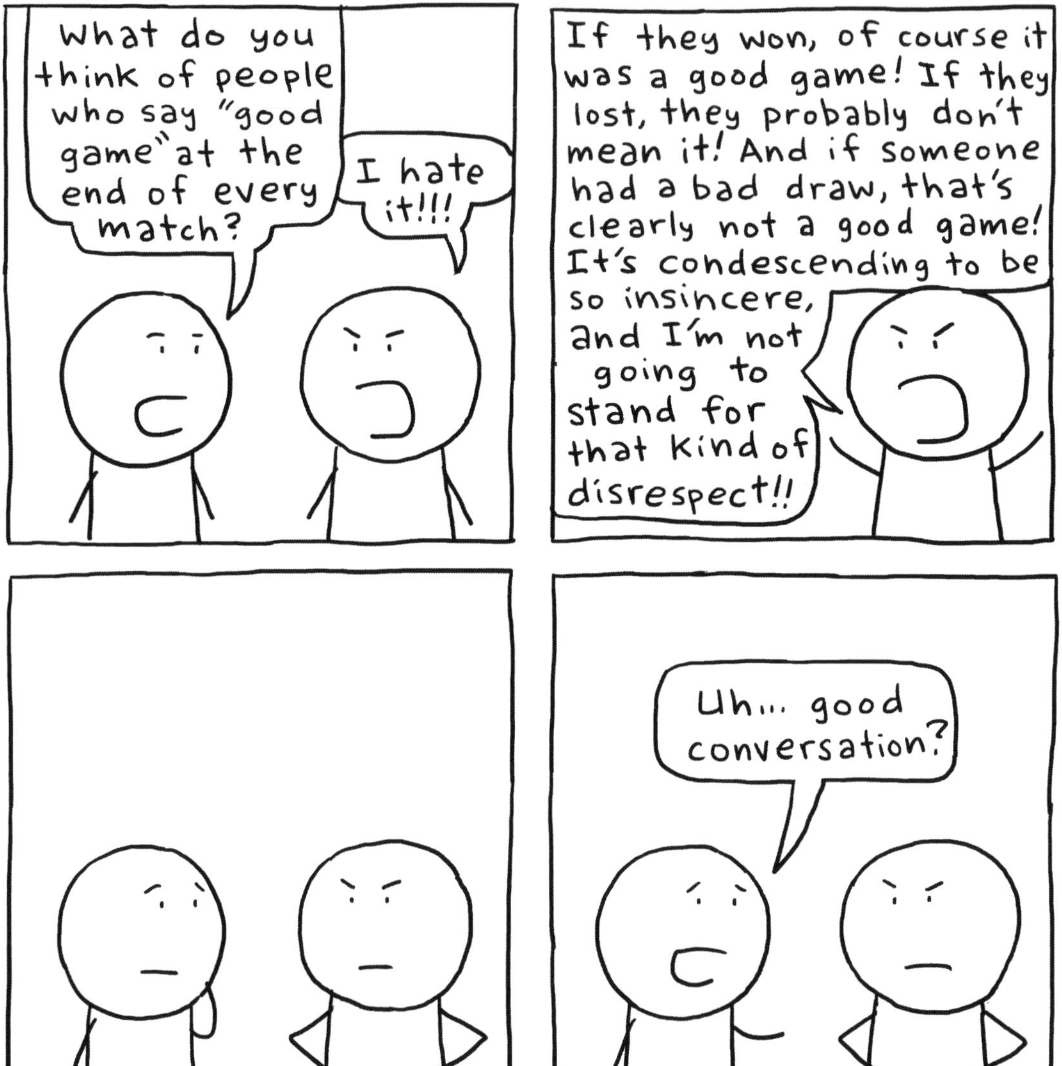
What do you think of people who say "good game" at the end of every match?
I hate it!!!
If they won, of course it was a good game! If they lost, they probably don't mean it! And if someone had a bad draw, that's clearly not a good game! It's condescending to be so insincere, and I'm not going to stand for that kind of disrespect!!
Uh... good conversation?

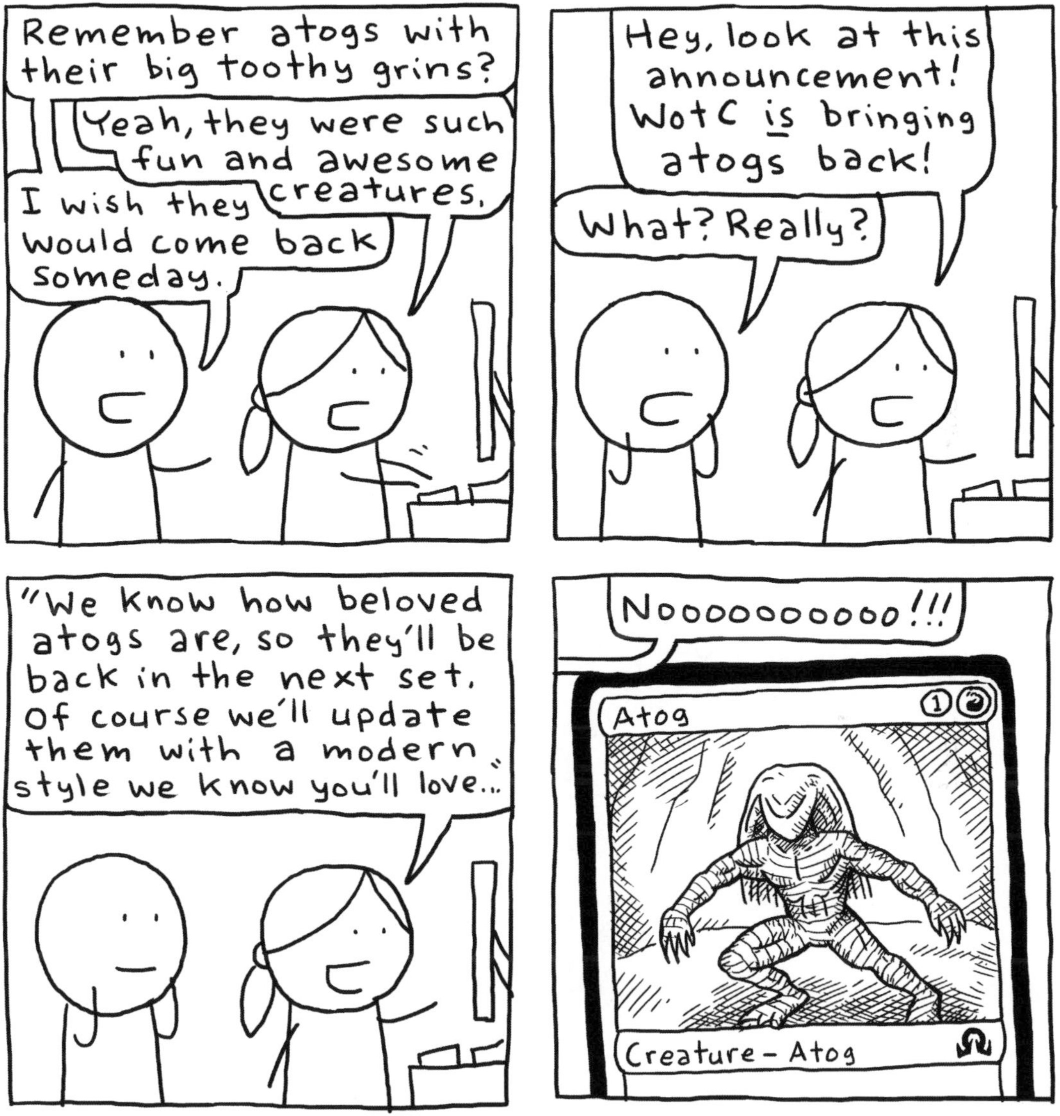
Remember atogs with their big toothy grins?
Yeah, they were such fun and awesome creatures.
I wish they would come back someday.
Hey, look at this announcement! WotC is bringing atogs back!
What? Really?
"We know how beloved atogs are, so they'll be back in the next set. Of course we'll update them with a modern style we know you'll love..."
Nooooooooooo!!!
Atog
1
Creature – Atog

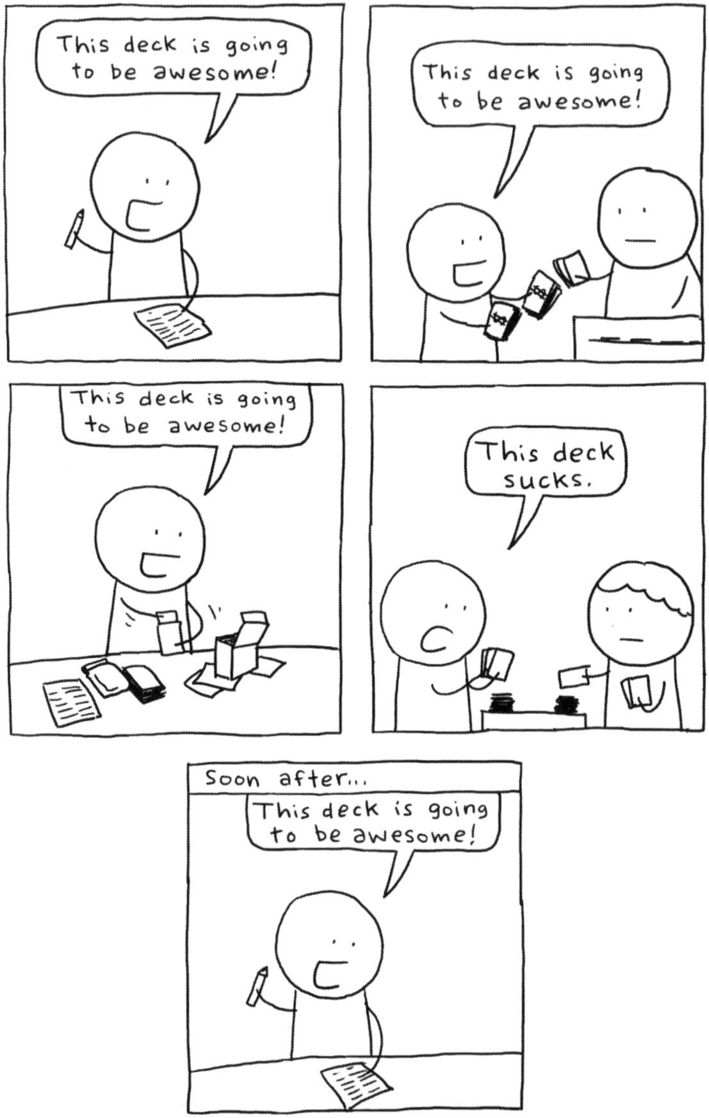
This deck is going to be awesome!
This deck is going to be awesome!
This deck is going to be awesome!
This deck sucks.
Soon after...
This deck is going to be awesome!

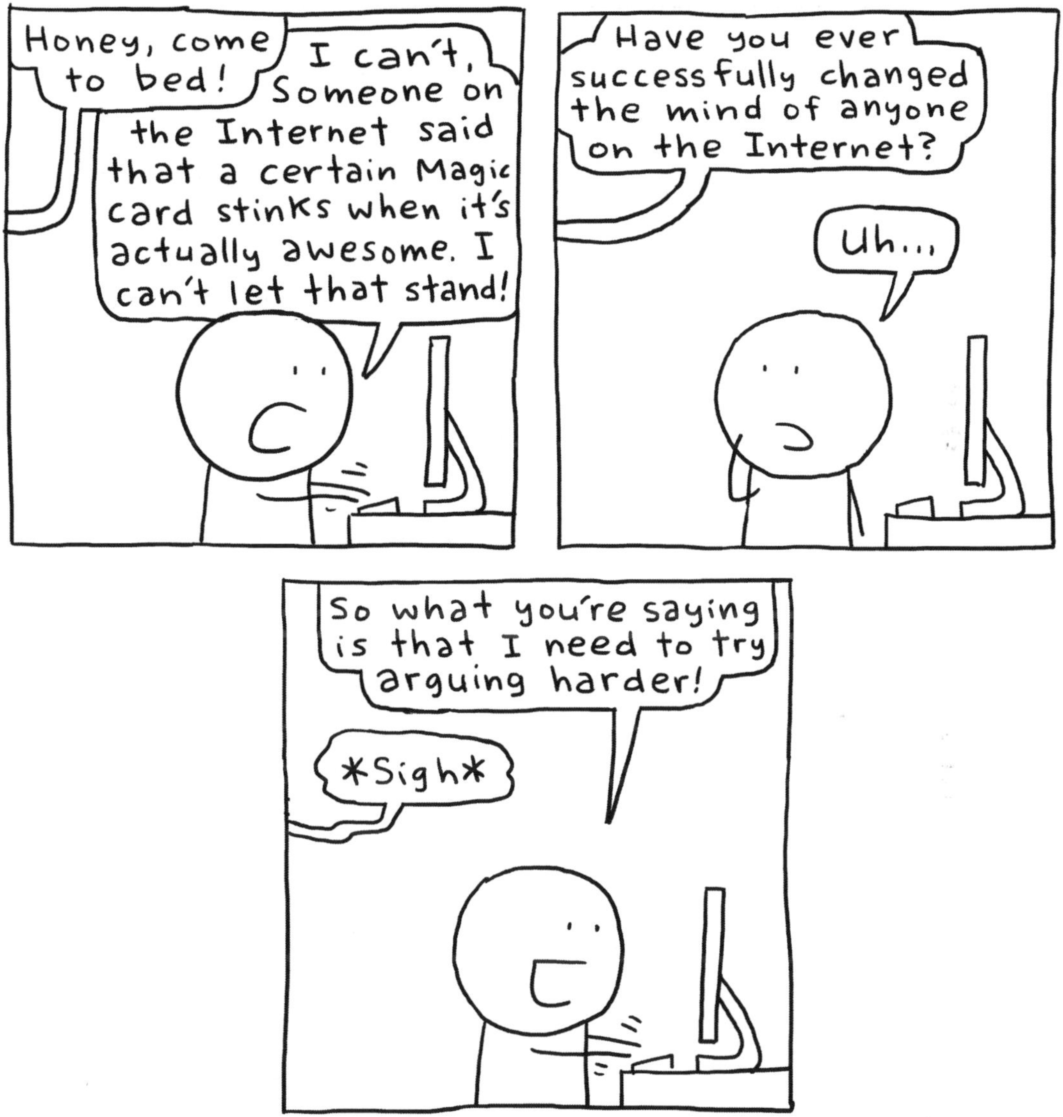
Honey, come to bed!
I can't, Someone on the Internet said that a certain Magic card stinks when it's actually awesome. I can't let that stand!
Have you ever successfully changed the mind of anyone on the Internet?
Uh...
So what you're saying is that I need to try arguing harder!
Sigh

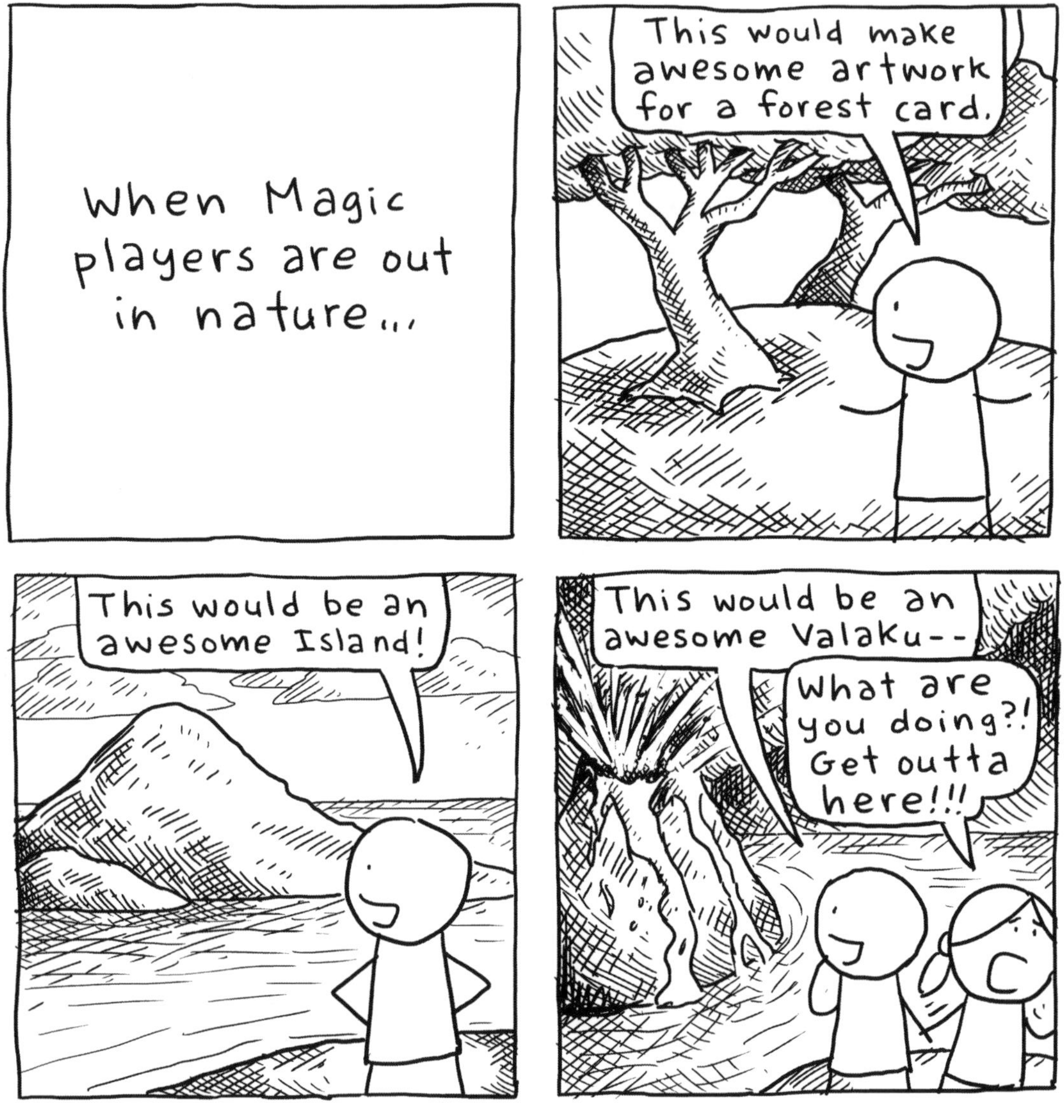

When Magic players are out in nature...
This would make awesome artwork for a forest card.
This would be an awesome Island!
This would be an awesome Valaku--
What are you doing?! Get outta here!!!

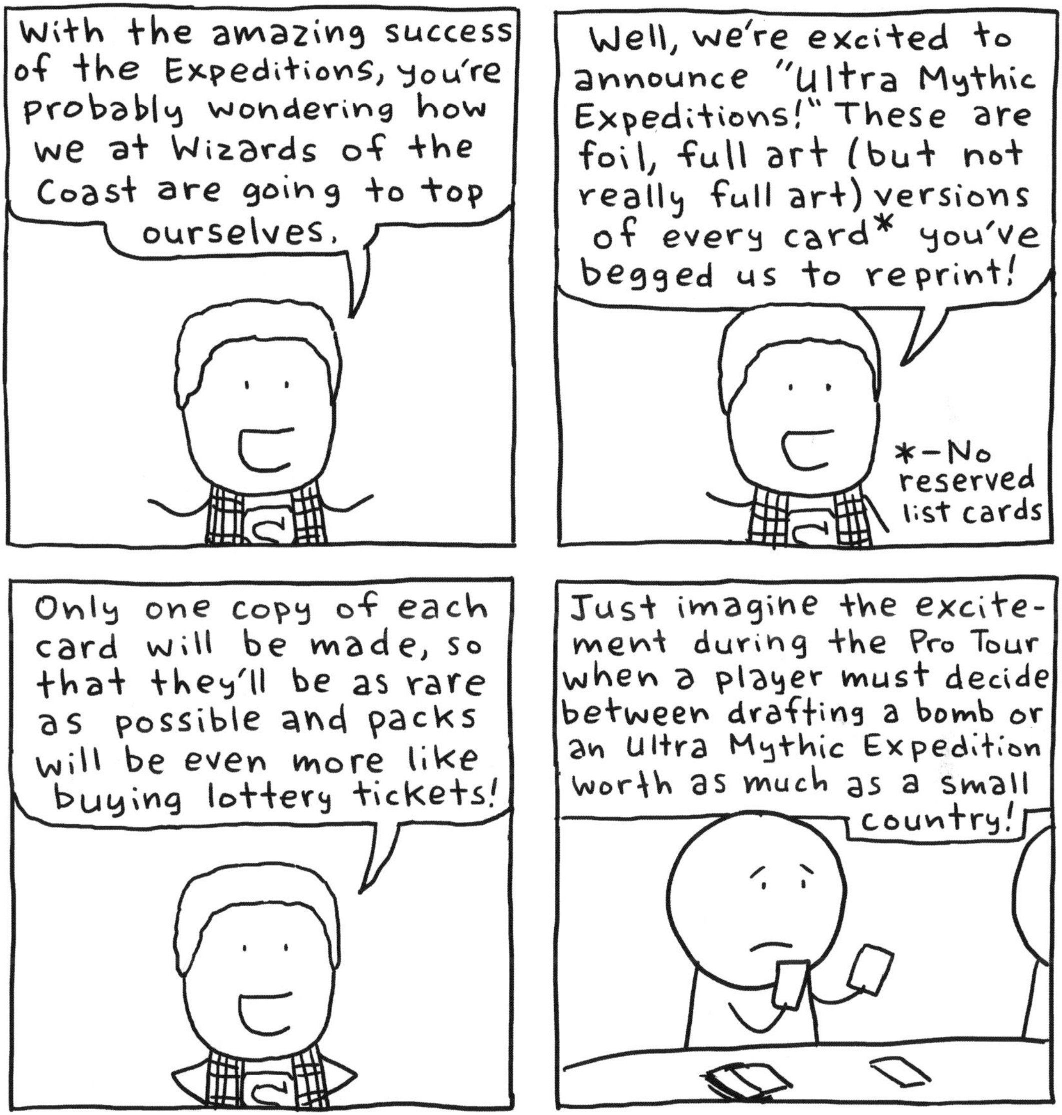
With the amazing success of the Expeditions, you're probably wondering how we at Wizards of the Coast are going to top ourselves.
Well, we're excited to announce "Ultra Mythic Expeditions!" These are foil, full art (but not really full art) versions of every card* you've begged us to reprint!
*—No reserved list cards
Only one copy of each card will be made, so that they'll be as rare as possible and packs will be even more like buying lottery tickets!
Just imagine the excitement during the Pro Tour when a player must decide between drafting a bomb or an Ultra Mythic Expedition worth as much as a small country!

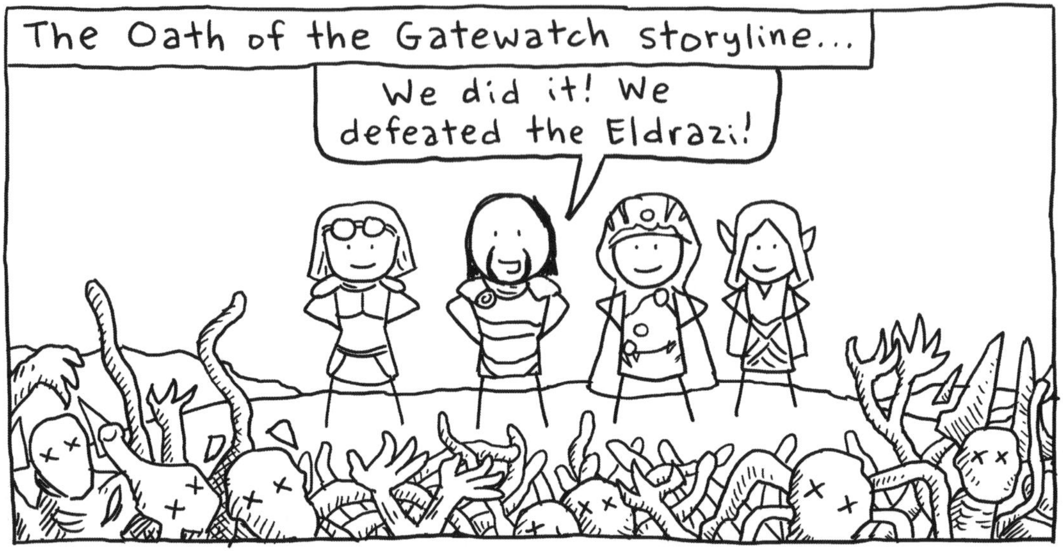
The Oath of the Gatewatch storyline...
We did it! We defeated the Eldrazi!

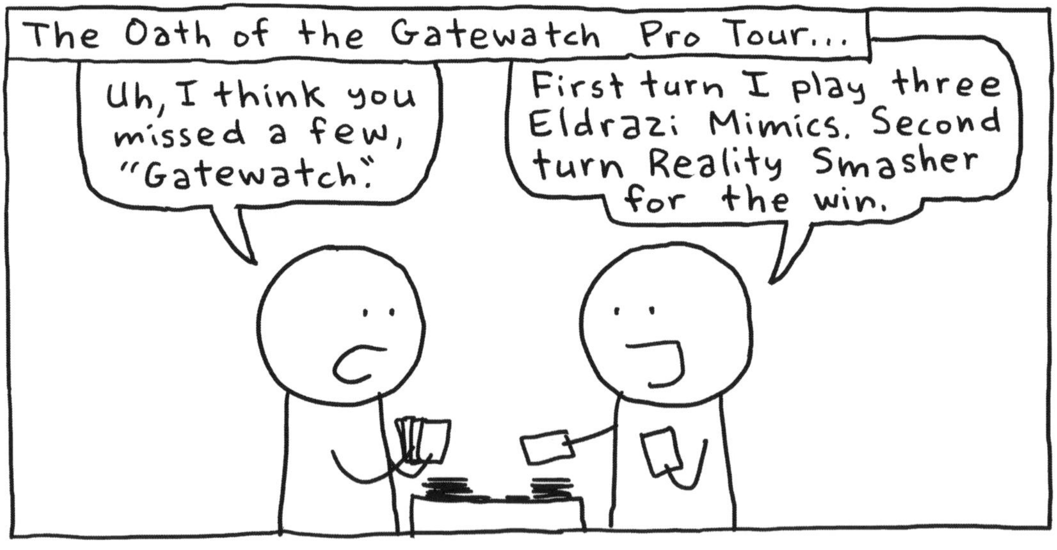
The Oath of the Gatewatch Pro Tour...
First turn I play three Eldrazi Mimics. Second turn Reality Smasher for the win.
Uh, I think you missed a few, "Gatewatch."

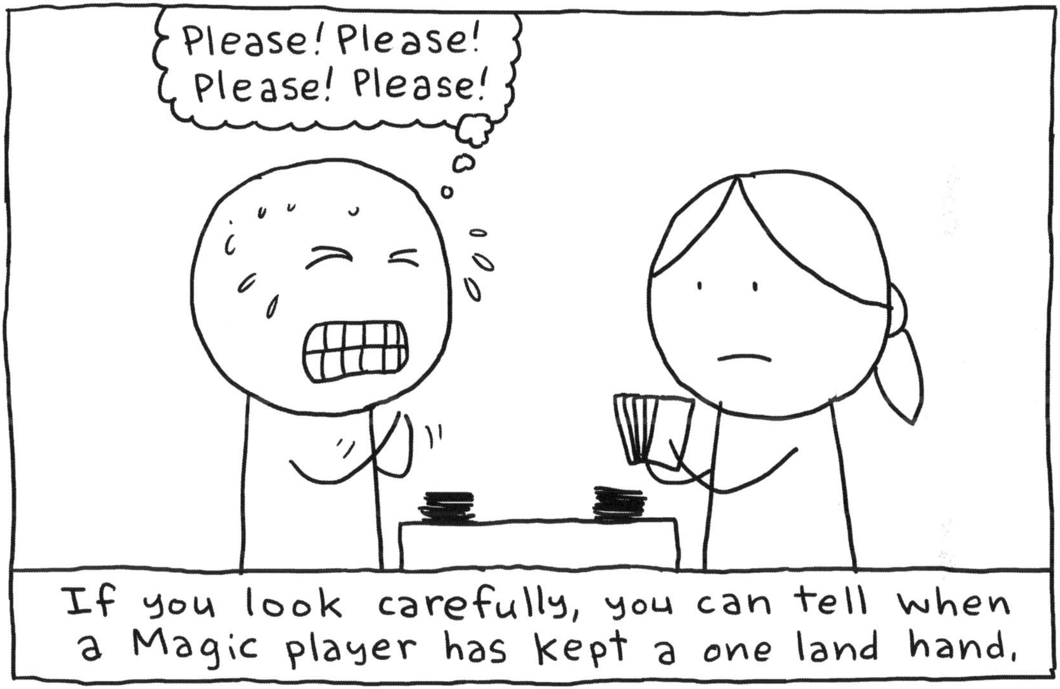
Please! Please!
Please! Please!
If you look carefully, you can tell when a Magic player has kept a one land hand.

Casting a Lightning Bolt will never feel the same again.

Rest in peace, Christopher Rush

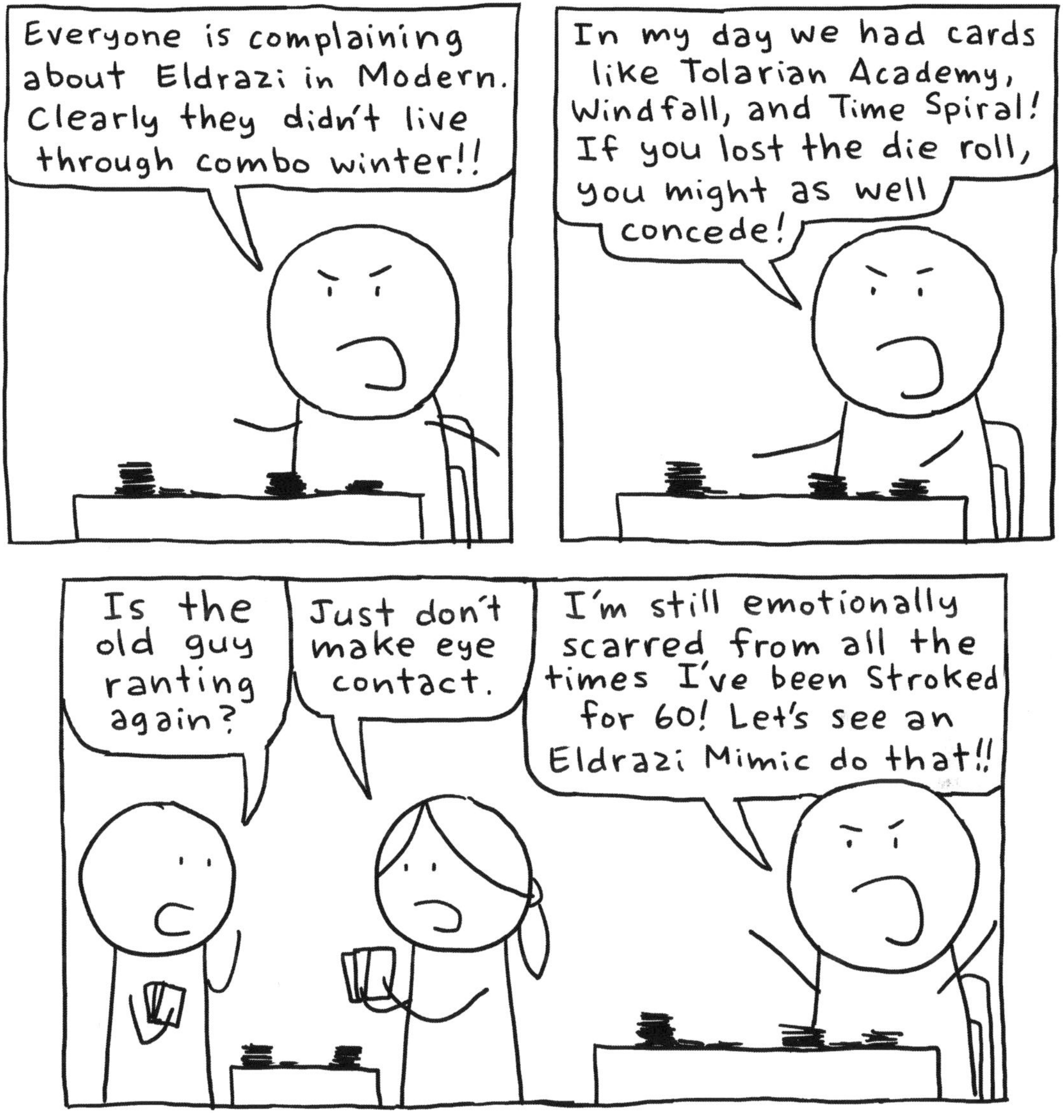
Everyone is complaining about Eldrazi in Modern. Clearly they didn't live through combo winter!!
In my day we had cards like Tolarian Academy, Windfall, and Time Spiral! If you lost the die roll, you might as well concede!
Is the old guy ranting again?
Just don't make eye contact.
I'm still emotionally scarred from all the times I've been Stroked for 60! Let's see an Eldrazi Mimic do that!!

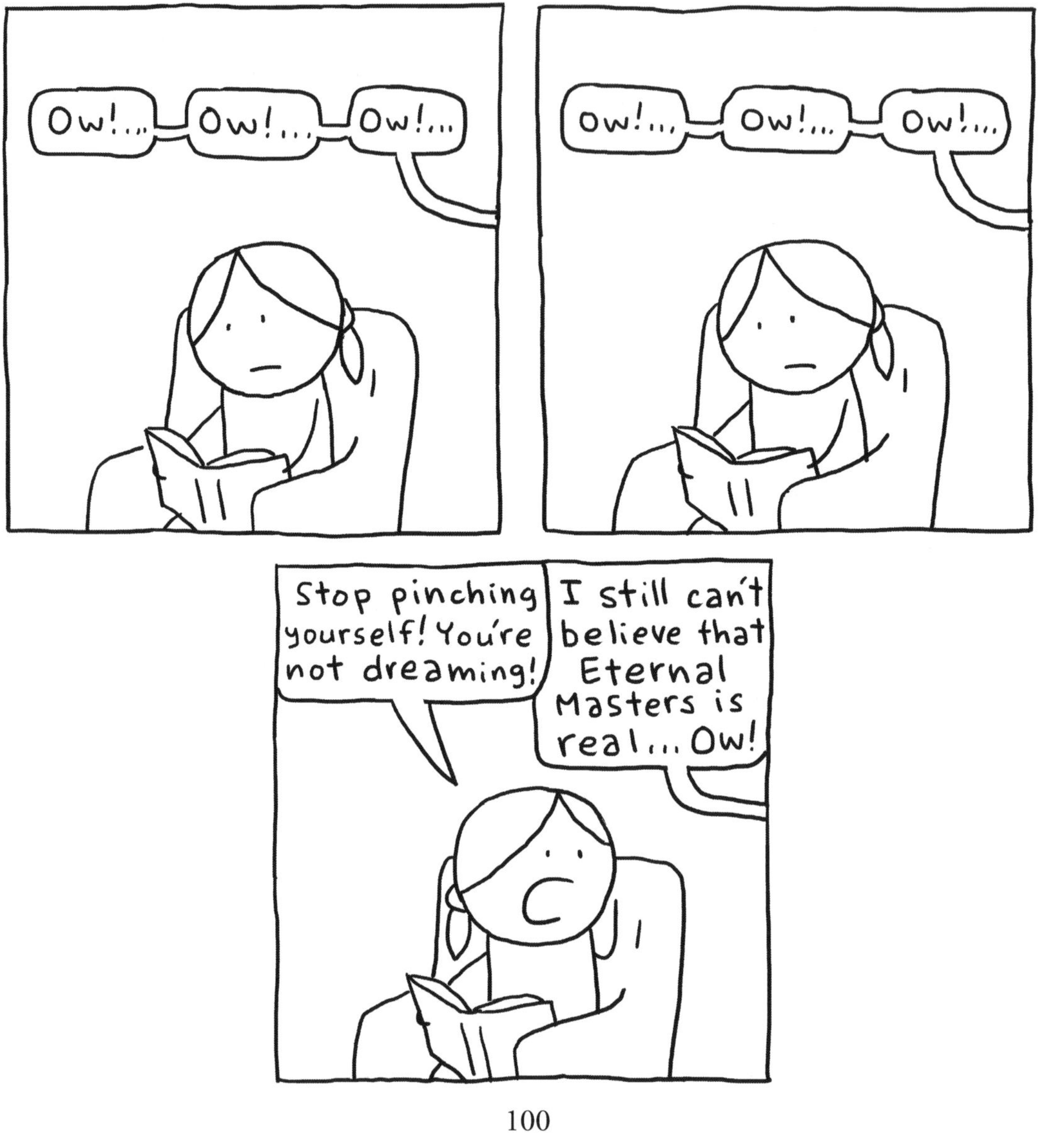
Ow!...
Ow!...
Ow!...
Ow!...
Ow!...
Ow!...
Stop pinching yourself! You're not dreaming!
I still can't believe that Eternal Masters is real... Ow!

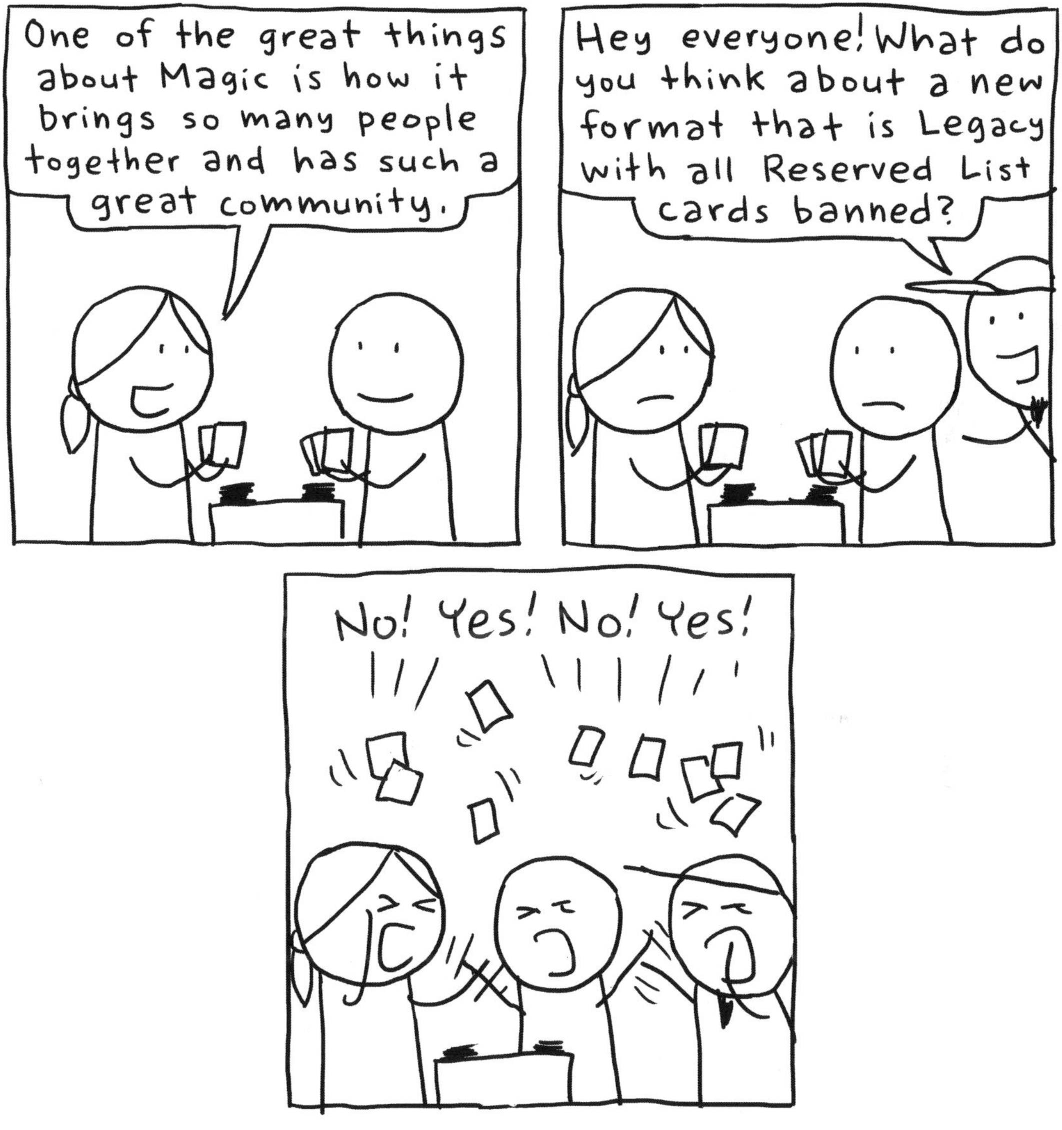
One of the great things about Magic is how it brings so many people together and has such a great community.
Hey everyone! What do you think about a new format that is Legacy with all Reserved List cards banned?
No! Yes! No! Yes!

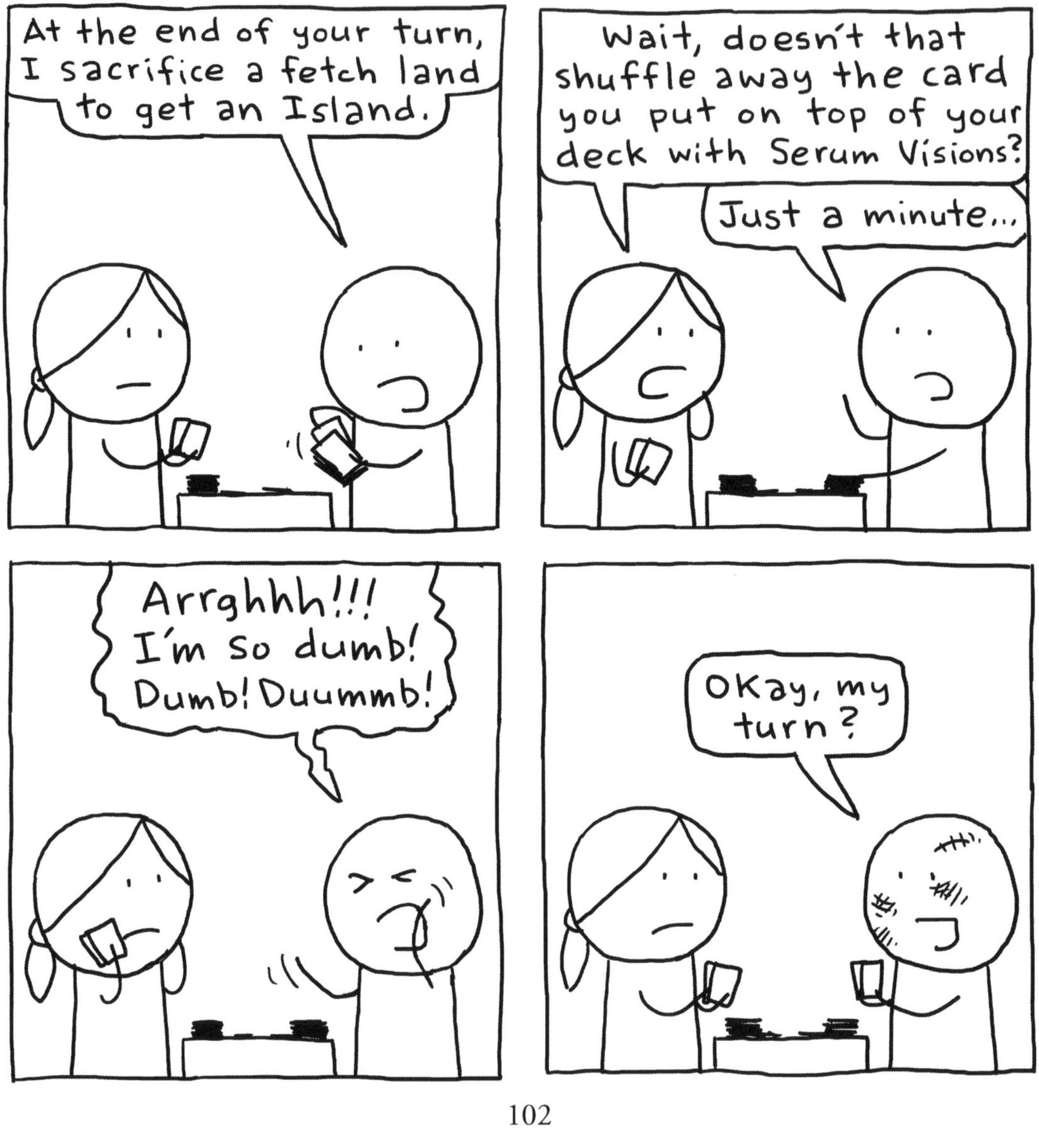
At the end of your turn, I sacrifice a fetch land to get an Island.
Wait, doesn't that shuffle away the card you put on top of your deck with Serum Visions?
Just a minute...
Arrghhh!!! I'm so dumb! Dumb! Duummb!
Okay, my turn?

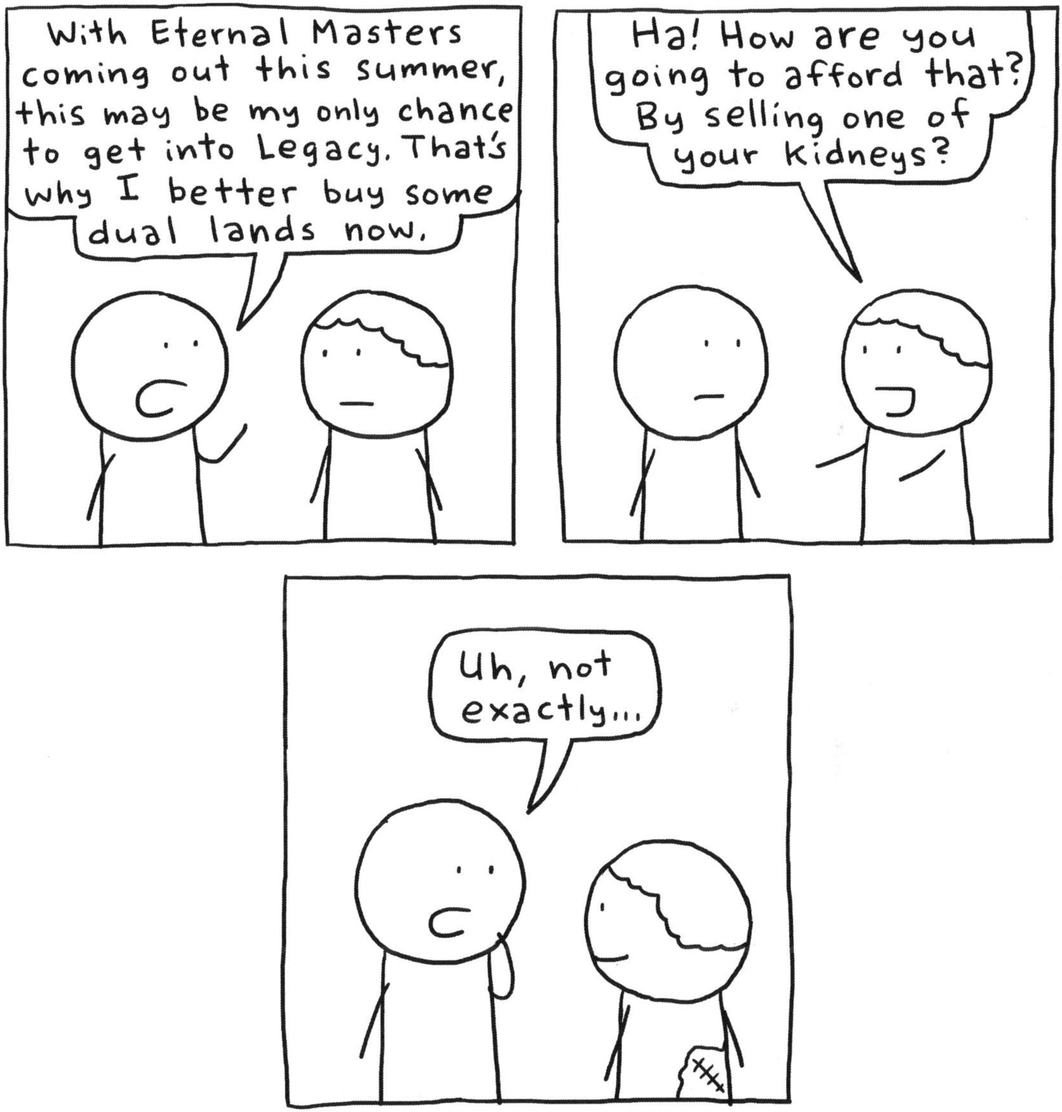
With Eternal Masters coming out this summer, this may be my only chance to get into Legacy. That's why I better buy some dual lands now.
Ha! How are you going to afford that? By selling one of your kidneys?
Uh, not exactly...

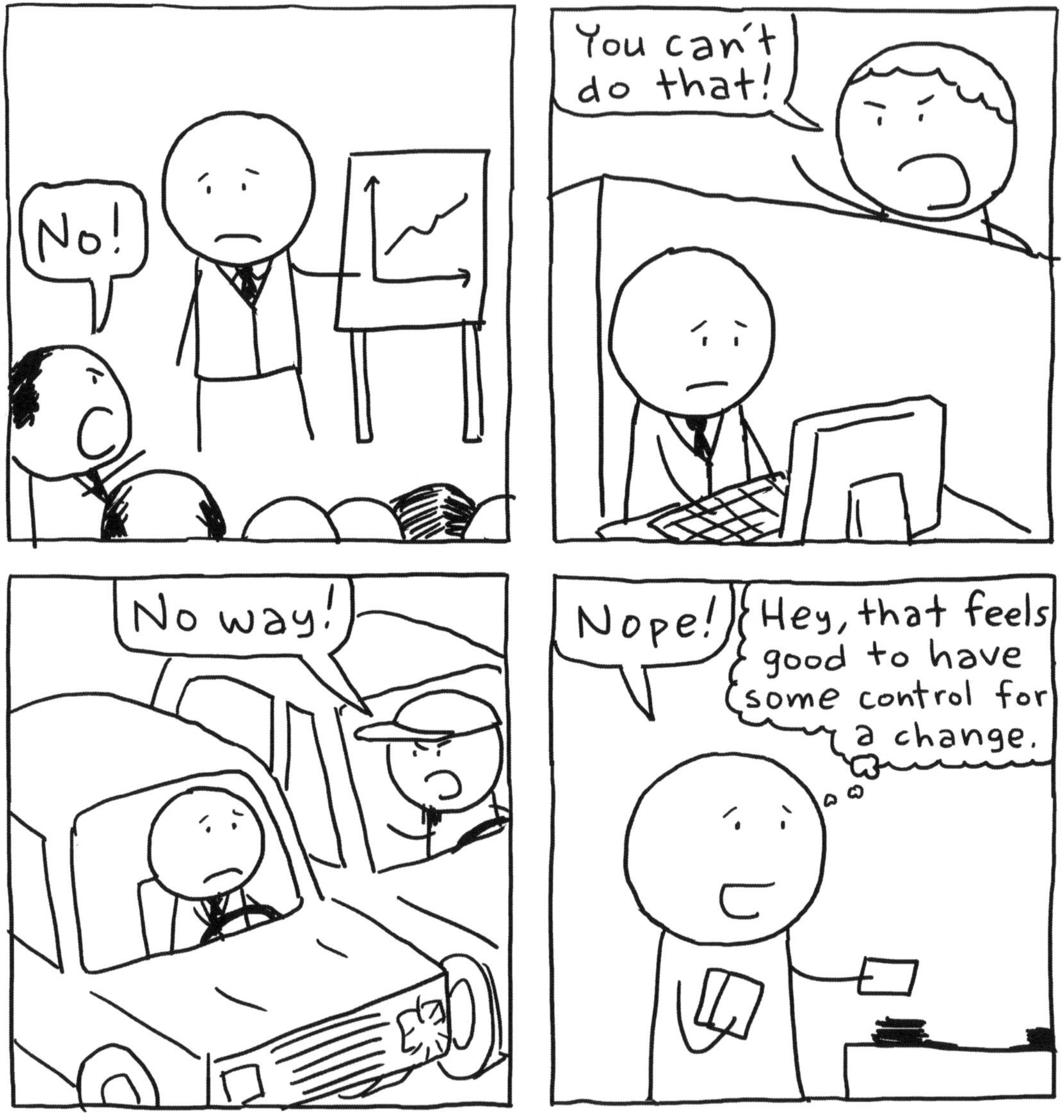
No!
You can't do that!
No way!
Nope!
Hey, that feels good to have some control for a change.

Modern players now...
I'm sick and tired of Eldrazi!!
Modern players after April 4th...
I'm sick and tired of Burn, Infect, and Affinity!!

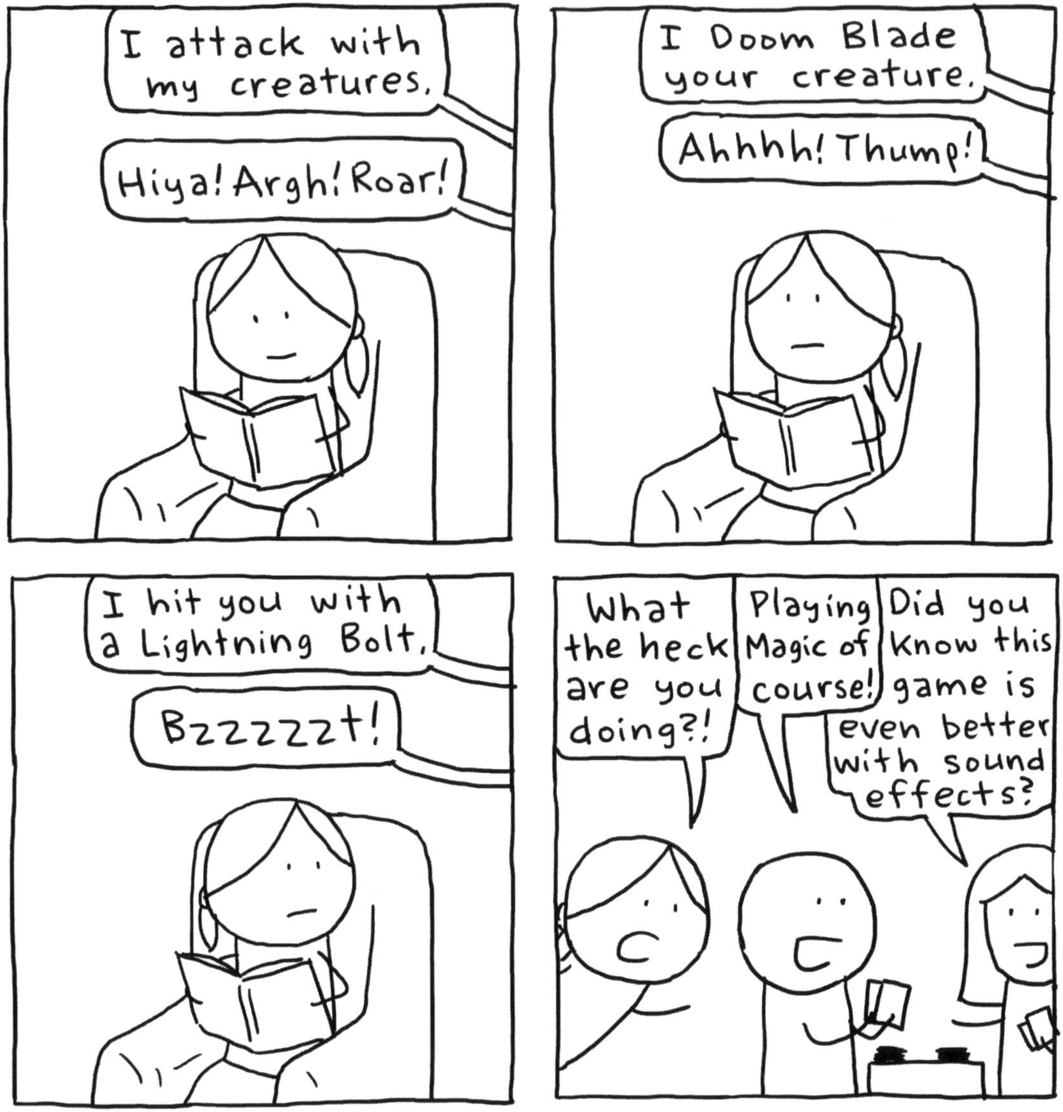
I attack with my creatures.
Hiya! Argh! Roar!
I Doom Blade your creature.
Ahhhh! Thump!
I hit you with a Lightning Bolt.
Bzzzzzt!
What the heck are you doing?!
Playing Magic of course!
Did you know this game is even better with sound effects?

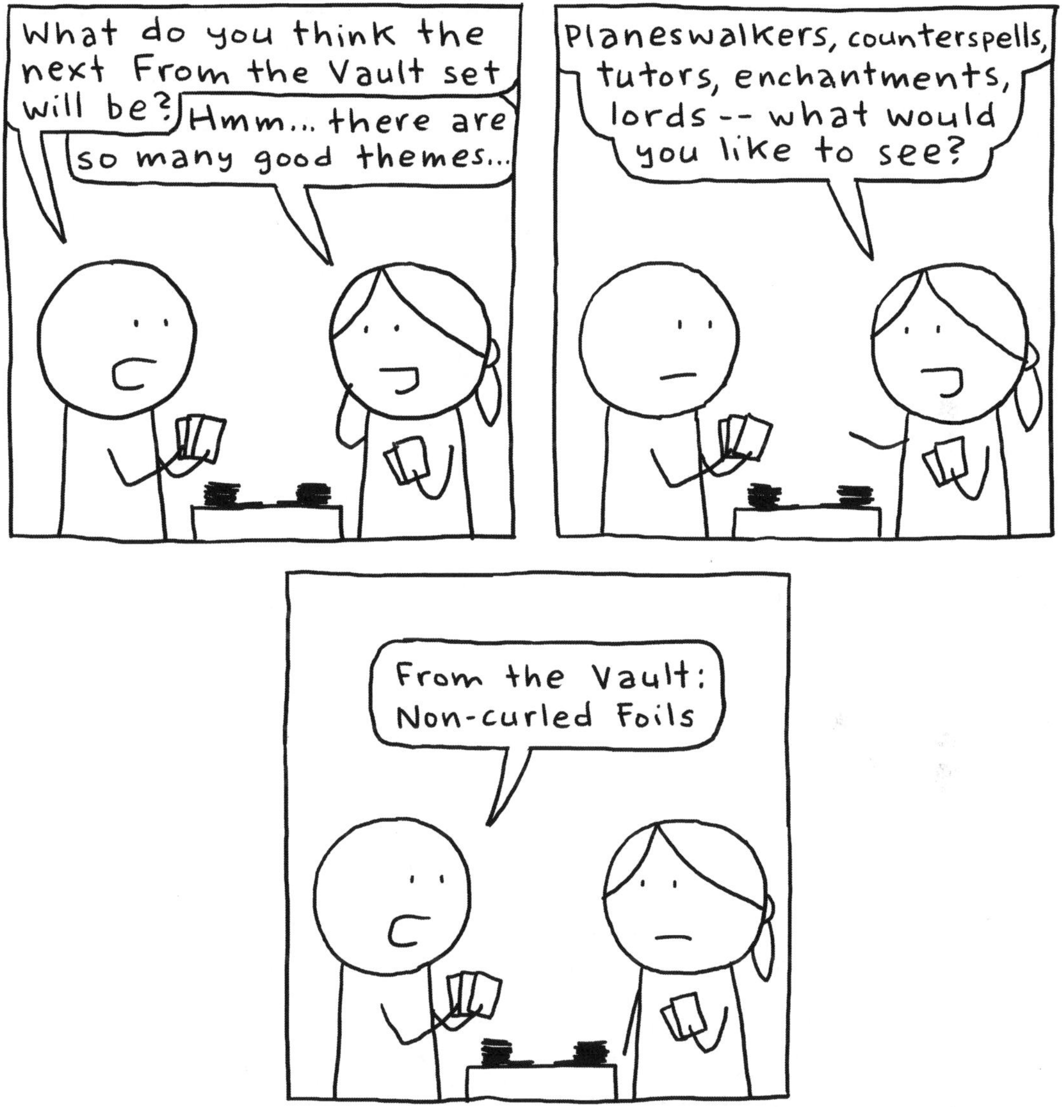
What do you think the next From the Vault set will be?
Hmm... there are so many good themes...
Planeswalkers, counterspells, tutors, enchantments, lords -- what would you like to see?
From the Vault: Non-curled Foils

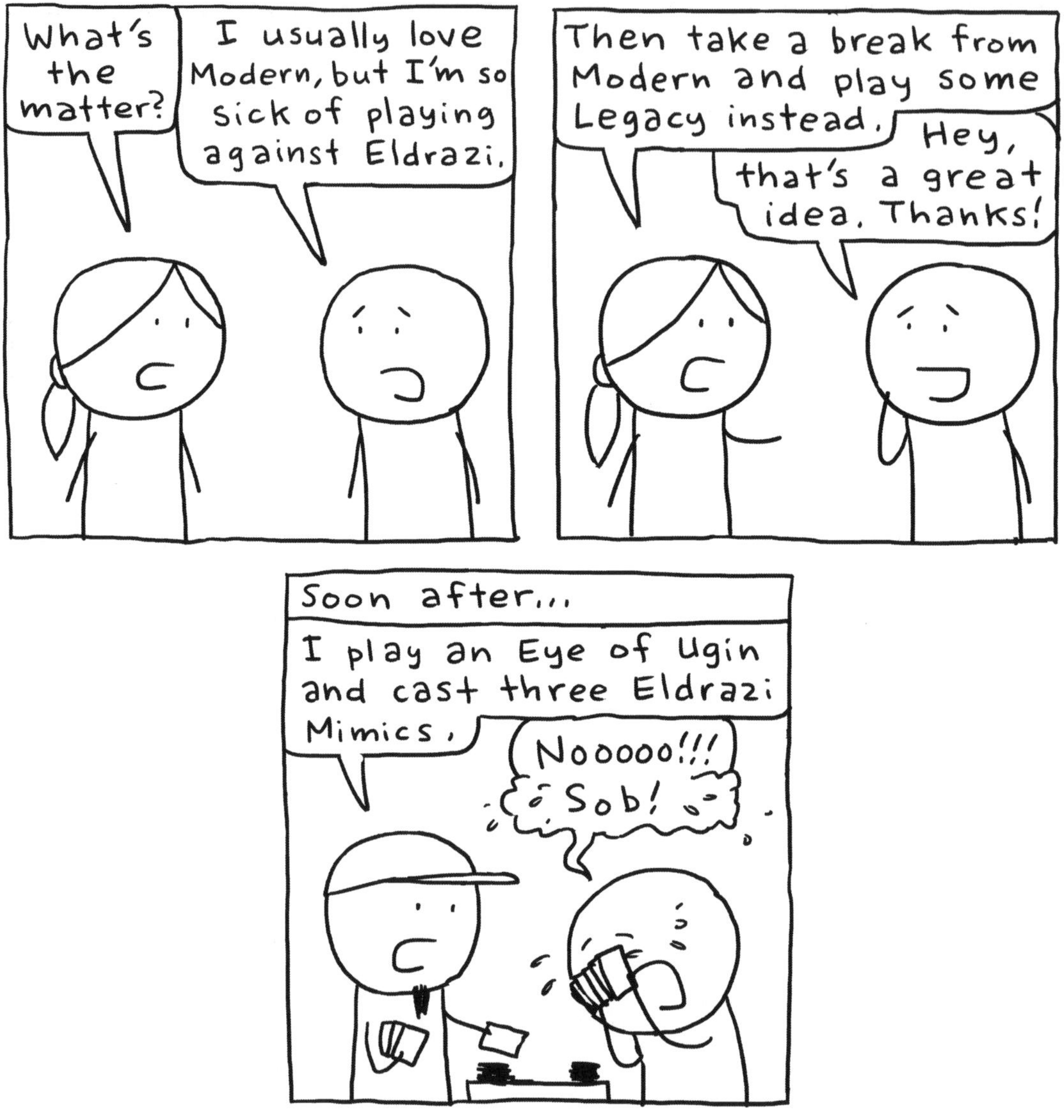
What's the matter?
I usually love Modern, but I'm so sick of playing against Eldrazi.
Then take a break from Modern and play some Legacy instead.
Hey, that's a great idea. Thanks!
Soon after...
I play an Eye of Ugin and cast three Eldrazi Mimics.
Nooooo!!! Sob!

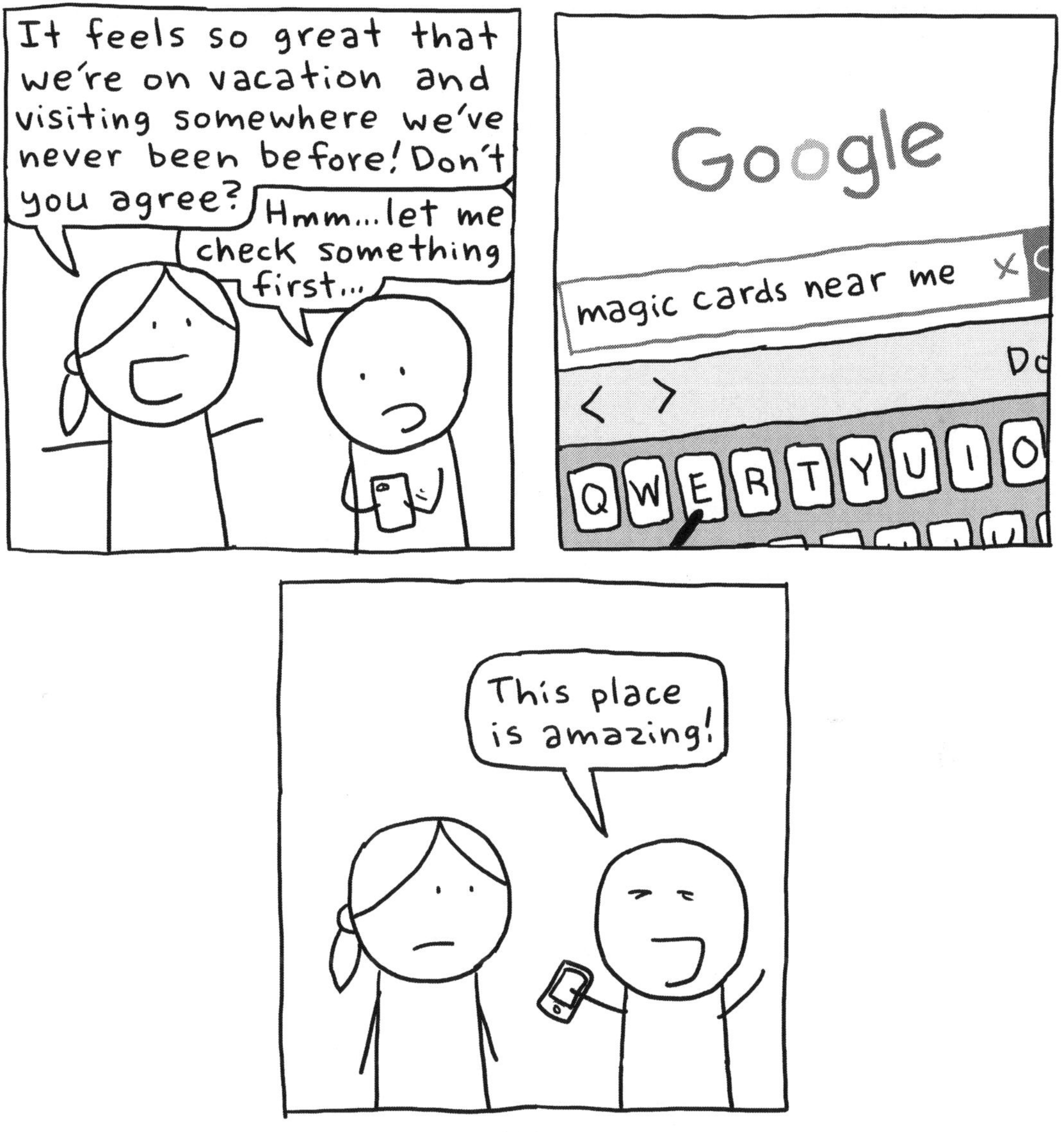
It feels so great that we're on vacation and visiting somewhere we've never been before! Don't you agree?
Hmm...let me check something first...
Google
magic cards near me
QWERTYUIO
This place is amazing!

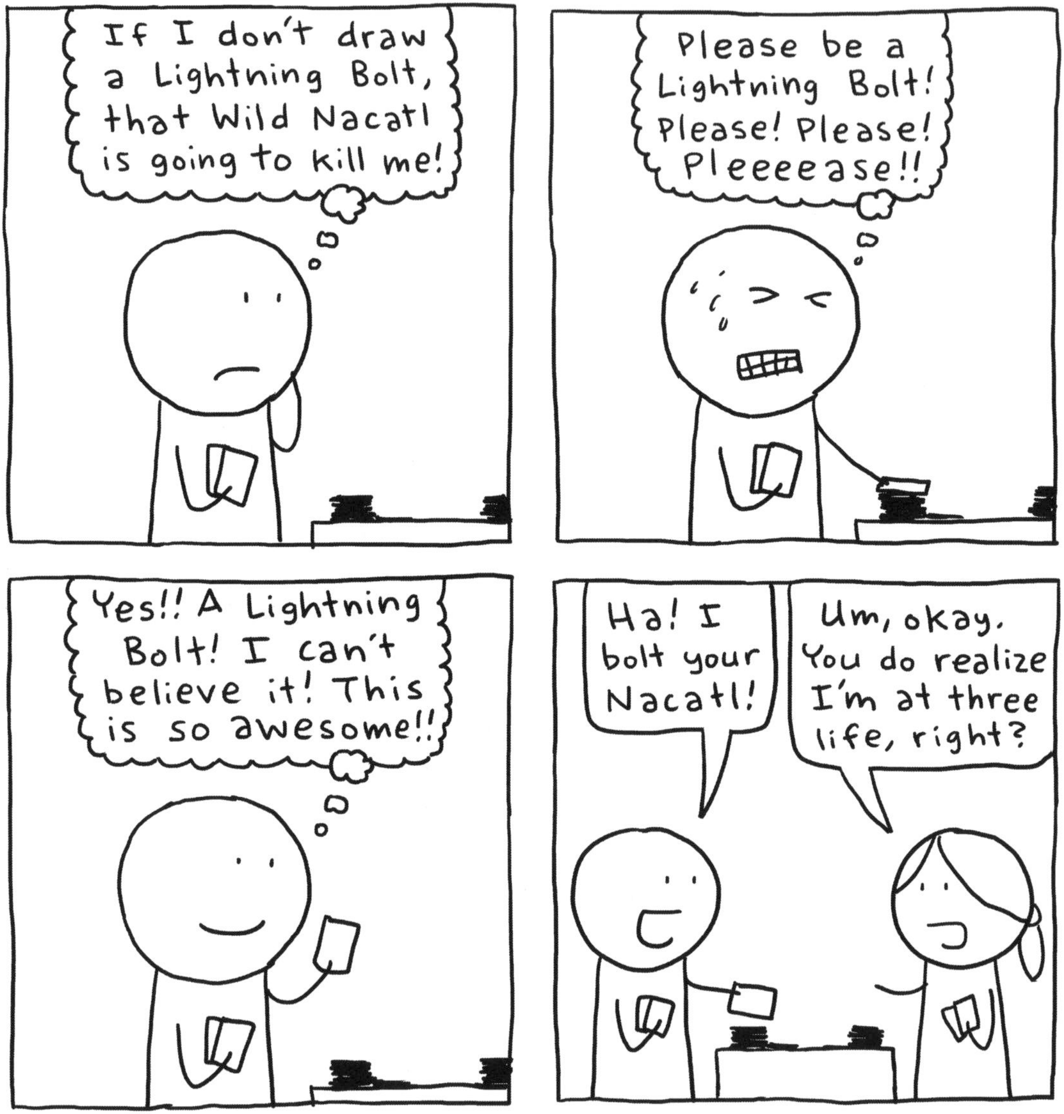
If I don't draw a Lightning Bolt, that Wild Nacatl is going to kill me!
Please be a Lightning Bolt! Please! Please! Pleeeeease!!
Yes!! A Lightning Bolt! I can't believe it! This is so awesome!!
Ha! I bolt your Nacatl!
Um, okay. You do realize I'm at three life, right?

Why is Nahiri like a drug dealer?
I don't know. Why?
If you cross her path, then you'll probably end up stoned!
We're no longer friends.

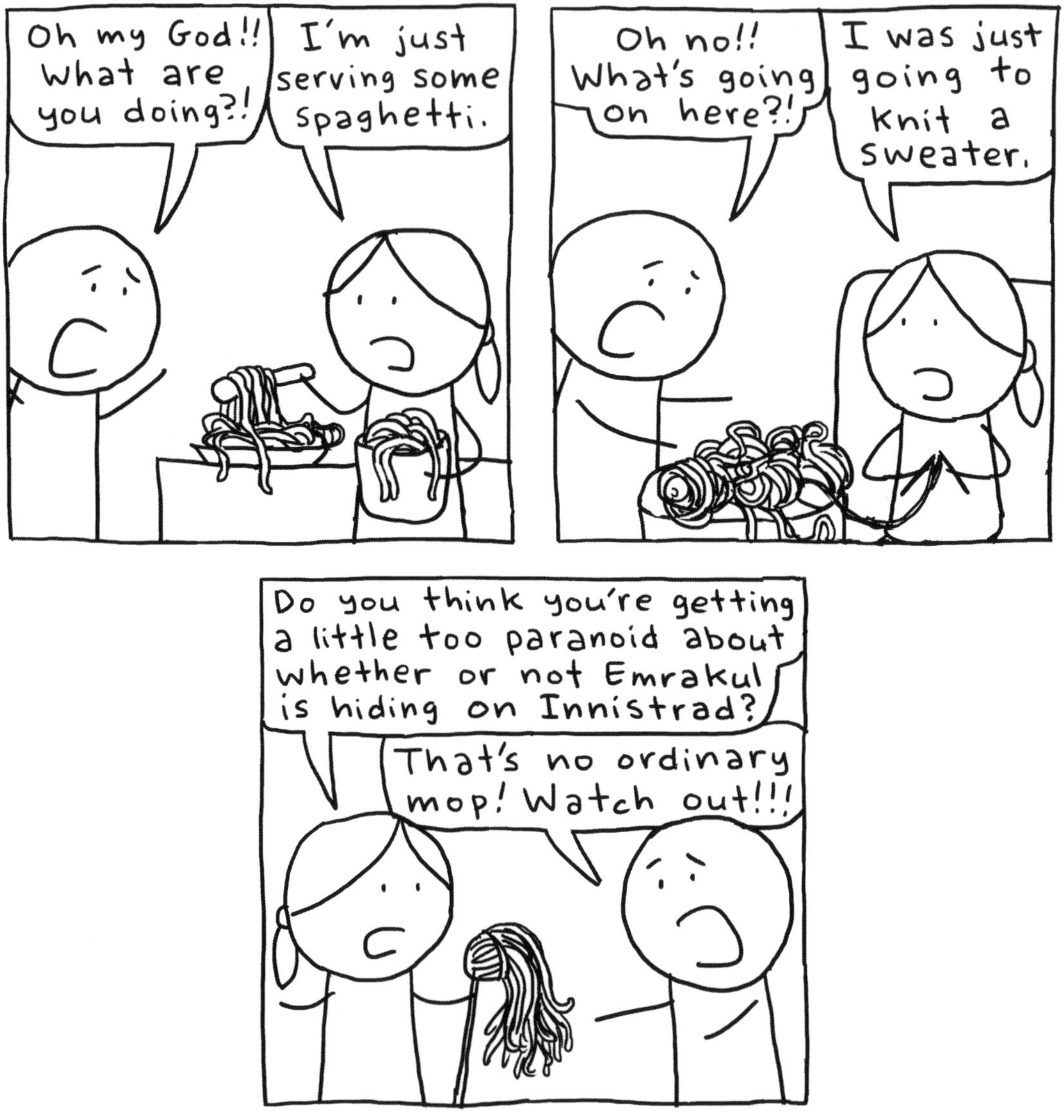

Oh my God!! What are you doing?!
I'm just serving some spaghetti.
Oh no!! What's going on here?!
I was just going to knit a sweater.
Do you think you're getting a little too paranoid about whether or not Emrakul is hiding on Innistrad?
That's no ordinary mop! Watch out!!!

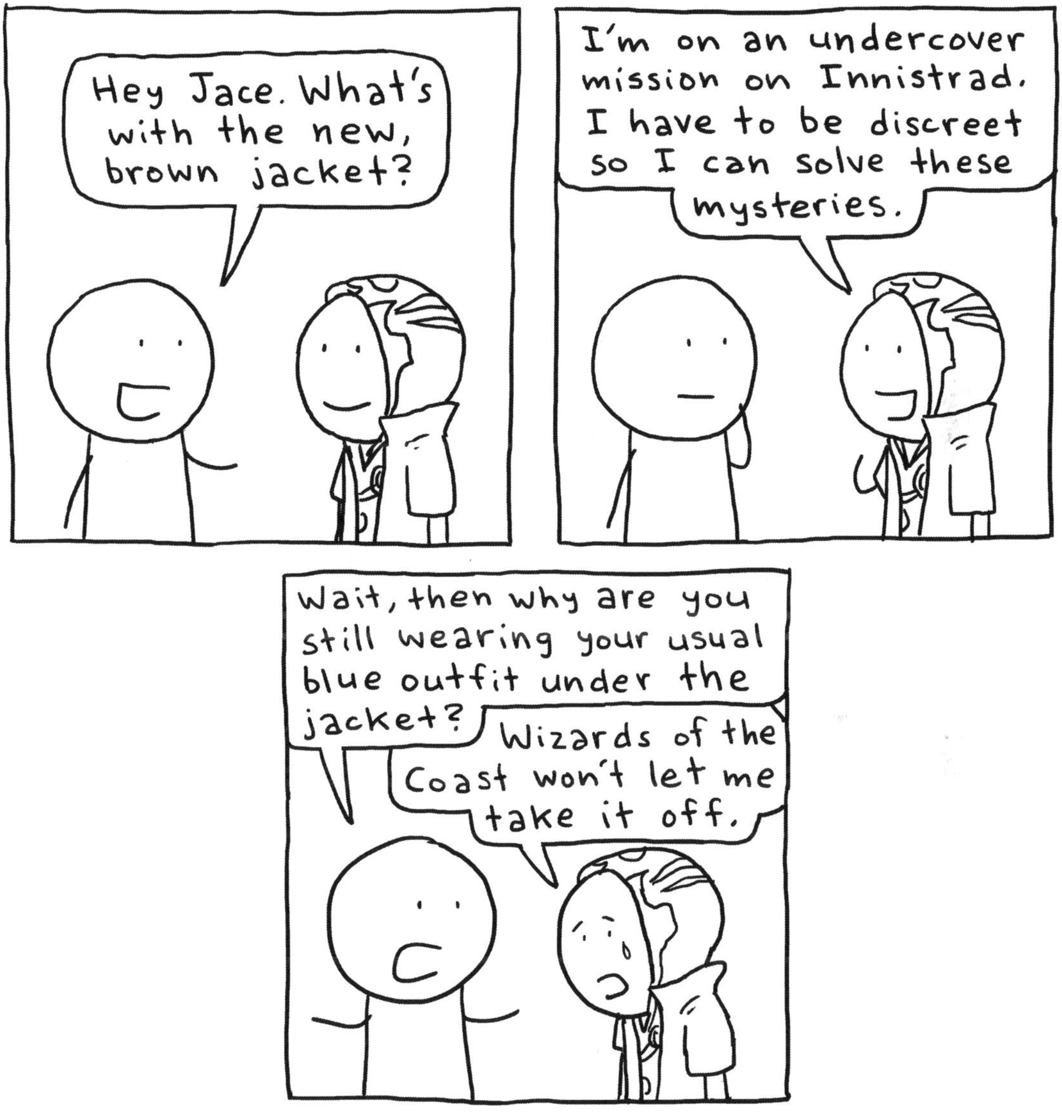
Hey Jace. What's with the new, brown jacket?
I'm on an undercover mission on Innistrad. I have to be discreet so I can solve these mysteries.
Wait, then why are you still wearing your usual blue outfit under the jacket?
Wizards of the Coast won't let me take it off.

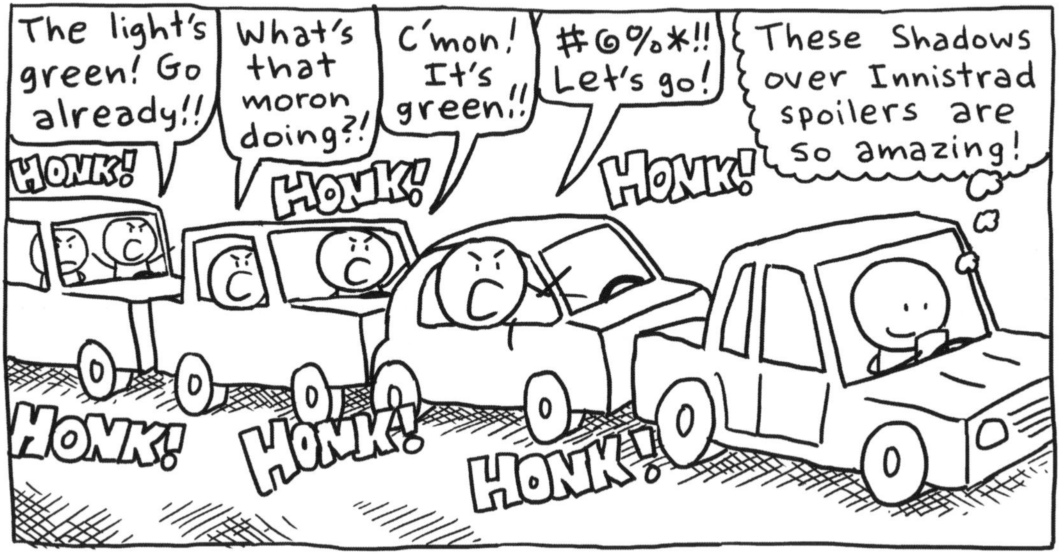
The light's green! Go already!!
What's that moron doing?!
C'mon! It's green!!
#@%*!! Let's go!
These Shadows over Innistrad spoilers are so amazing!
HONK!
HONK!
HONK!
HONK!
HONK!
HONK!

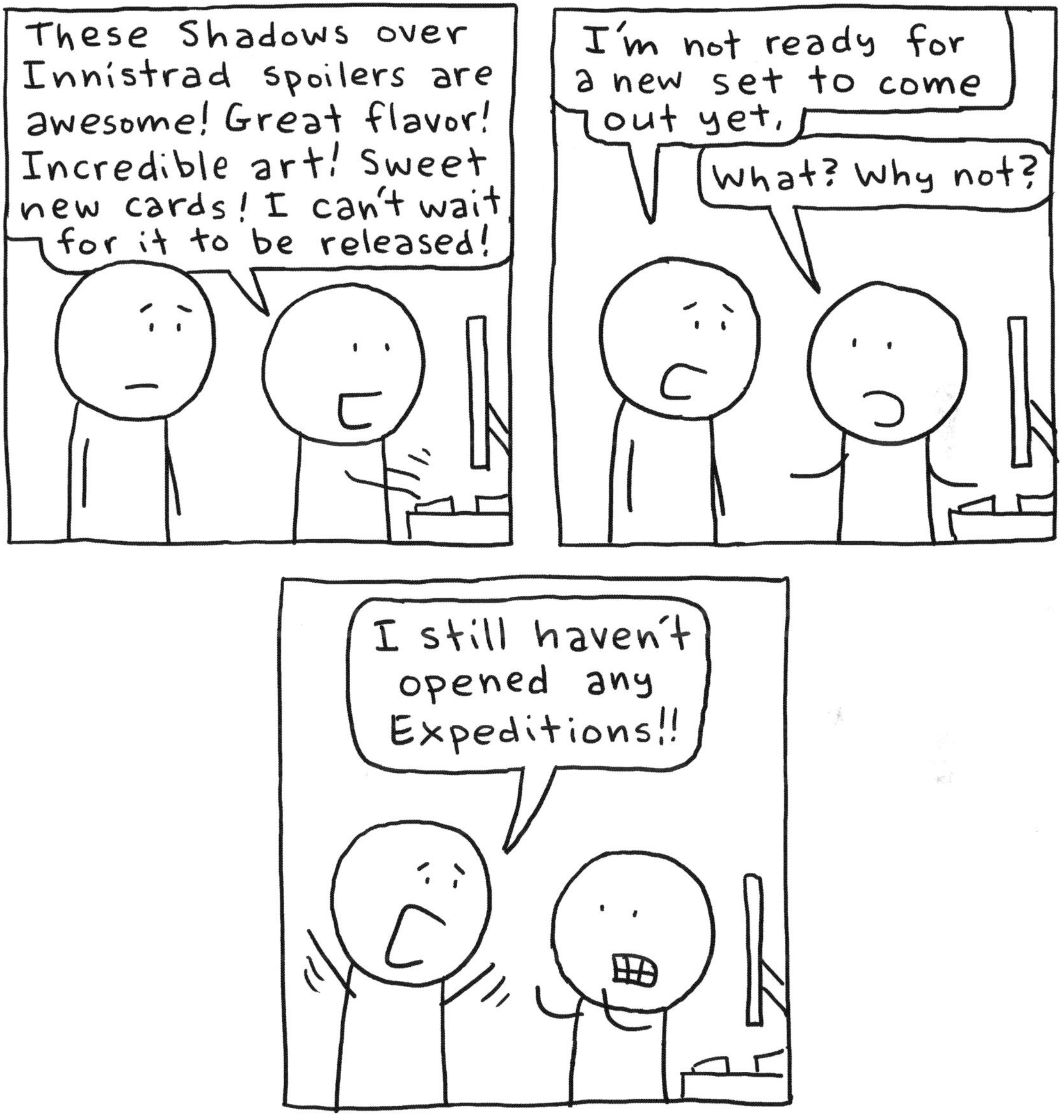
These Shadows over Innistrad spoilers are awesome! Great flavor! Incredible art! Sweet new cards! I can't wait for it to be released!
I'm not ready for a new set to come out yet,
What? Why not?
I still haven't opened any Expeditions!!

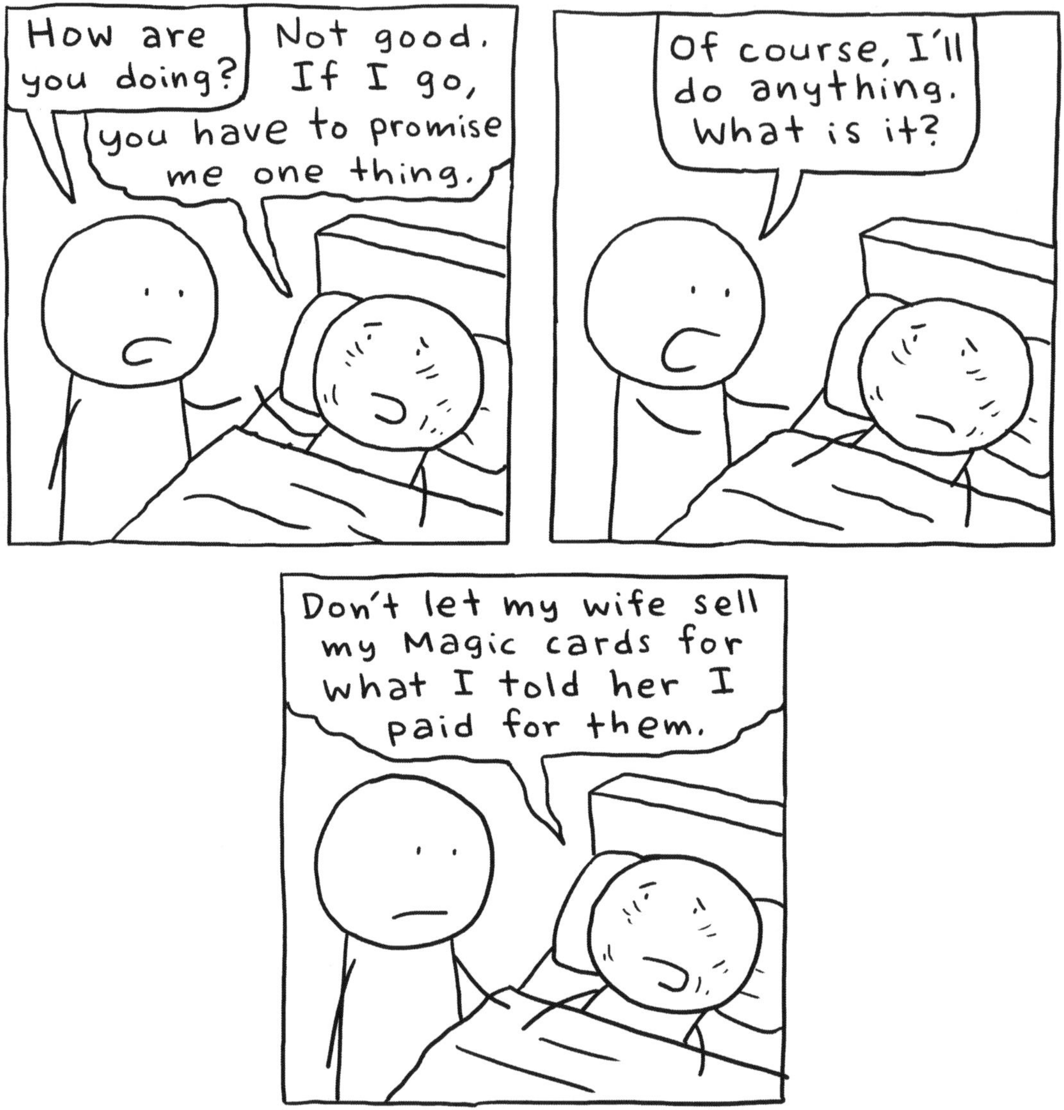
How are you doing?
Not good. If I go, you have to promise me one thing.
Of course, I'll do anything. What is it?
Don't let my wife sell my Magic cards for what I told her I paid for them.

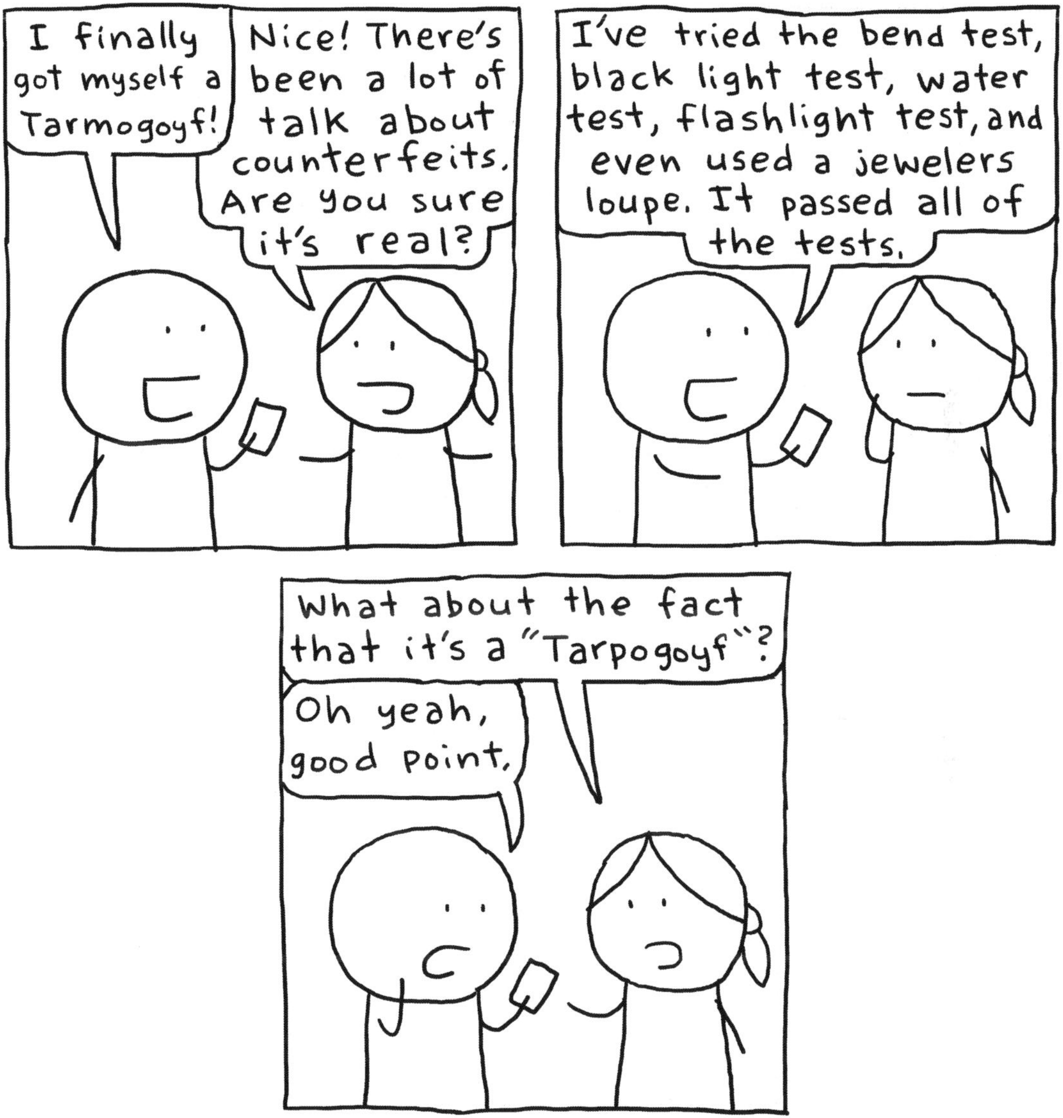
I finally got myself a Tarmogoyf!
Nice! There's been a lot of talk about counterfeits. Are you sure it's real?
I've tried the bend test, black light test, water test, flashlight test, and even used a jewelers loupe. It passed all of the tests.
What about the fact that it's a "Tarpogoyf"?
Oh yeah, good point.

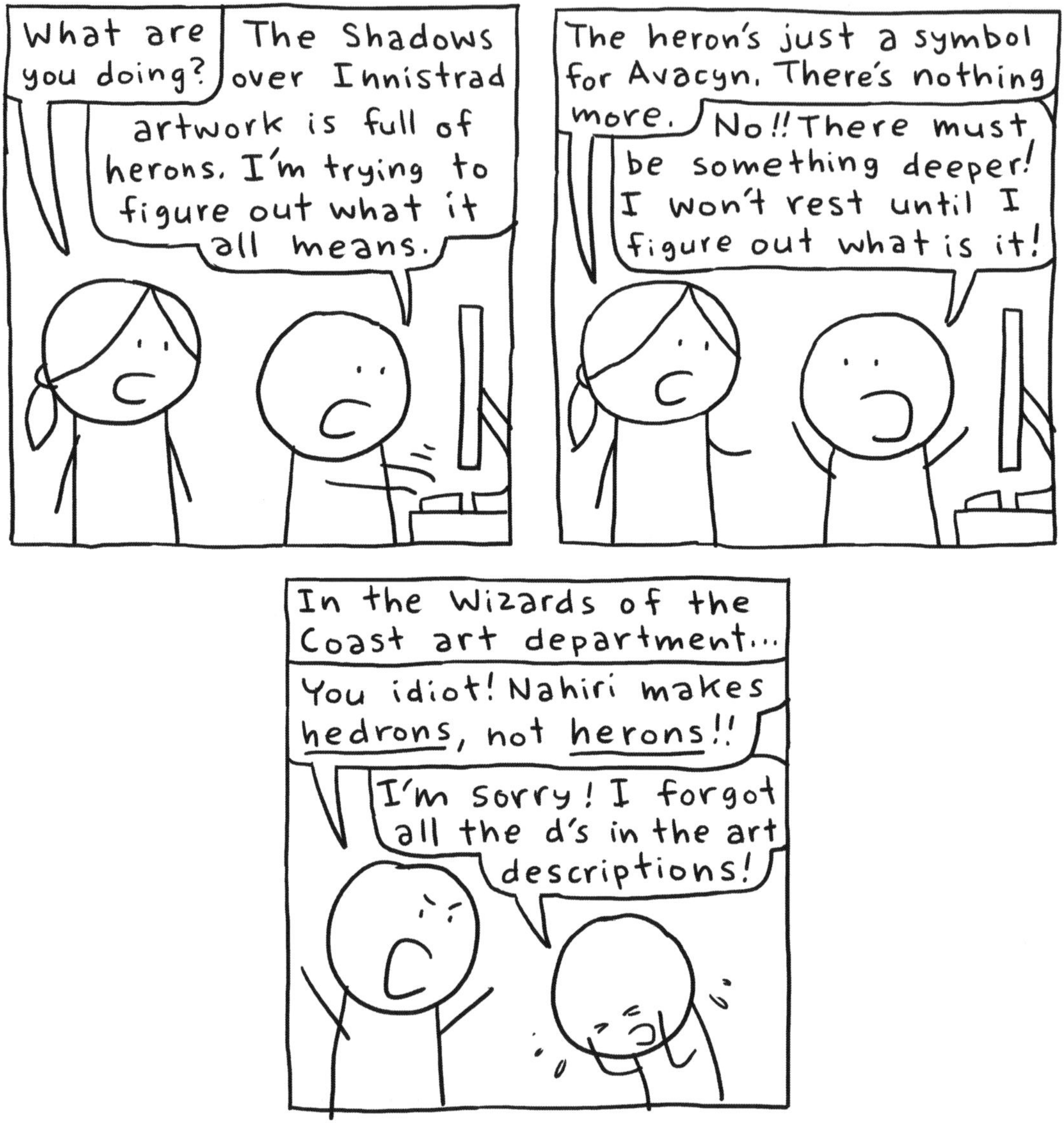
What are you doing?
The Shadows over Innistrad artwork is full of herons. I'm trying to figure out what it all means.
The heron's just a symbol for Avacyn. There's nothing more.
No!! There must be something deeper! I won't rest until I figure out what is it!
In the Wizards of the Coast art department...
You idiot! Nahiri makes hedrons, not herons!!
I'm sorry! I forgot all the d's in the art descriptions!

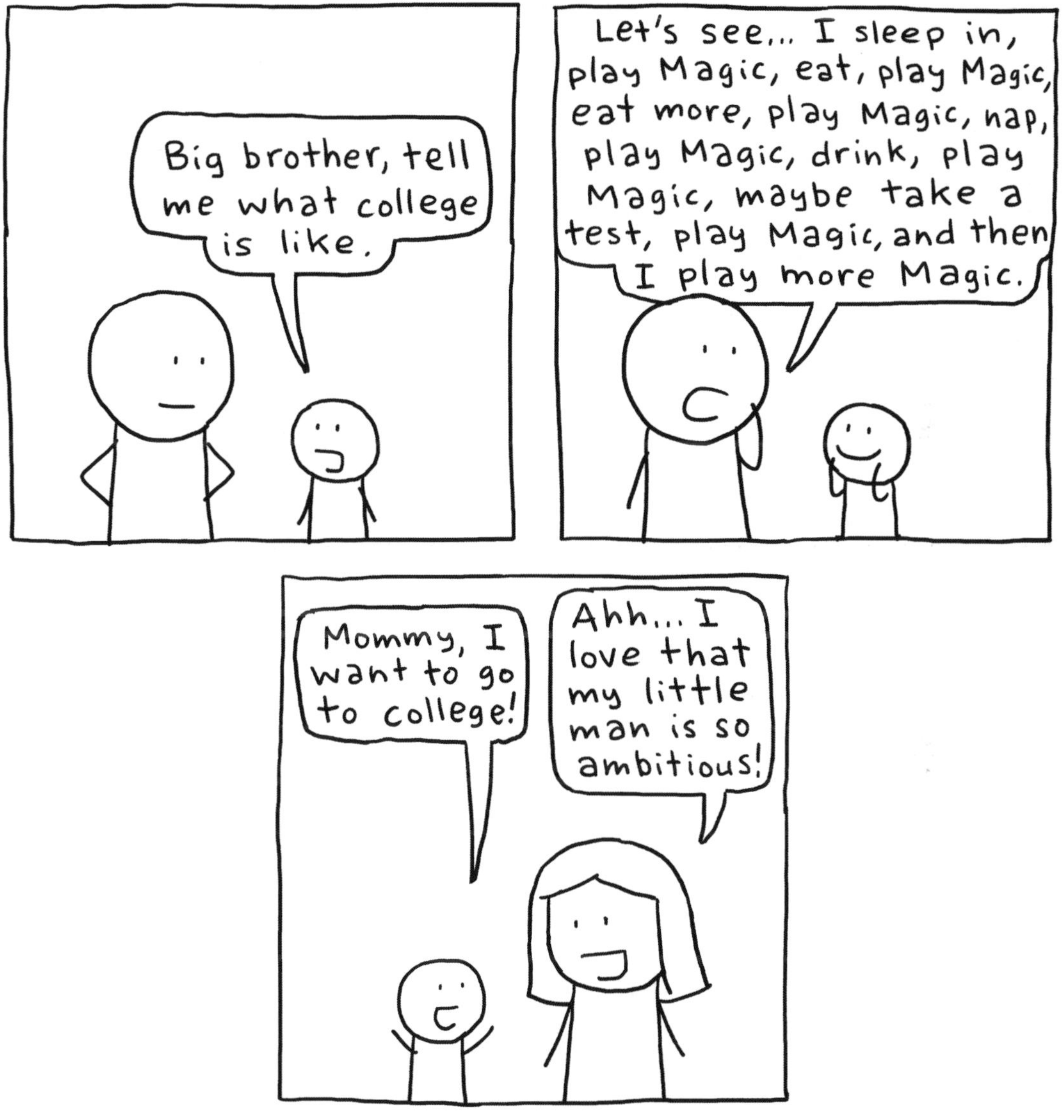
Big brother, tell me what college is like.
Let's see... I sleep in, play Magic, eat, play Magic, eat more, play Magic, nap, play Magic, drink, play Magic, maybe take a test, play Magic, and then I play more Magic.
Mommy, I want to go to college!
Ahh... I love that my little man is so ambitious!

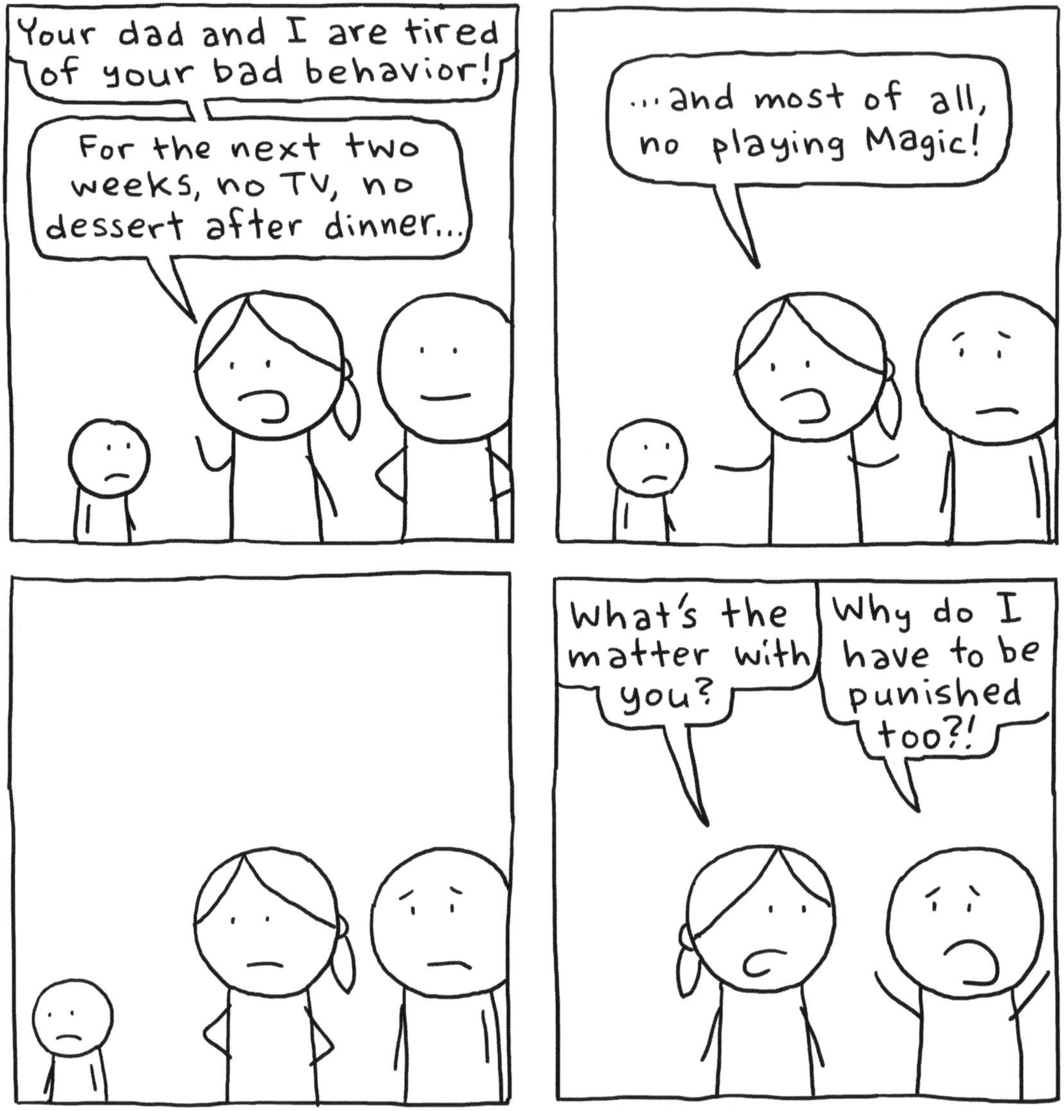
Your dad and I are tired of your bad behavior!
For the next two weeks, no TV, no dessert after dinner...
...and most of all, no playing Magic!
What's the matter with you?
Why do I have to be punished too?!

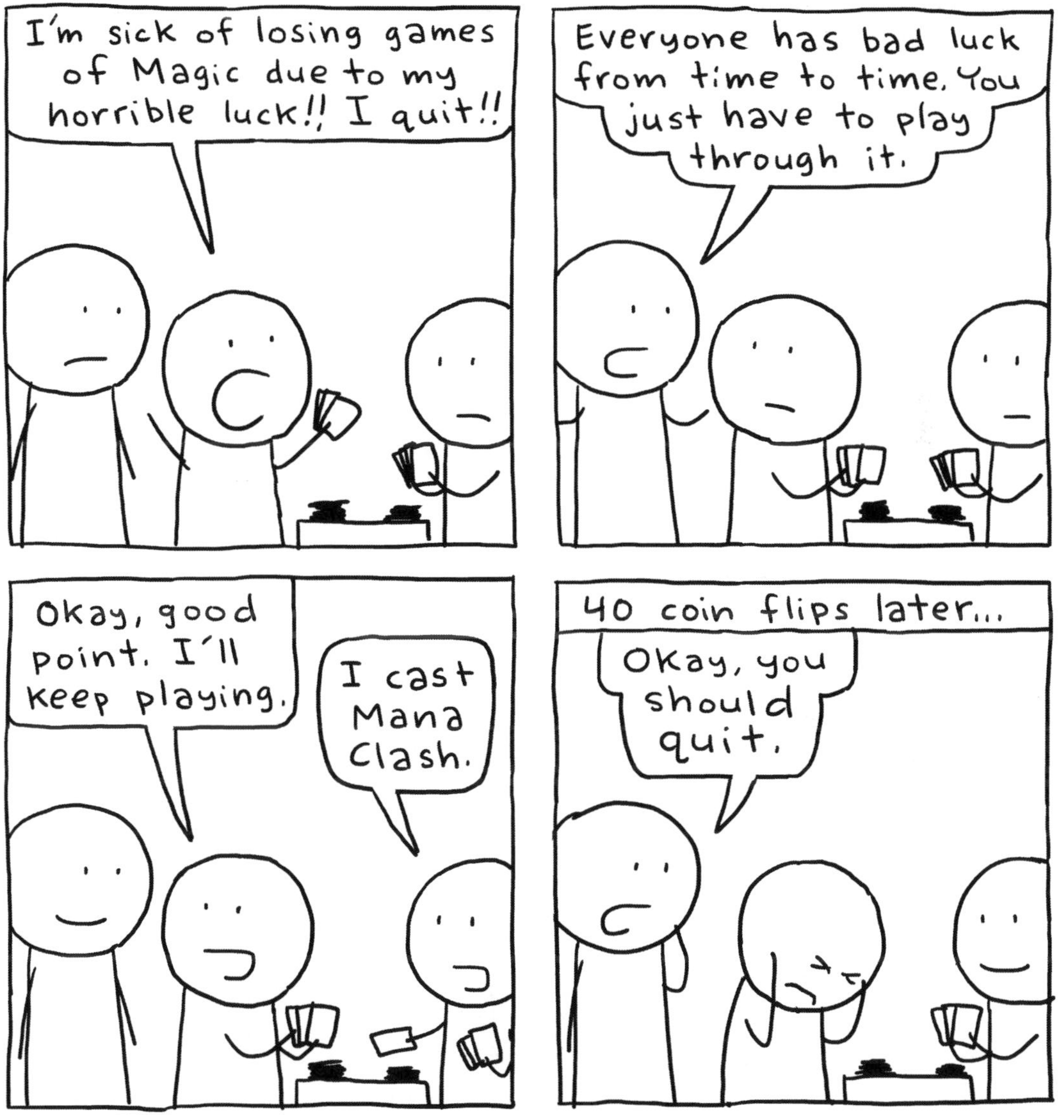
I'm sick of losing games of Magic due to my horrible luck!! I quit!!
Everyone has bad luck from time to time. You just have to play through it.
Okay, good point. I'll keep playing.
I cast Mana Clash.
40 coin flips later...
Okay, you should quit.

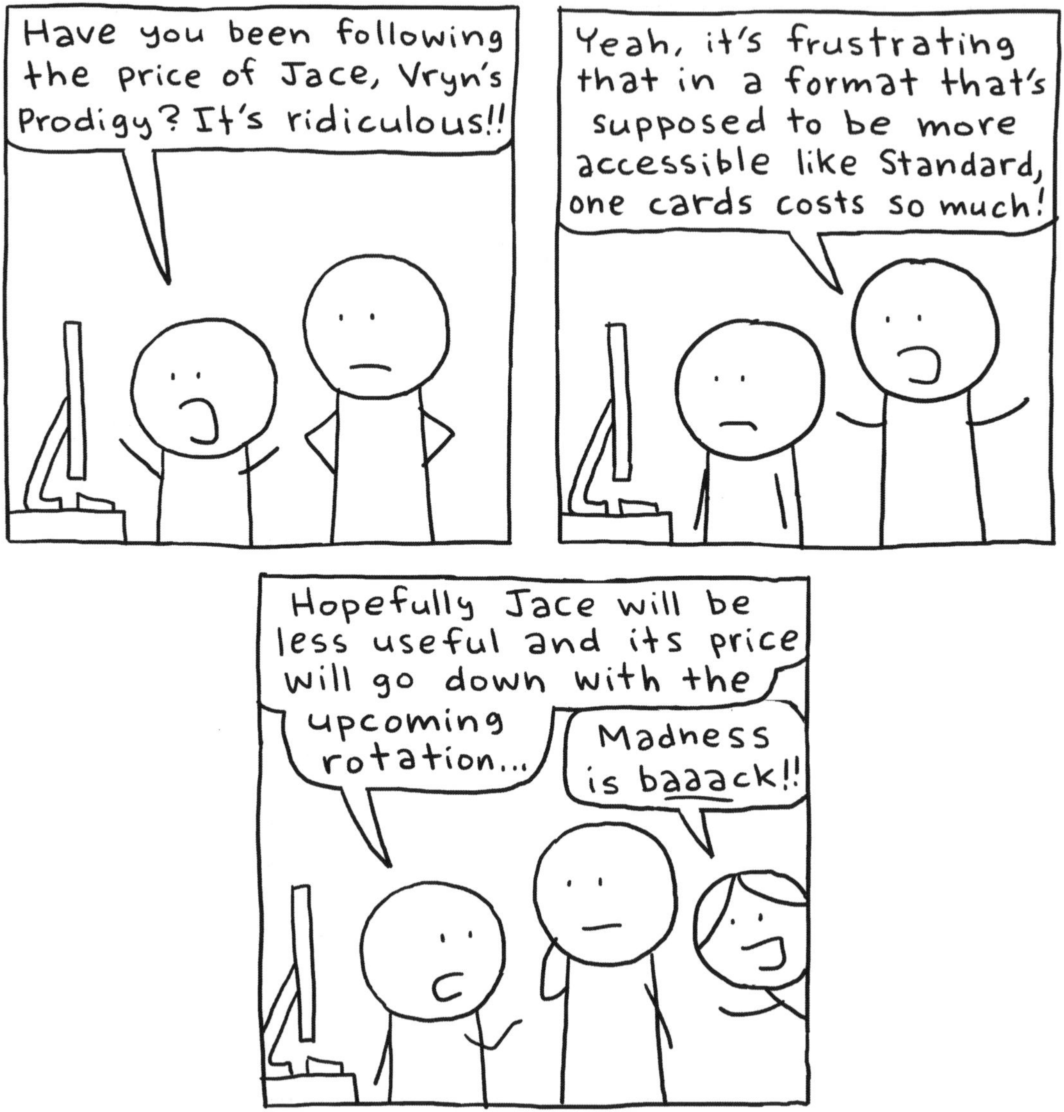
Have you been following the price of Jace, Vryn's Prodigy? It's ridiculous!!
Yeah, it's frustrating that in a format that's supposed to be more accessible like Standard, one cards costs so much!
Hopefully Jace will be less useful and its price will go down with the upcoming rotation...
Madness is baaack!!

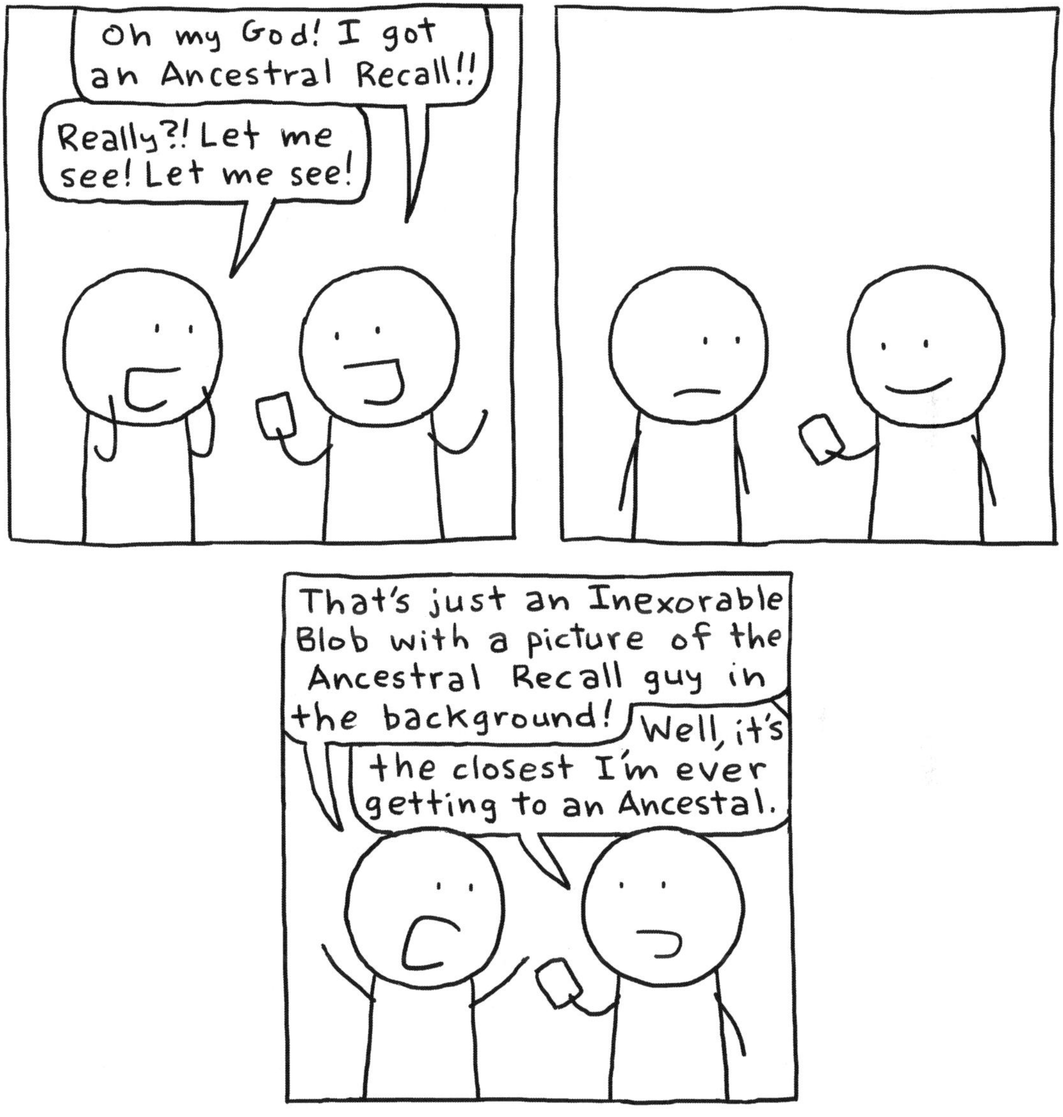
Oh my God! I got an Ancestral Recall!!
Really?! Let me see! Let me see!
That's just an Inexorable Blob with a picture of the Ancestral Recall guy in the background!
Well, it's the closest I'm ever getting to an Ancestal.

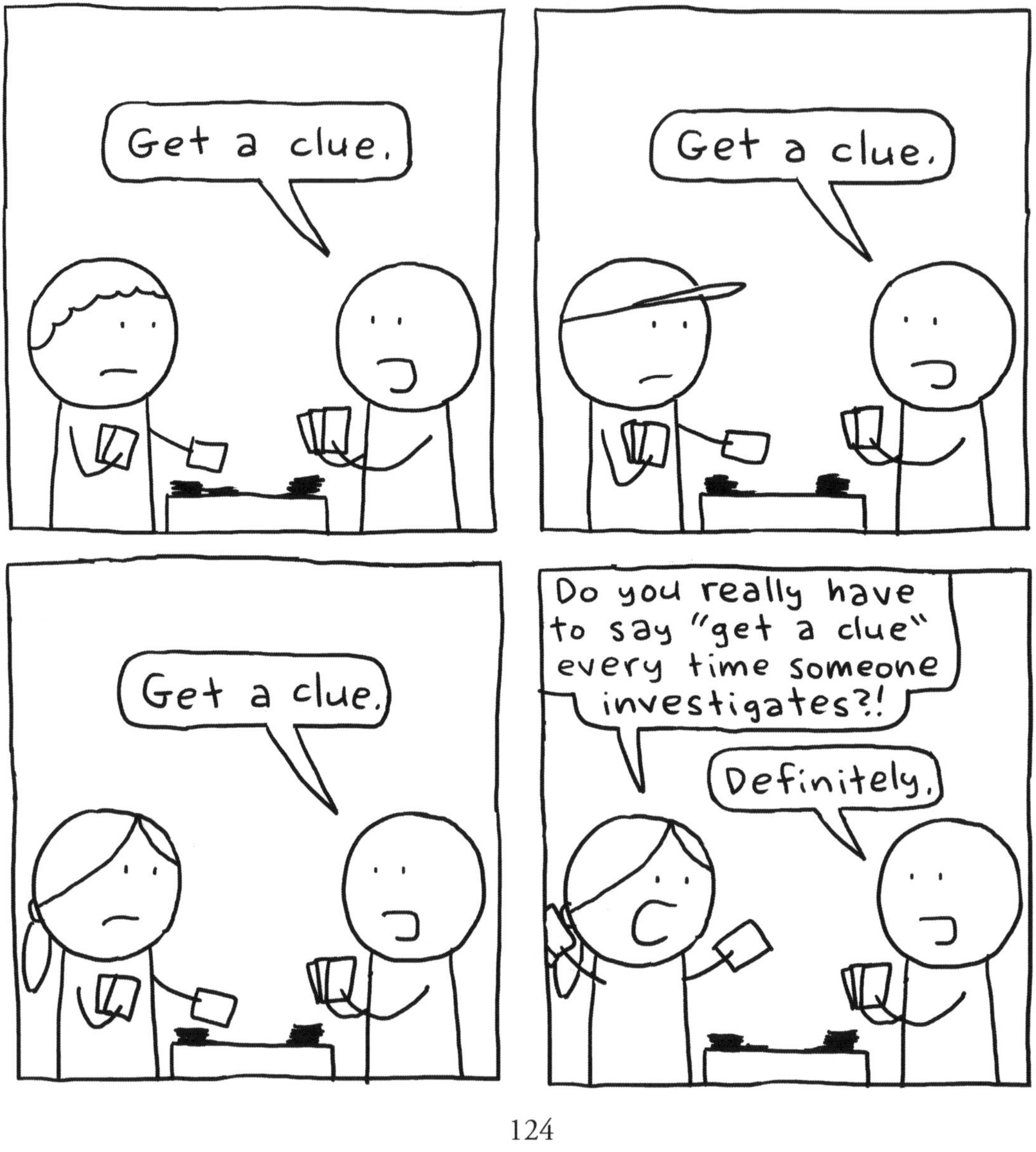
Get a clue.
Get a clue.
Get a clue.
Do you really have to say "get a clue" every time someone investigates?!
Definitely.

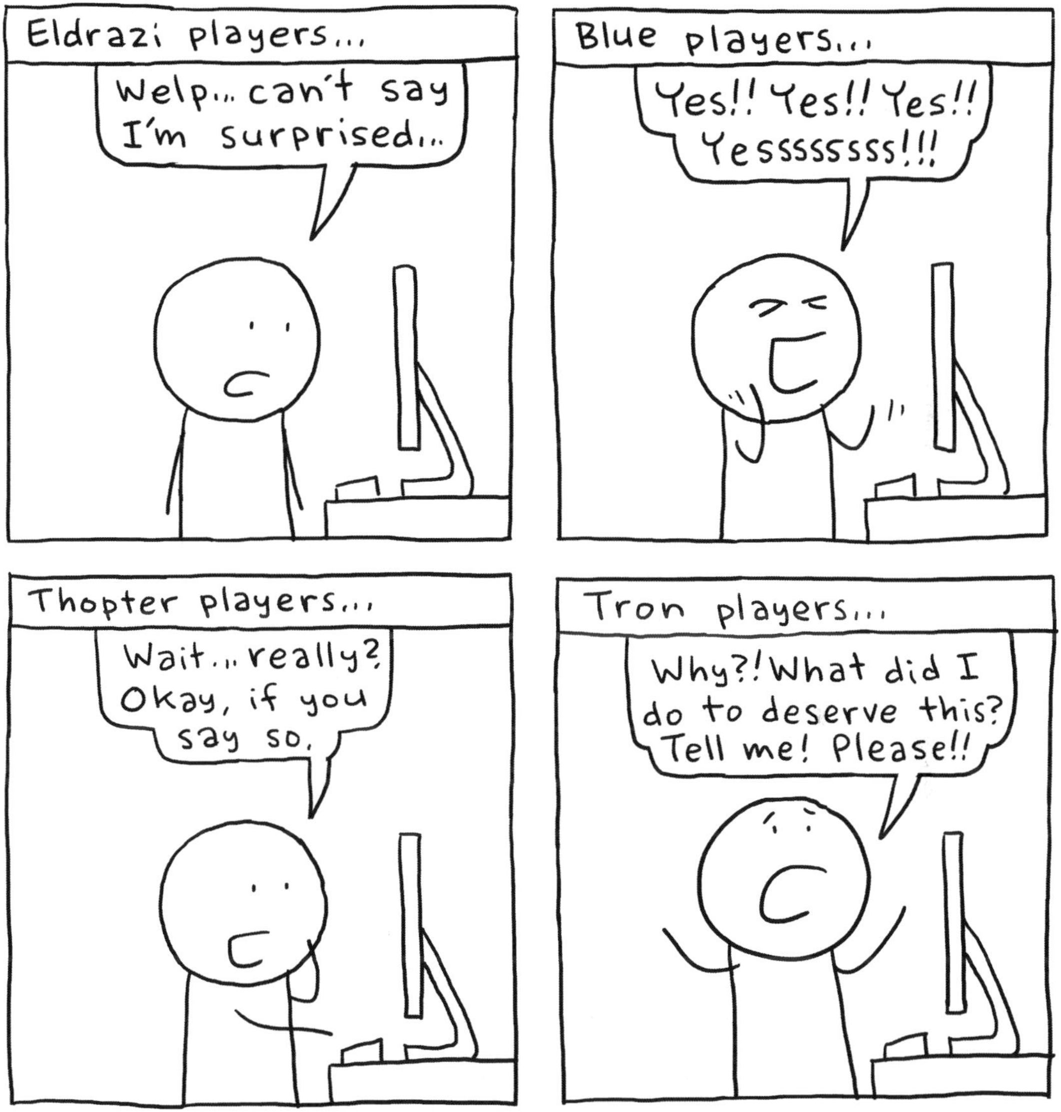

Eldrazi players...
Welp... can't say I'm surprised...
Blue players...
Yes!! Yes!! Yes!! Yessssssss!!!
Thopter players...
Wait... really? Okay, if you say so.
Tron players...
Why?! What did I do to deserve this? Tell me! Please!!

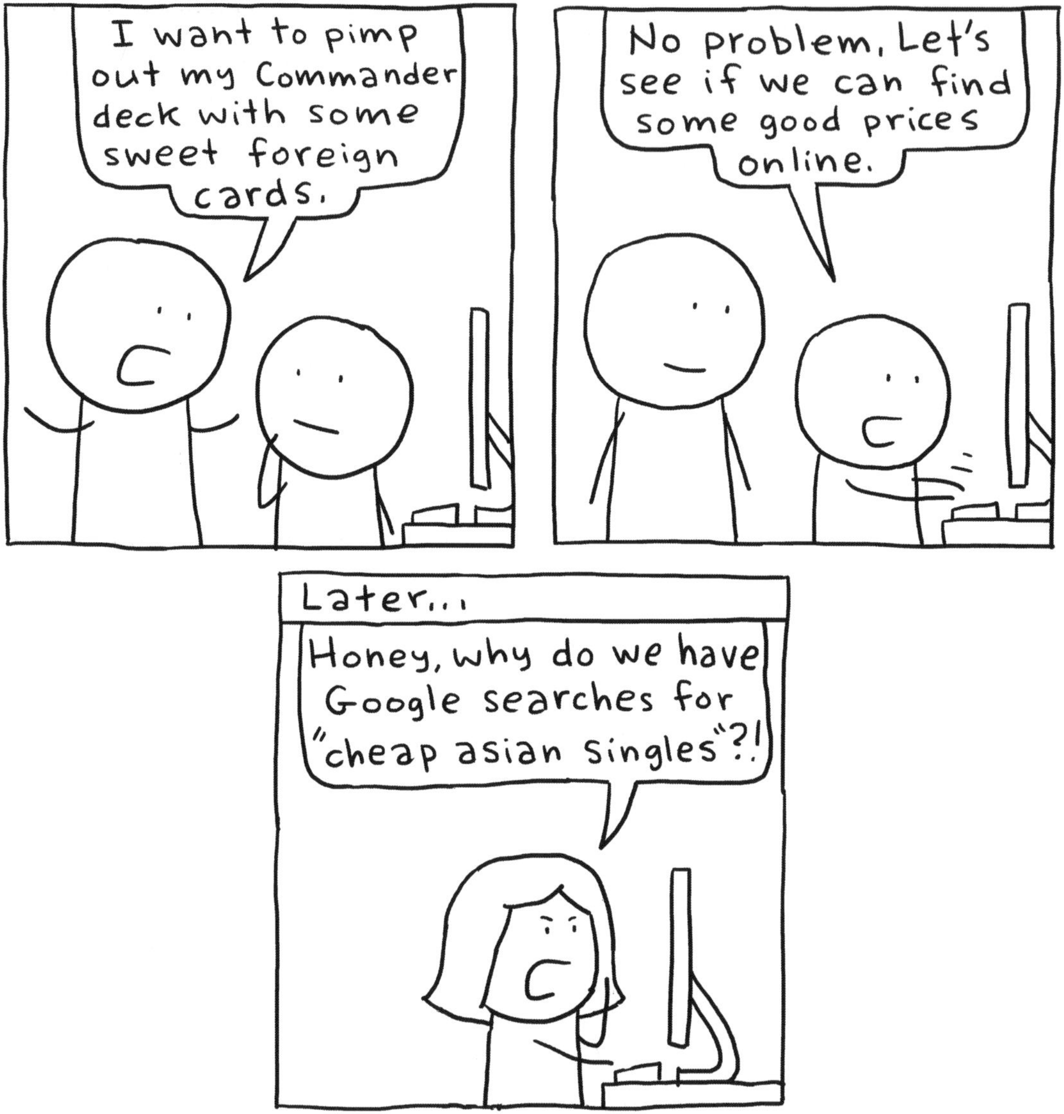
I want to pimp out my Commander deck with some sweet foreign cards.
No problem. Let's see if we can find some good prices online.
Later...
Honey, why do we have Google searches for "cheap asian singles"?!

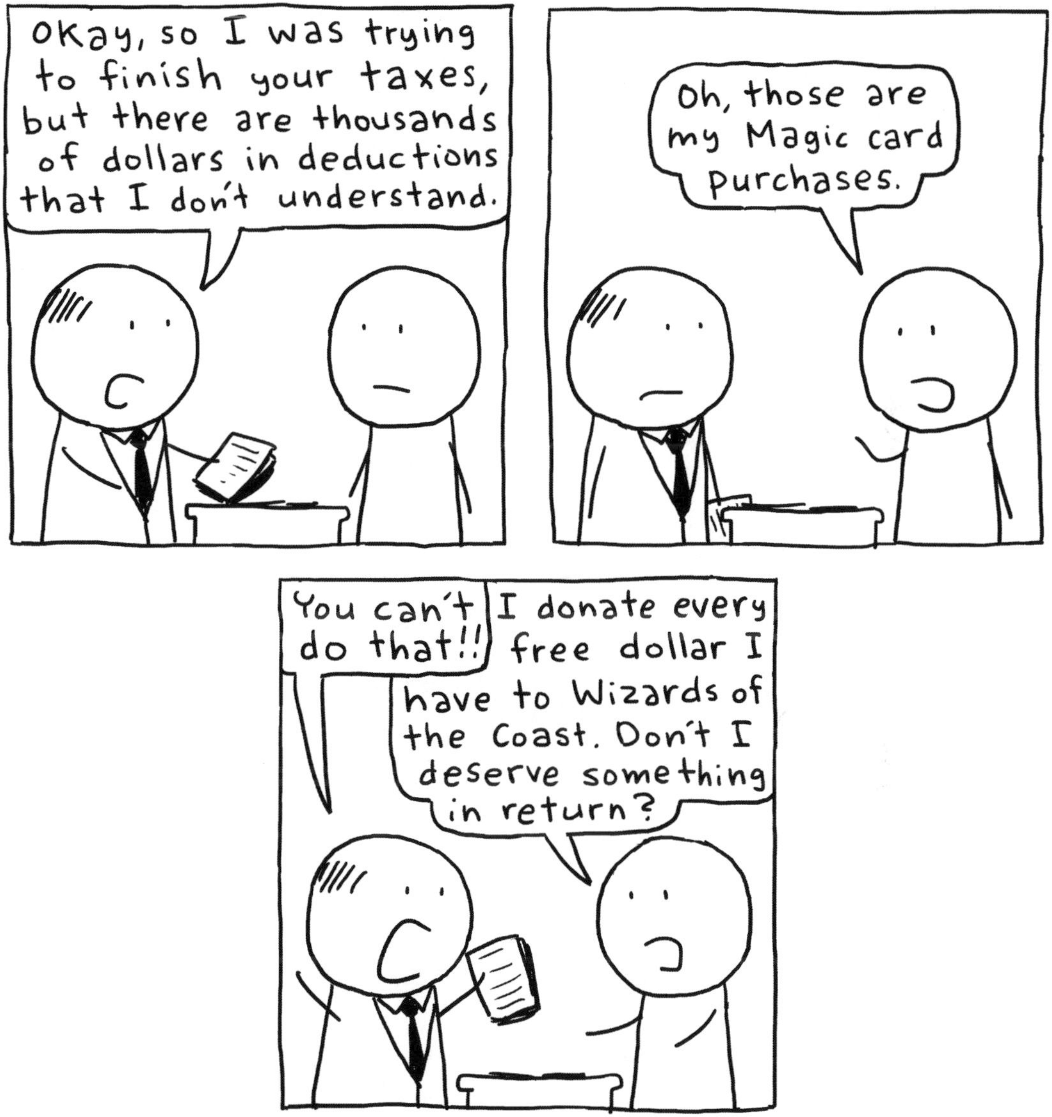
Okay, so I was trying to finish your taxes, but there are thousands of dollars in deductions that I don't understand.
Oh, those are my Magic card purchases.
You can't do that!!
I donate every free dollar I have to Wizards of the Coast. Don't I deserve something in return?

Panel 1: What is this? Black border, white border, Ice Age Unglued -- your lands are completely mismatched!

So what?

Panel 2: So what?! What if I play Thoughtseize, so I know what's in your hand? If during your next turn you play a land I didn't see before, then I still know what's in your hand and I can play around it!

Panel 3: Do you even have a way to look at my hand?

No, but that's besides the point! You should do everything to maximize your win percentage!...

Panel 4: Seriously, what could be the advantage of playing mismatched lands and driving me crazy?!

I think you answered your own question.

Magic in 1997....

Wait, why isn't Serra Angel in 5th Edition?

4/4 flying vigilance for only 5 mana? That's way too strong!

Magic now...

Archangel Avacyn is 4/4 flying vigilance for 5 mana.

That's it?

And flash, and makes your creatures indestructible until end of turn, and flips into a 6/5, and deals 3...

Bonus Comics

The following pages feature comics that have never appeared on the Cardboard Crack website. I hope you enjoy the chance to see them here for the first time!

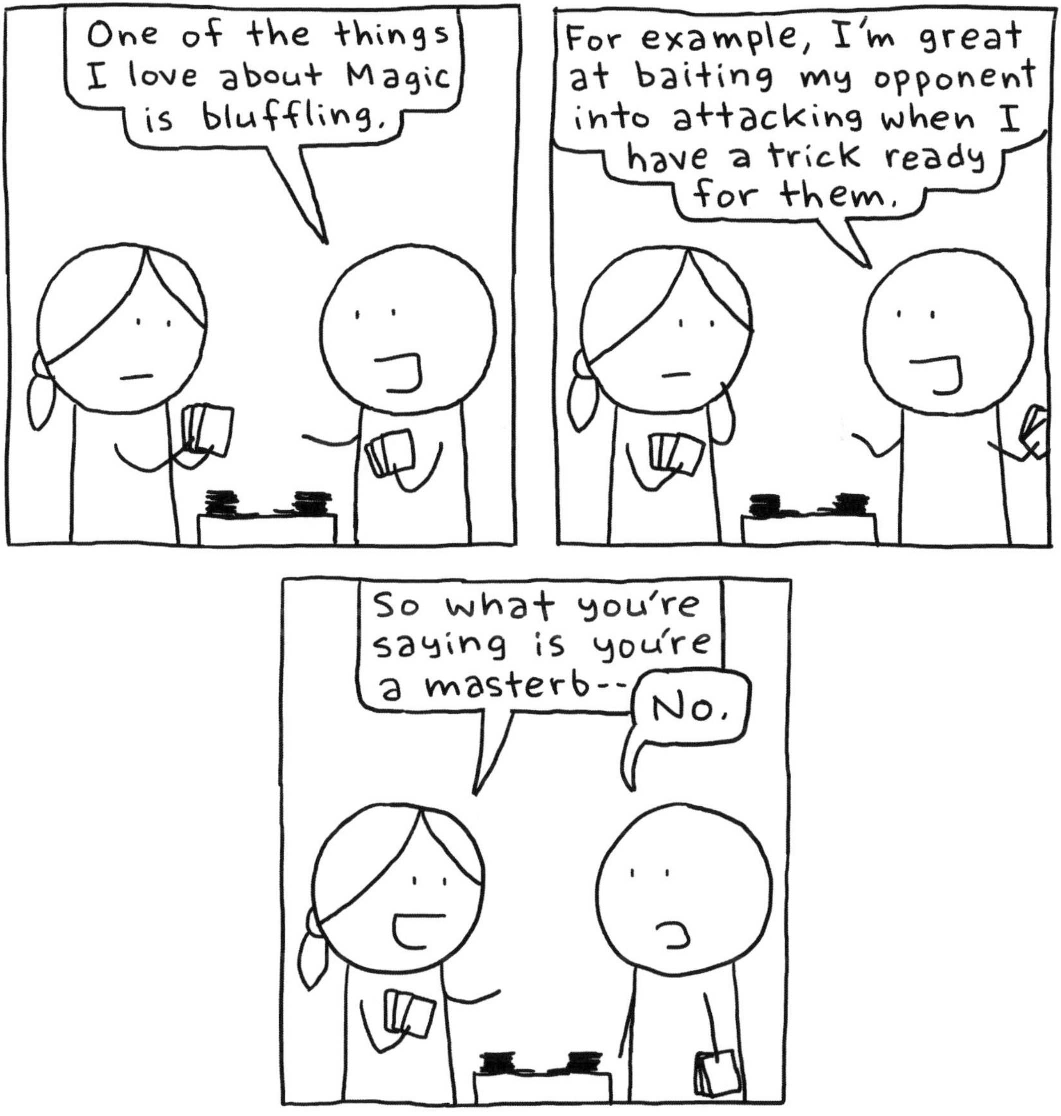
One of the things I love about Magic is bluffling.
For example, I'm great at baiting my opponent into attacking when I have a trick ready for them.
So what you're saying is you're a masterb--
No.

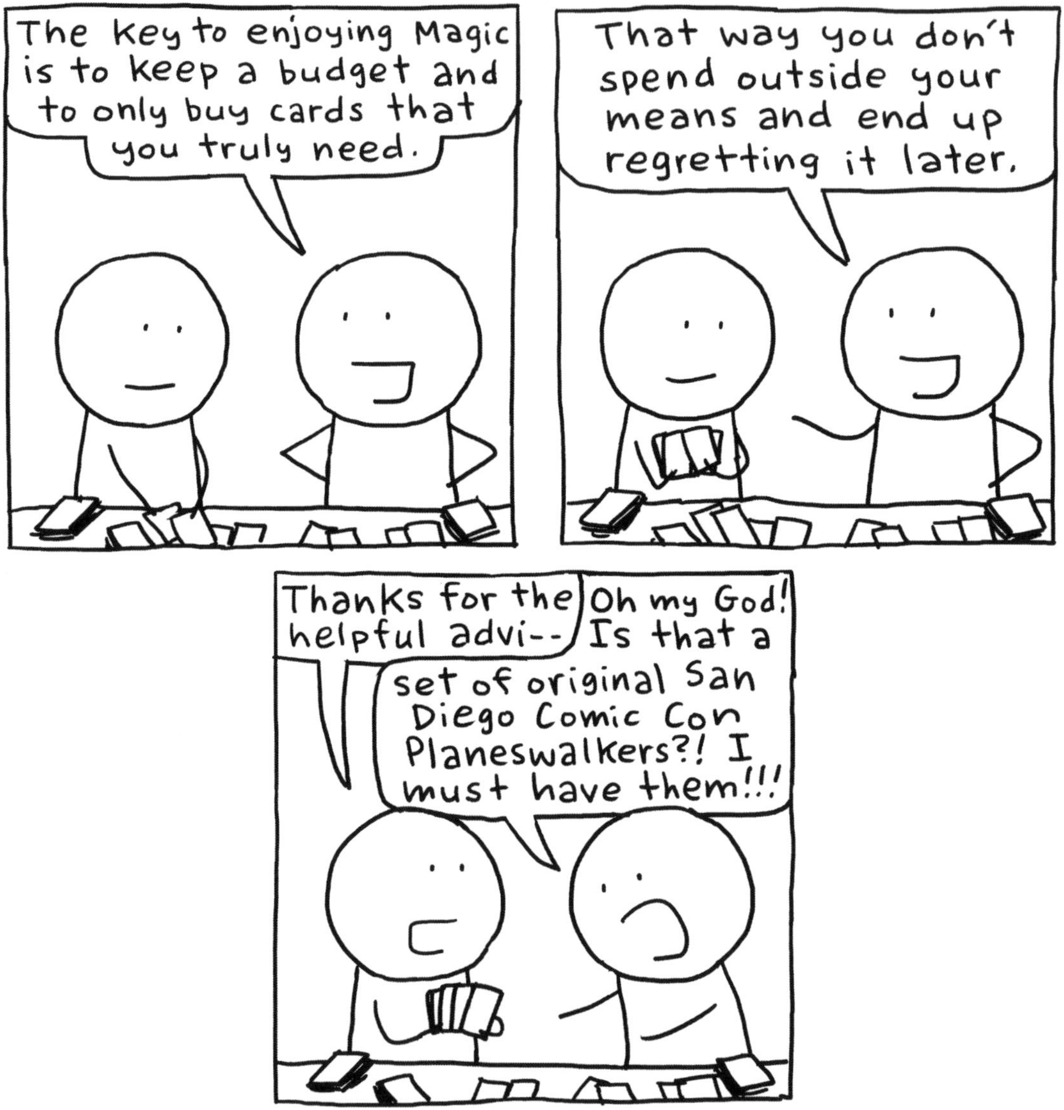
The key to enjoying Magic is to keep a budget and to only buy cards that you truly need.
That way you don't spend outside your means and end up regretting it later.
Thanks for the helpful advi--
Oh my God! Is that a set of original San Diego Comic Con Planeswalkers?! I must have them!!!

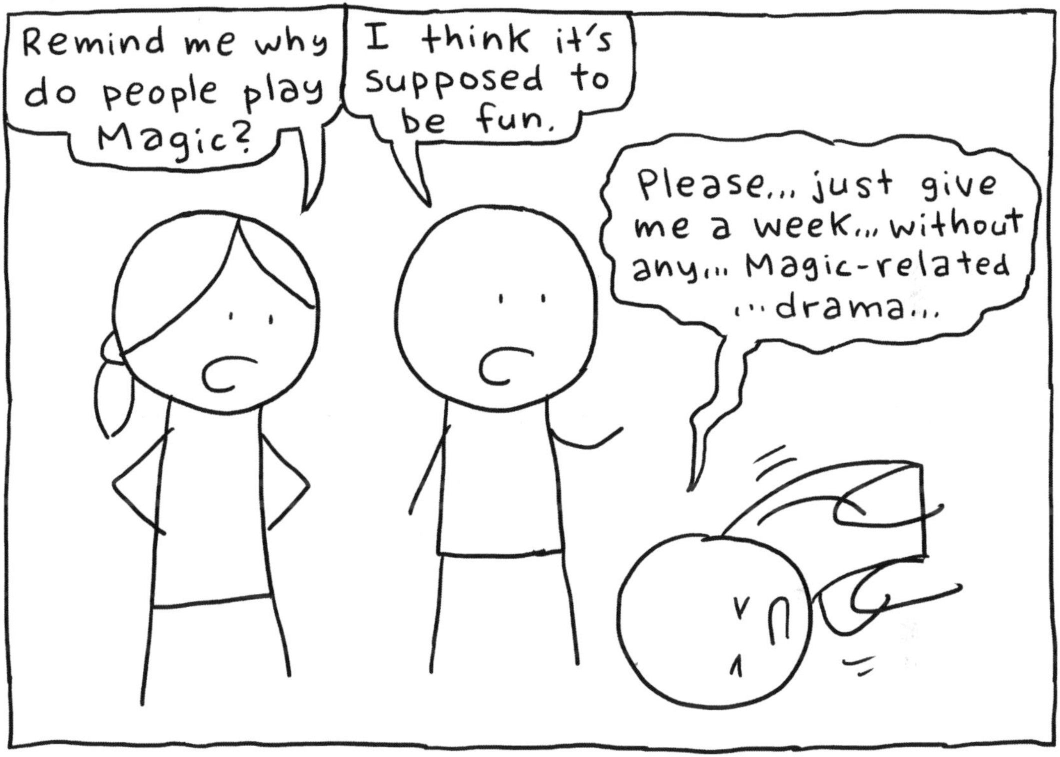
Remind me why do people play Magic?
I think it's supposed to be fun.
Please... just give me a week... without any... Magic-related ...drama...

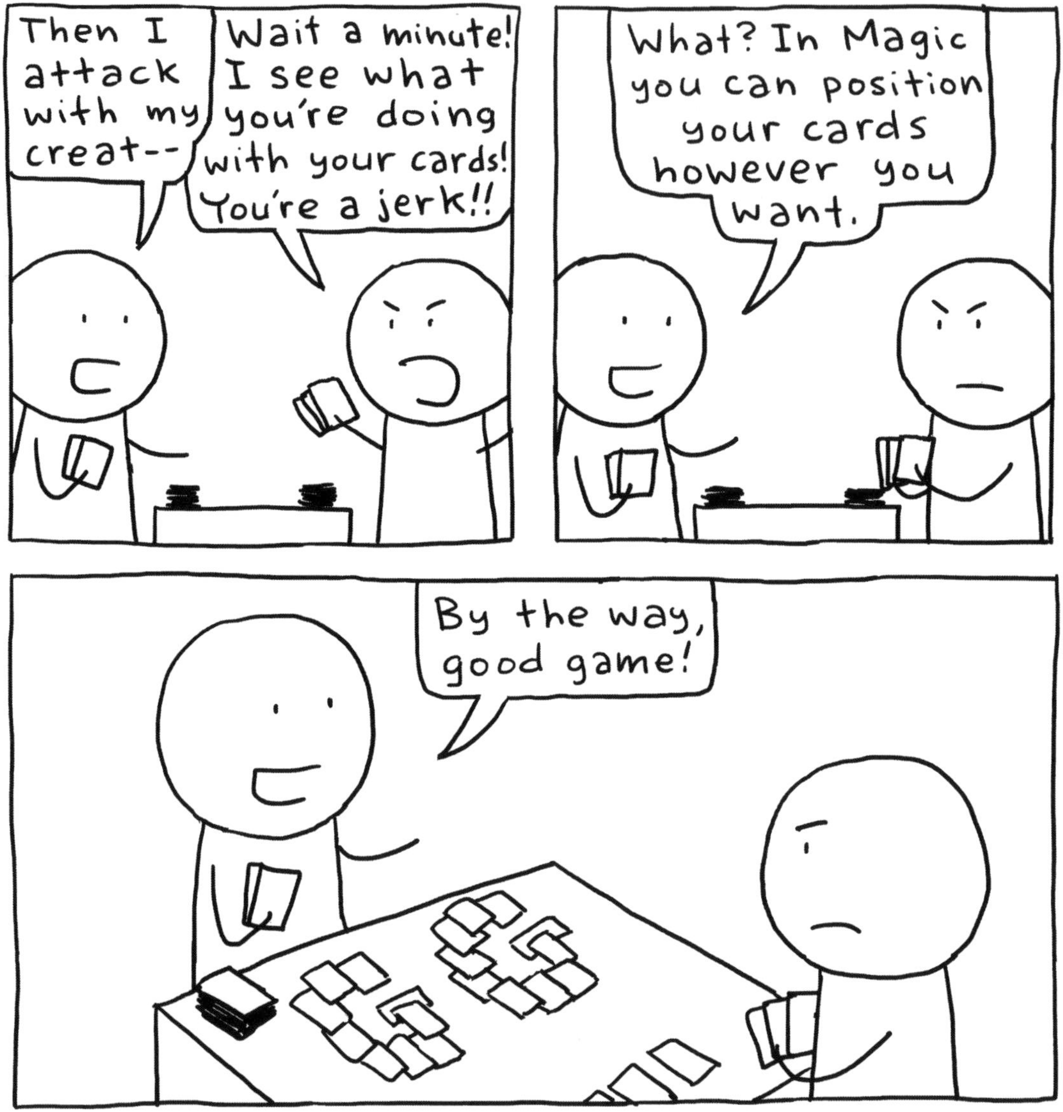
Then I attack with my creat--
Wait a minute! I see what you're doing with your cards! You're a jerk!!
What? In Magic you can position your cards however you want.
By the way, good game!

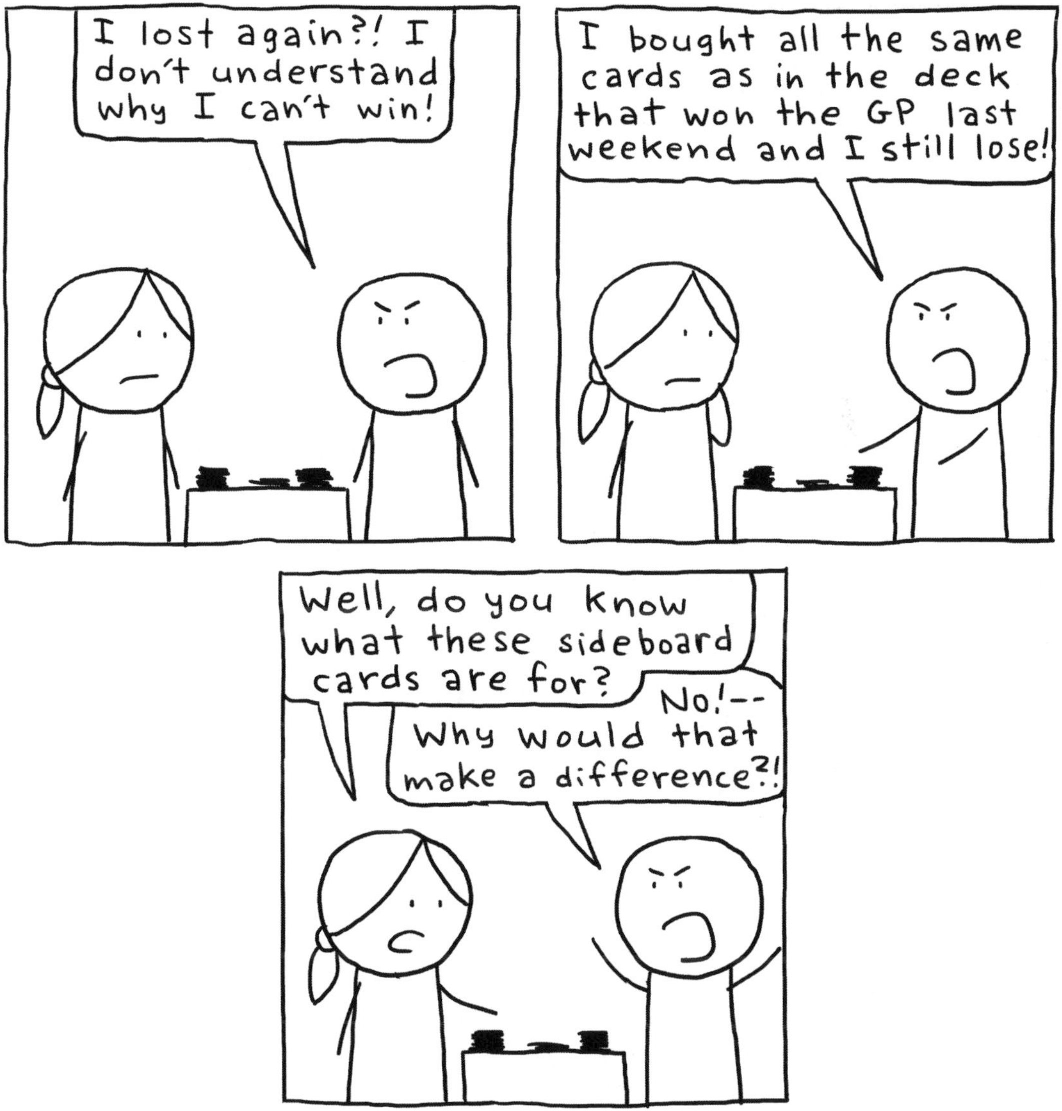
I lost again?! I don't understand why I can't win!
I bought all the same cards as in the deck that won the GP last weekend and I still lose!
Well, do you know what these sideboard cards are for?
No!-- Why would that make a difference?!

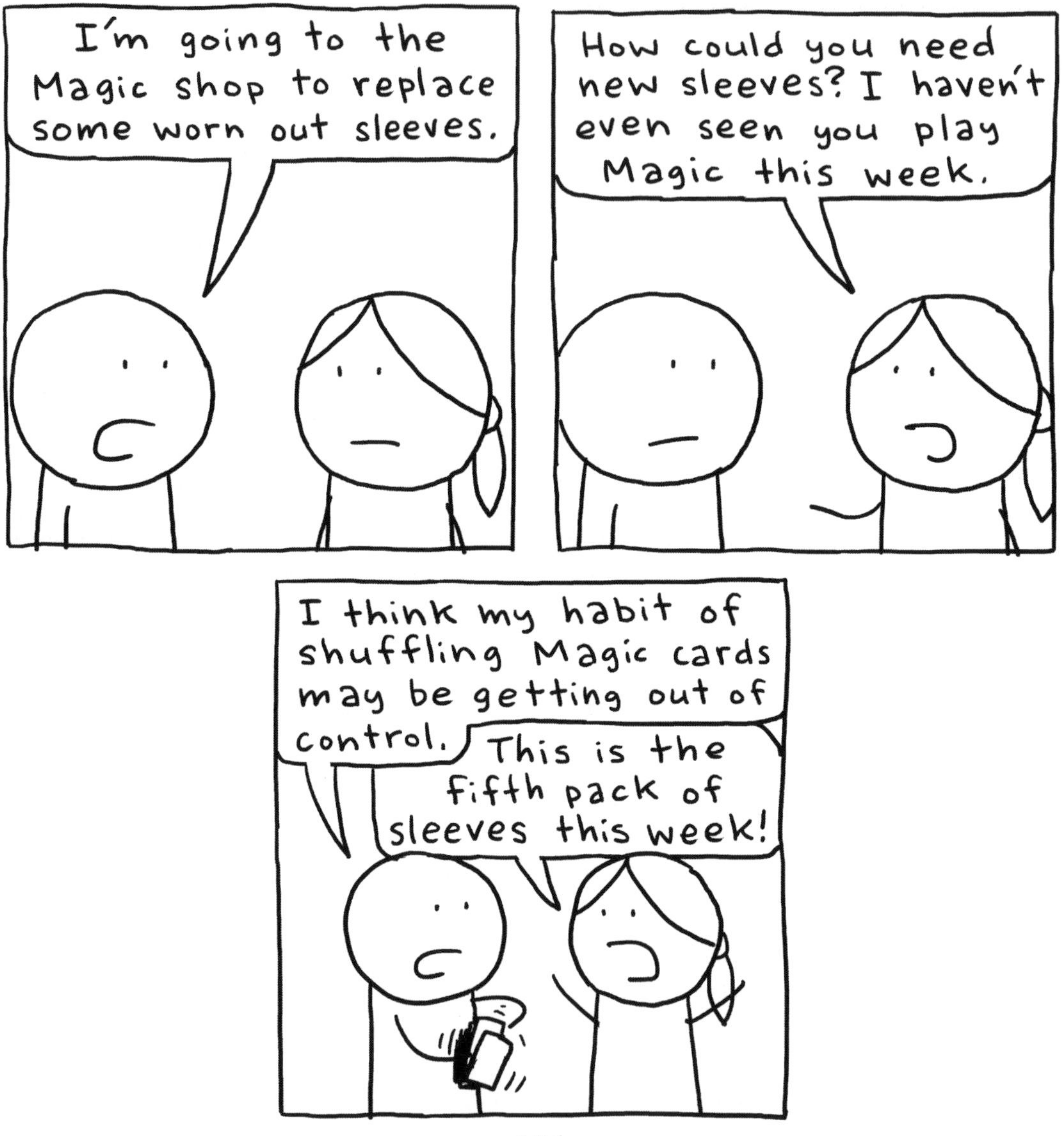
I'm going to the Magic shop to replace some worn out sleeves.
How could you need new sleeves? I haven't even seen you play Magic this week.
I think my habit of shuffling Magic cards may be getting out of control.
This is the fifth pack of sleeves this week!

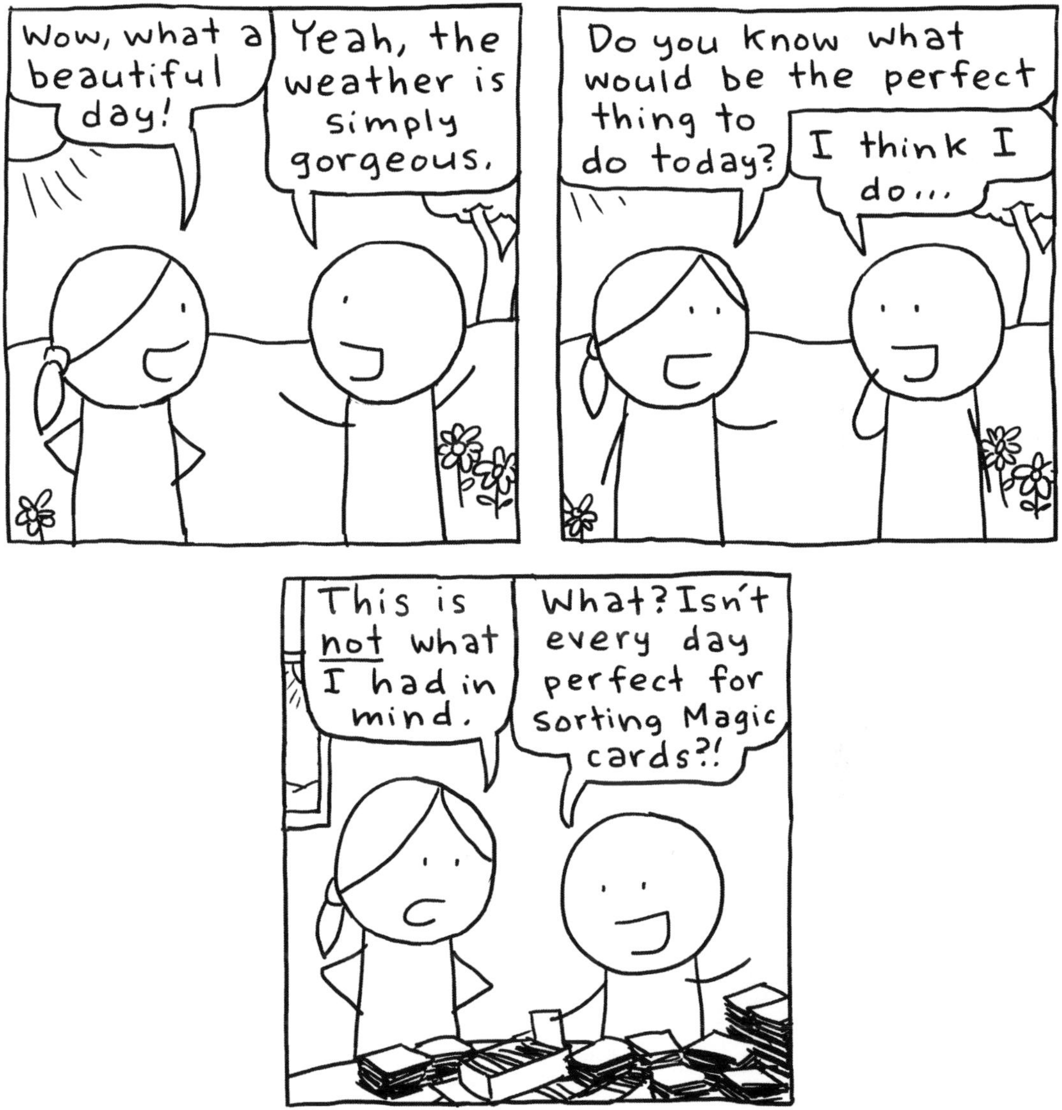
Wow, what a beautiful day!
Yeah, the weather is simply gorgeous.
Do you know what would be the perfect thing to do today?
I think I do...
This is not what I had in mind.
What? Isn't every day perfect for sorting Magic cards?!

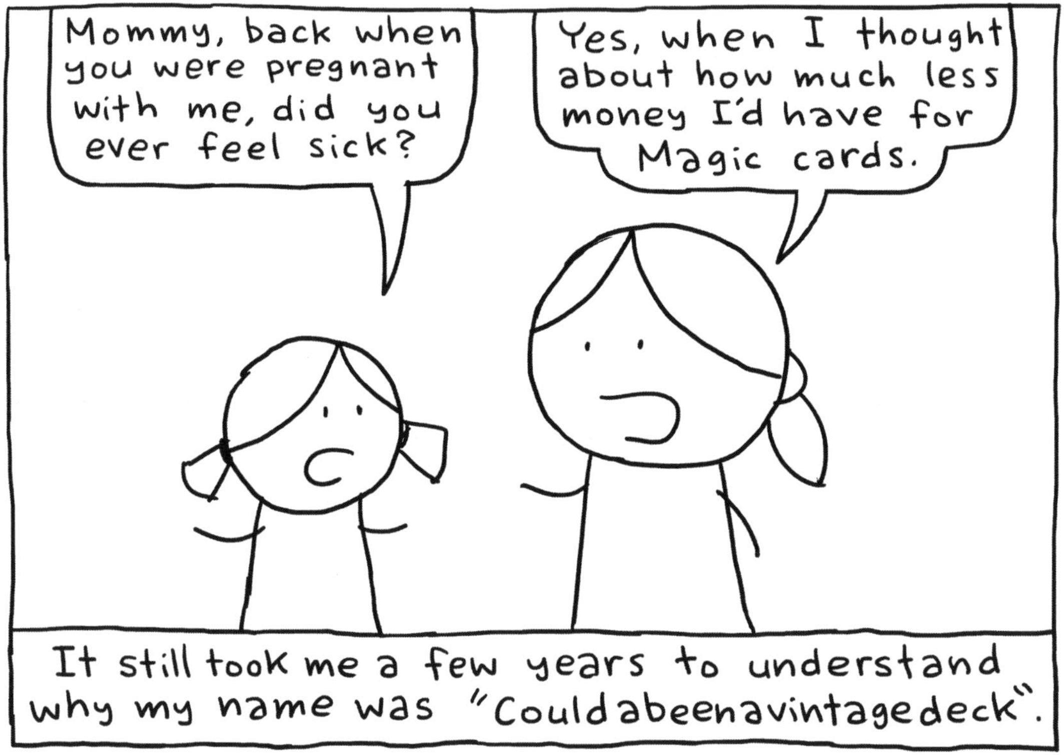

Mommy, back when you were pregnant with me, did you ever feel sick?
Yes, when I thought about how much less money I'd have for Magic cards.
It still took me a few years to understand why my name was "Couldabeenavintagedeck".

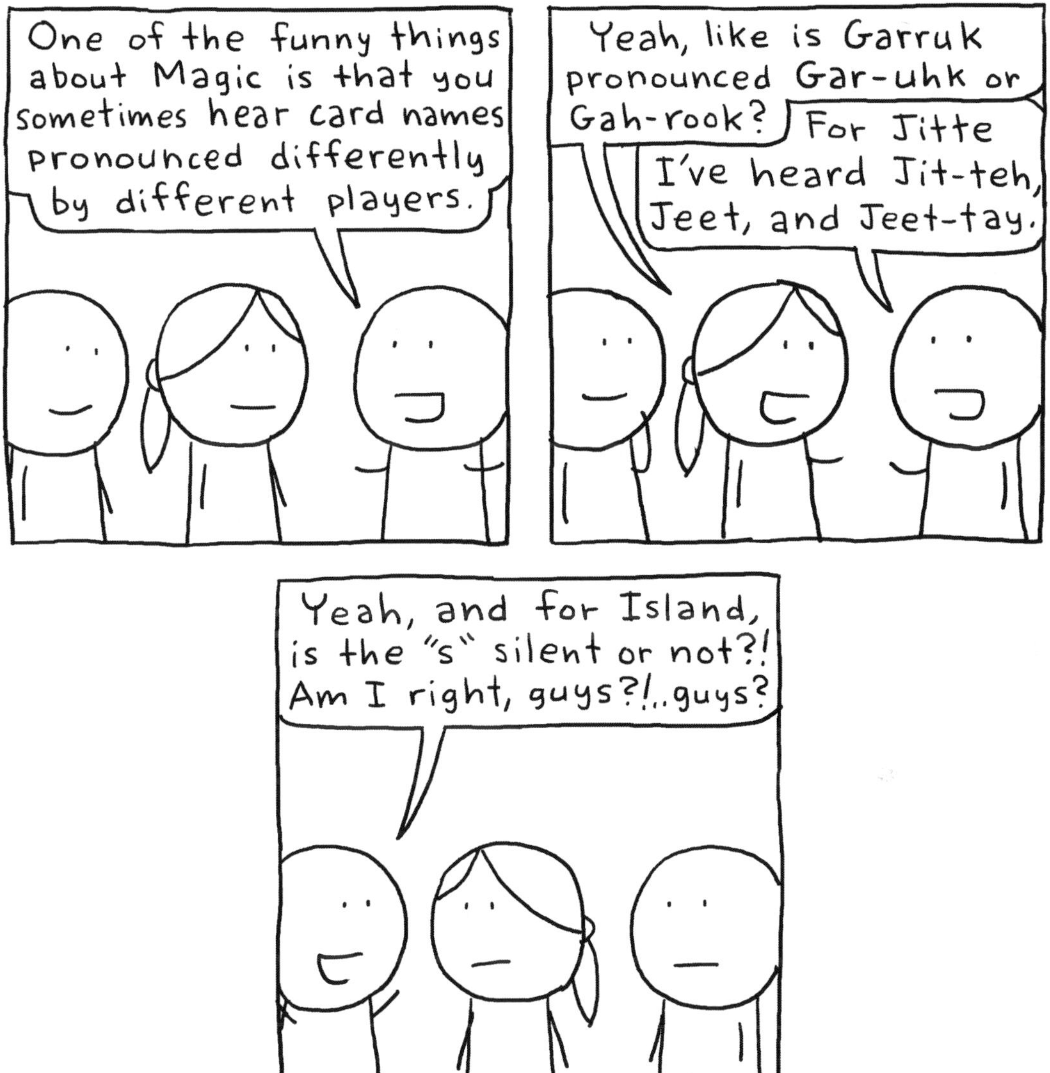
One of the funny things about Magic is that you sometimes hear card names pronounced differently by different players.
Yeah, like is Garruk pronounced Gar-uhk or Gah-rook?
For Jitte I've heard Jit-teh, Jeet, and Jeet-tay.
Yeah, and for Island, is the "s" silent or not?! Am I right, guys?!..guys?

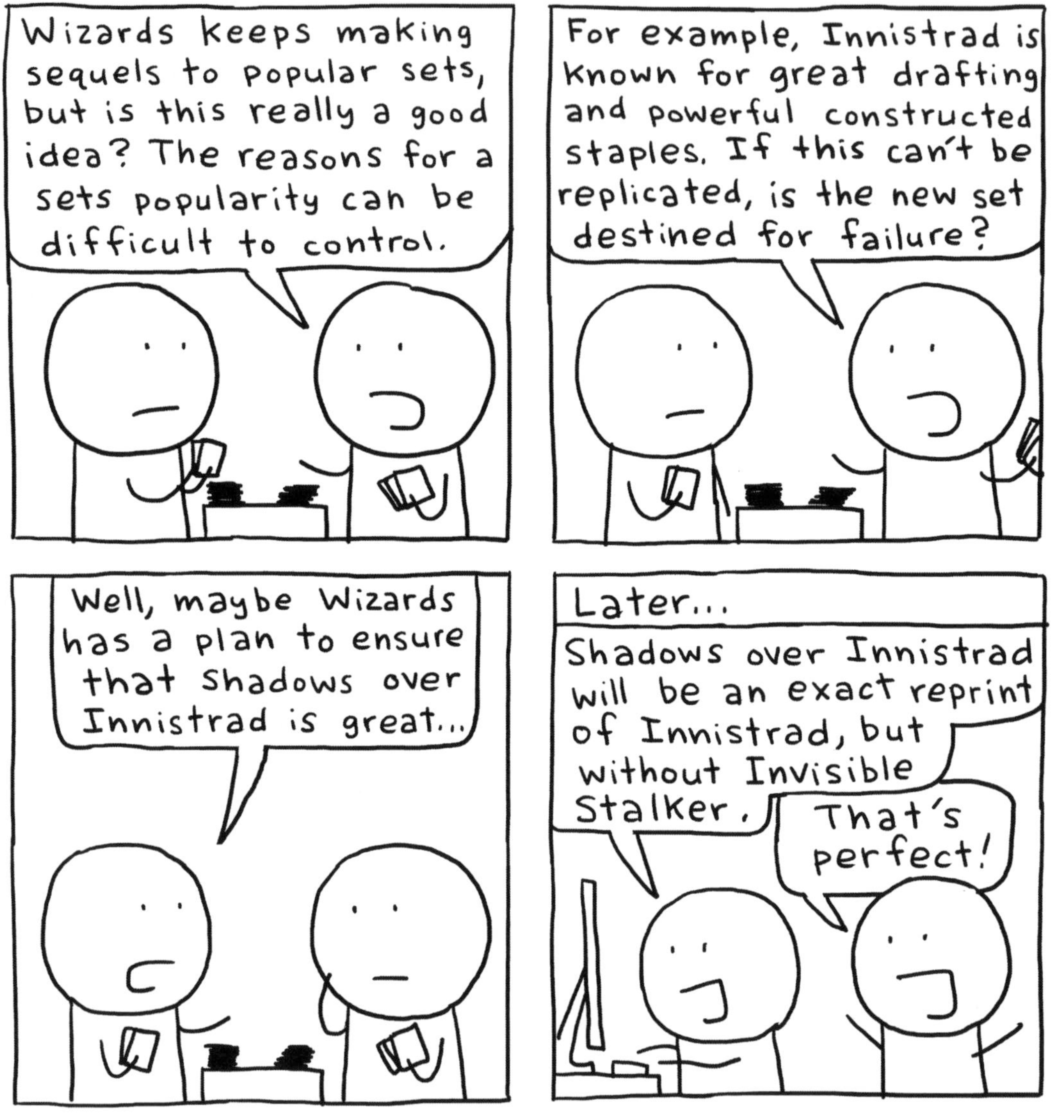
Wizards keeps making sequels to popular sets, but is this really a good idea? The reasons for a sets popularity can be difficult to control.
For example, Innistrad is known for great drafting and powerful constructed staples. If this can't be replicated, is the new set destined for failure?
Well, maybe Wizards has a plan to ensure that Shadows over Innistrad is great...
Later...
Shadows over Innistrad will be an exact reprint of Innistrad, but without Invisible Stalker.
That's perfect!

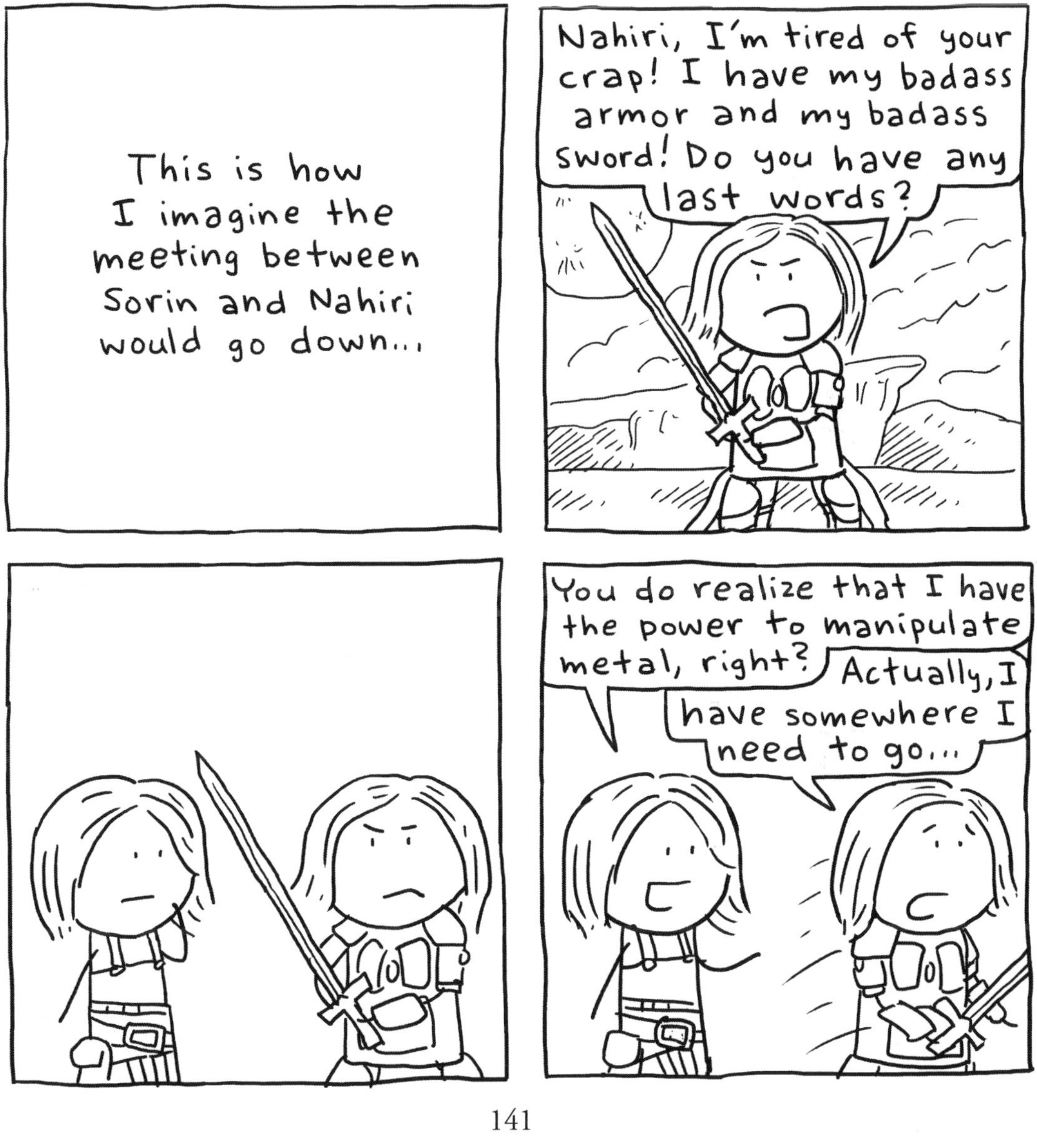
This is how I imagine the meeting between Sorin and Nahiri would go down...
Nahiri, I'm tired of your crap! I have my badass armor and my badass sword! Do you have any last words?
You do realize that I have the power to manipulate metal, right?
Actually, I have somewhere I need to go...

Cardboard Crack has been online since 2013, featuring comics exclusively about the world's most addictive game, Magic: The Gathering. Since that time, the Cardboard Crack website has gained many thousands of followers and many millions of page views. It has received links from a wide variety of prominent personalities in the Magic community, from Aaron Forsythe (current director of Magic: The Gathering R&D) to Jon Finkel (widely regarded as one of the greatest Magic players of all-time).

New comics can be found regularly at:
cardboard-crack.com
facebook.com/CardboardCrack

Check out these other Cardboard Crack books:
Cardboard Crack
I will never quit Cardboad Crack
Cardboard Crack anytime, anywhere
Cardboard Crack until the day I die
I'm always thinking about Cardboard Crack
Cardboard Crack is an intellectual sport

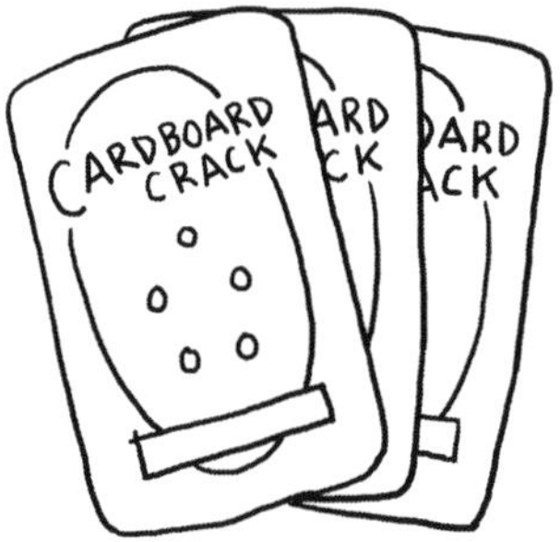
CARDBOARD CRACK

Made in the USA
San Bernardino, CA
20 December 2016